"Theatricals of Day"

"THEATRICALS OF DAY"

EMILY DICKINSON AND NINETEENTH-CENTURY AMERICAN POPULAR CULTURE

SANDRA RUNZO

UNIVERSITY OF MASSACHUSETTS PRESS
AMHERST & BOSTON

ISBN 978-1-62534-442-7 (paper); 481-6 (hardcover)

Designed by adam b. bohannon
Set in Fairfield
Printed and bound by Maple Press, Inc.

Cover design by adam b. bohannon
Cover art: Detail from a broadside for Franconi's Colossal Hippodrome in Worcester, Massachusetts,
1853. Courtesy of the American Antiquarian Society.

Library of Congress Cataloging-in-Publication Data

Names: Runzo, Sandra, author.
Title: "Theatricals of day" : Emily Dickinson and nineteenth-century
American popular culture / Sandra Runzo.
Description: Amherst : University of Massachusetts, [2019] | Includes
bibliographical references and index. |
Identifiers: LCCN 2019019889 | ISBN 9781625344816 (hardcover) | ISBN
9781625344427 (paperback) | ISBN 9781613767252 (ebook) | ISBN
9781613767245 (ebook)
Subjects: LCSH: Dickinson, Emily, 1830–1886—Knowledge—Popular culture. |
Popular culture—United States—19th century.
Classification: LCC PS1541.Z5 R78 2019 | DDC 811/.4—dc23
LC record available at https://lccn.loc.gov/2019019889

British Library Cataloguing-in-Publication Data
A catalog record for this book is available from the British Library

An earlier version of chapter one, "Emily Dickinson's American Museum," was previously published in *ESQ: Journal of the American Renaissance* (51.4 [2005]). The author's
essay "Popular Culture" in *Emily Dickinson in Context*, edited by Eliza Richards (Cambridge UP, 2013) includes part of the discussion of "I cannot dance opon my toes"
from chapter three as well as a few general ideas drawn from this project.

CONTENTS

ACKNOWLEDGMENTS

My gratitude extends far—to scores of people: scholars, teachers, colleagues, friends, and family. My most humble appreciation to all those who ventured down new roads in Dickinson studies. Although it is dangerous to mention any because there are so many who have paved a way, I name a few whose scholarly work has been galvanizing for me: Sandra Gilbert and Susan Gubar, Shira Wolosky, David S. Reynolds, Daneen Wardrop, Barton Levi St. Armand, Cristanne Miller, and Jay Leyda.

Over the years, librarians and curators at a number of universities and museums have generously assisted me in finding materials for this project. I am extremely grateful to them all: Susan Amann and Jo-Ann Roy, Wadleigh Memorial Library, Milford, New Hampshire; Patricia J. Albright, Archives and Special Collections, Mt. Holyoke College Library; Margaret R. Dakin and Daria D'Arienzo, Archives and Special Collections, Amherst College Library; Tevis Kimball and Kate Boyle, Special Collections, Jones Library, Amherst, Massachusetts; Janet Stewart, University of Massachusetts Library; Christine Jacobson, Susan Halpert, Emily Walhout, and Mary Haegert, Houghton Library, Harvard University; Jane Wald, Emily Dickinson Museum, Amherst, Massachusetts; Judith Marshall, Lynn Museum and Historical Society, Lynn, Massachusetts; Marie E. Lamoureux, American Antiquarian Society, Worcester, Massachusetts. Also, my appreciation to Philip F. Gura for permission to include the albumen photograph he discovered of a woman who might be Emily Dickinson, and to the private collector who granted permission to include a daguerreotype of two women, speculated to be Emily Dickinson and her friend Kate Anthon.

Mary Dougherty has been a wonderfully enthusiastic editor, for which I sincerely thank her. In addition, the anonymous reviewers of the book manuscript offered astute commentary, and I am grateful for their care and attention.

The librarians and staff members, past and present, at Denison University's William Howard Doane Library have been extremely helpful. My thanks especially to Susan Rice, Stephanie Kays, Earl Griffith, Pam Magelaner, Susan Scott, and Heather Lyle. The marvelous Cheryl Johnson with Denison's information technology department is a true hero.

As these chapters were finding their final form, I had the benefit of the keen minds and eyes of a few people. Thank you, Sylvia Brown, Linda Krumholz, and Cris Miller.

With much gratitude, I offer thanks to a wonderful group of friends and colleagues who have supported this project in various ways: David Baker, Mark Brown, Sylvia Brown, Christopher Bruhn, the late Jim Davis, Linda Frost, Karen Graves, Linda Hess, Mark Jeffreys, Linda Krumholz, Lisa McDonnell, Anna Nekola, Fred Porcheddu, Dennis Read, Mitchell Snay, Liz Stanton, Ann Townsend, Marlene Tromp, Mary Tuominen, and James Weaver. With your spirit, wit, humor, kindness, and generosity, you all inspire me.

Thank you to James Brown, Jonathan Brown, and Anna Nekola for sharing in conversation some of their musical expertise. I probably owe a lifetime of thanks to my sister, Cynthia Runzo Wignall, herself a marvelous painter, who helped me to contemplate the visual language of portraiture. Undoubtedly, no amount of thanks is ever enough to express full appreciation for one's parents. My first models of people who loved music and books, my parents, JoAnne Runzo and the late Robert Runzo, are two of the finest people to ever take a breath. Finally, my thanks (again and again) to Sylvia, with whom every day is fun and to whom I dedicate this book. Thank you for being a singer, a dreamer, a wonder-worker, and an inspiration.

"Theatricals of Day"

INTRODUCTION

Ne'er saw I such a wondrous scene —
(F13)

In her own private ways, Emily Dickinson participated in the popular entertainments of her time. Dickinson was an enthusiast of the traveling circus, a performer of popular musical numbers on her piano, a collector of sheet music of popular songs, and—earlier in her life—an occasional audience member of performances by musicians such as the Germania Serenade Band, the popular singer Jenny Lind, and, likely, the Hutchinson Family Singers, one of the most prominent of the family singing groups of the nineteenth century. Dickinson read current fiction and verse, some brought into the Dickinson home in the pages of local and national newspapers and magazines, such as the *Springfield Republican, Harper's,* and the *Atlantic Monthly.* As a person living in nineteenth-century America, Dickinson experienced the popular culture that infused and shaped "ordinary life." The proliferating sites of popular amusement and mass culture in nineteenth-century America—such as circuses, traveling shows, dime museums, minstrelsy, literary fiction, and early photography—provided abundant opportunities to contemplate the host of troubles, struggles, and anxieties that pervaded the nation. America obsessively examined forms of freedom and captivity, categories of human identity, and definitions of normality and aberration, yet these persistent and pressing issues of the nineteenth century were more like puzzles than clear-cut questions, and so it is perhaps not surprising that these matters were taken up and dramatized in varied formats, including the open world of popular entertainments.

1

Whatever her aspirations were or were not regarding participation in a public arena, the rich world of popular culture offered Dickinson access to public discussions regarding the key social and political struggles of her time.

My concern in this study is Emily Dickinson in her own time. My attention is to the social and historical context of the nineteenth century, especially the place of mass popular entertainments, and the presence of this context in her experience, perspective, and writing. I examine how popular culture and popular entertainments of her time are seen, heard, and felt in Dickinson's writing. Taking into account the place of popular entertainments in the perception and comprehension of the many troubled, muddled, and perplexing issues and situations that shaped life in the nineteenth century, I propose that an understanding of (or even recognition of) the presence of popular entertainment in Dickinson's life opens our eyes to new dimensions of Dickinson's writing, illuminating ways that Dickinson was attentive to social and political matters of her time.

The titular phrase "Theatricals of Day" comes from a poem of about 1862 (as dated by Dickinson scholar Thomas Johnson) or spring 1863 (according to scholar Ralph W. Franklin) in which Dickinson's tropes of the theatre invoke seasonal or diurnal transformations as well as dramatic events of the times, even quite plausibly scenes of violence and bloodshed. In the poem, references to stage productions emphasize the public's attention to scenes playing out around them, suggesting that an unspecified fiery "Red" serves as a "Mighty" spotlight, illuminating what is happening in individual settings and, more pointedly, in the nation.

> Like Mighty Foot Lights — burned the Red
> At Bases of the Trees —
> The far Theatricals of Day
> Exhibiting — to These —
>
> 'Twas Universe — that did applaud —
> While Chiefest — of the Crowd —

Enabled by his Royal Dress —
Myself distinguished God —
                    (F507)

It is easy and even sensible to understand the poem as a paean to autumnal changes in New England, the colorful shifts in the landscape and trees celebrated by the entire "Universe." While the audience for this show is vast, the speaker manages to spy God in the "Crowd." This kind of all's-right-with-the-world reading of the poem sets aside the potentially disturbing imagery, opting for a reassuring description of seasonal regularity and ignoring likely connotations that would be apparent to readers in the 1860s. In the first line, the phrase "burned the Red" might suggest vibrant autumn foliage, but it as readily suggests passion or rage or blood, and, by extension, those injured and killed in war. The word "burned" is key: What kind of burn is this? Are there embers or flashes or fevers or fires? The word "burned" suggests that something has been ignited. Something inflamed exists in plain sight ("At Bases of the Trees — "), and its visibility must extend far and wide, with the burning projected as "Foot Lights" while the modifier "Mighty" furthers the impression that these Lights have exceptional power. In addition, for the "Universe" to "applaud," one imagines that the burning must be extremely grand, more of a conflagration than a small contained blaze. Seen from this angle, the Universe and the God who watch and delight in the "show" seem perverse, detached from the horrifying reality, entertained by the incendiary spectacles staged by human beings. We are told that other "far Theatricals of Day" are "Exhibiting"; these other dramas and narratives are illumined by the "Mighty Foot Lights" for an audience's viewing.

What are the "Theatricals" of Dickinson's day? Played out within both public settings and private spaces, they are the turbulent narratives regarding human rights and human identity, the variations of captivity that stole or constrained people's lives, and a civil war, all of which entranced yet rived the nation. In the nineteenth century (as perhaps in all times), the world of exhibition and entertainment

addressed the most vital debates, these dramatizations central to popular culture of the nineteenth century, evident, for example, in dime
museums, circuses, minstrel shows, literary fiction, and early photography. The imaginative creations and marvels of popular entertainment
provided vehicles whereby matters of most serious significance were
brought to the attention of mass audiences—virtually anyone and everyone—for engagement and contemplation.

In scholarly studies, some have presented Dickinson as excessively reclusive, perceived her as unconcerned with material life,
or claimed, as Thomas Johnson did, that "she did not live in history
and held no view of it, past or current" (Introduction to *Letters* xx).
In his 1979 volume *The Only Kangaroo among the Beauty,* Karl Keller
presents an Emily Dickinson detached from American history and
American experience: "Except for an embarrassingly few instances,
we cannot tell from her references that she wrote in America!" (102).
In her essay on Dickinson and social class, Betsy Erkkila seeks to
"make visible the historical and specifically class formations of
Dickinson's life and work," proposing that it is Dickinson's class status and "economic privilege" that allow her to write poems, while
also arguing that Dickinson herself was "retreating from historical
time," by which she avers that Dickinson showed "little concern"
for the social injustices around her and withdrew from the world
(156–57, 166, 174–75). In her study of "twentieth-century critical
thought about lyric subjectivity," Virginia Jackson explores the critical impulses that transformed Dickinson from a particular person in
an historical context into an "abstract person accessible to modern
readers" (90, 92). Jackson further observes that as Dickinson was
converted into the "representative of the lyric," she became more
"fictive" (92).

I am writing in the tradition and spirit of such scholars as Jay
Leyda, David S. Reynolds, Barton Levi St. Armand, Shira Wolosky,
Cristanne Miller, and others, all of whom contend that Dickinson
is not detached from the political and social struggles of her time.
Acting on his claim that the "closest juxtaposition of her poems

4

with a complete chronology of her life and times . . . would reveal how much a part of her world she was" (Leyda 1: xxi), Jay Leyda established an invaluable foundation for investigating the contexts of Dickinson's life with the assemblage of materials published in his 1960 volume *The Years and Hours of Emily Dickinson*. Shira Wolosky's 1984 *Emily Dickinson: A Voice of War,* which explores the presence of the Civil War in Dickinson's poems, was vital to opening a pathway to examinations of Dickinson within the context of social and political realities of the nineteenth century. Numerous excellent scholars have followed Wolosky, investigating Dickinson in connection with the Civil War and perceiving Dickinson as a witness of and commentator on the great struggles of the age: slavery and abolition, the constraints on women's lives as well as war. Visual biographers such as Polly Longsworth (*The World of Emily Dickinson* in 1990) and Jerome Liebling (*The Dickinsons of Amherst* in 2001) have assembled photographs and other materials to document the daily lives of the Dickinsons. More recently, *Emily Dickinson in Context,* edited by Eliza Richards in 2013, and the 2016 annotated volume of Dickinson's poems edited by Cristanne Miller, *Emily Dickinson's Poems: As She Preserved Them,* aim to expand and clarify the contexts of Dickinson's life and writing. Interest in Dickinson's herbarium (a facsimile edition published in 2006) and in the physical scraps of paper and envelopes on which she wrote (reproduced in 2013's *Emily Dickinson: The Gorgeous Nothings*) further attests to the widening and intense occupation with the contexts and details of Dickinson's life. In this spirit, a 2017 exhibit at the Morgan Library and Museum emphasized the "rich intellectual and cultural environment in which Dickinson lived and worked."[1]

This is all to say that scholars, curators, and historians continue to press forward, step by step, exploring the life and writing of Emily Dickinson, with ever more interest in personal, social, and political contexts. Are these signs of a flourishing Dickinson fever? Our current moment is engaging—or re-engaging—with an Emily Dickinson who seems freshly present to us as well as newly mysterious.

Like many of the scholars and biographers mentioned above, I, too, place Dickinson in a place and in a time, focusing on the mass popular entertainments and popular culture of nineteenth-century America, in particular, dime museums, traveling circuses, minstrel shows, popular music, popular fiction, and early photography. I address Dickinson's personal engagement with these various forms of popular culture and examine how their iconography and spectacle resonate in Dickinson's writing. Dickinson's fascination with the world of the circus perhaps reflects the allure for her of "curiosities" that crisscross realms as well as her affinity with the mysterious, the quizzical, and the otherworldly. Circuses and dime museums thrived on the exhibition of human riddles: "attractions" that represented bodies that were "different," ambiguous, or excessive, conundrums of human identity that set forth and queried what was normal, desirable, frightening, even dangerous. Blackface minstrelsy was a tremendously popular entertainment throughout much of the century, with blackface performers regularly appearing in many venues—circuses, dime museums, Christmas parades and other holiday pageants, and minstrel shows; while it would be improbable for Dickinson to be unaware of this form of popular culture, Dickinson's familiarity with blackface minstrel performance is evidenced partly through her sheet music collection. That components of the minstrel show appear in many of her poems (through references to song, dance, masquerade, crossed identities, satire, and riddles) suggests that Dickinson was attracted to the expressions of misrule and rebellion that characterized minstrel performance. Several pieces of music in Dickinson's personal album of sheet music are associated with reform movements of the day, possibly indicating that she was interested in these debates, or, at the very least, she was aware of them. Popular fiction that Dickinson read in the publications that came into the family household was a continuing source of information on the perils, confinements, and battles abounding in the nation. The new wondrous visual technology of photography contributed different terms to cultural conversations about personal and public identity.

In my examination of Emily Dickinson's engagements with these forms of popular culture, questions of perception and of comprehension repeatedly arise. An issue that runs through this study regards the difficulties in understanding what one sees and what one hears. In the nineteenth century, what did audience members at the circus think they were witnessing, either at the sideshow or at the big show? Standing in front of Joice Heth, one of P. T. Barnum's money-making marvels, did anyone believe they were viewing (and perhaps talking to) a 161-year-old slave woman who had been the nursemaid of George Washington? If this seemed a dubious proposition, what did a visitor to the museum see when he or she stared at Joice Heth? At a blackface minstrel show, what did audience members believe they were seeing (and what did they not see)? When the songs of the minstrel repertoire were enlisted, with new lyrics, in the cause of social reform or abolition, how were they heard by nineteenth-century ears? In regard to objects with important ties to Emily Dickinson herself, one can ask the same questions: What have different viewers perceived in a portrait of Emily Dickinson, or in a white dress, or in a house? These uncertainties of what one sees or might see were also surprisingly overt in the worlds of daguerreotypy and early photography, in which the question of what was made visible in a portrait, so mysteriously produced, is exactly what was deliberated.

Just as importantly, what did these various exhibitions and entertainments, songs and fictions, images and objects mean to Emily Dickinson? Moreover, with the distance of time, how do different people perceive and assess these songs, curiosities, stories, artifacts, and performers and performances of the nineteenth century? One answer is that different people see and hear different things. Another answer, perhaps equally as unsatisfying, is that it is hard to know. Dickinson has left her poems and letters as clues to her own perceptions and perspectives on the culture of her day.

These complexities of perception, manifest in many displays of popular culture, inevitably point to other conundrums, every sight and every situation potentially mystifying. If empirical knowledge is so unsettled, one's sense of reality might also feel eerily unstable, easily undermined, about to break apart. One is left to wonder what is actual

7

and what is illusory, what is trustworthy and what is deceptive. Alongside these basic tests of empirical reality stand real-life people and situations, the unclarity of perceptions and of understanding creating the most weighty of consequences as a culture ponders what is normal and what is aberrant, and who is human and who is not-wholly-human. These kinds of questions, repeatedly scrutinized and dramatized in the nineteenth century, circled around other tensions of definition and experience involving such issues as freedom and captivity. So many forms of captivity persisted in the nineteenth-century United States that its forceful presence touched every community, household, and imagination. Stories of captivity in its many forms—slavery, Indian captivity, high-seas kidnapping, mill work, constrictions of women's lives—were widely narrated, with tropes of freedom and captivity commonly imagined in productions of popular culture. These perceptual and epistemological confusions over concepts or values that one might presume to be obviously distinct were displayed in seemingly endless variation on the stages, in the tents, in the auditoriums, and on the printed pages so popular in the century.

Questions about perception and comprehension have been posed about Emily Dickinson by people who knew her, by scholars, biographers, and readers. How can one read, see, and understand her? One could argue that Emily Dickinson herself has held a long-standing place among public and private exhibitions, she herself a living curiosity, on display, so to speak—someone to be studied, interpreted, managed, and presented. Letters, memoirs, biographies, and critical studies of Dickinson offer a miscellany of reminiscences and views, many stressing her mysterious and enigmatic ways. Mabel Loomis Todd is not the only person who has promoted an image of Dickinson as a "character" or "Myth," as she writes in a letter to her parents (Leyda 2: 357). In his *The Village of Amherst*, Frank Prentice Rand records the image of Dickinson as a hermit, and an unusually eccentric one at that: "This is the woman who spent nearly her entire mature life in virtual seclusion behind a hedge on Main Street, and was regarded by friendly, but uncomprehending, neighbors as 'a little cracked'" (230). Martha Dickinson Bianchi recalls that "various fantastic tales were circulated about" her Aunt Emily (*Face to Face* 37). As noted before, Jackson posits that the Dickinson generated by twentieth-century literary criticism became "fictive"; in Todd's preface to the 1931 *Letters of Emily Dickinson,* she writes that "the Emily legend has assumed a shape unrecognizable to one who knew her" (x). The Emily Dickinson portrayed in critical studies and biographies often seems at least partly fictional or apocryphal, someone not quite real or tangible, someone "strange" (as Higginson pronounced), as much a specter or shadow as a real person, glimpsed with wonder by curious neighbors, readers, and scholars.

This phenomenon whereby the person we think of as Emily Dickinson is accepted as a combination of fact and fiction is vividly demonstrated in stories regarding visual images of her. Disagreements among family members about the authenticated 1846/1847 daguerreotype of Dickinson centered on whether the portrait was a sufficiently "truthful" depiction, the judgments of "truth" sometimes based on clearly fictional or intangible details. There have been occasional discoveries of photographic images of a woman (or women) speculated to be Emily Dickinson, each of these finds met with much fanfare and much suspicion. The fascination with the discovered "Dickinson" portraits taps into resilient hopes and expectations: that there are existing photographic images of Dickinson to be found, that such images will assist in our understanding of her, that a photographic image can connect us to a person and to an extraordinary mind. The talismanic energy of these photographic images is so great that even photographs of a woman (or women) merely conjectured to be Emily Dickinson can be treated as revelatory of her.

Many "Emily Dickinson"s have entered contemporary popular culture in the form of novels, plays, and a recent film,[2] all extensions of this compulsion to ponder her life and writing from different angles and to consider new possibilities, however fantastical, to account for her. Contemporary fictional renderings of Dickinson include Judith Farr's 1996 *I Never Came to You in White,* Joanne Dobson's 1997 *Quieter Than Sleep,* Jerome Charyn's 2010 *The Secret Life of Emily Dickinson,* Nuala O'Connor's 2015 *Miss Emily,* and Susan Snively's 2015 *The Heart Has Many Doors.* Although Rand claims that by 1958 there had been three plays written about Emily Dickinson (229),[3] stage portrayals of Dickinson more apparently begin with William Luce's *The Belle of Amherst*, a 1976 play that offers a Dickinson who teeters between the "strange" and the "normal." Luce's Dickinson is a games-playing wit, a whimsical storyteller who entertains herself by deliberately deciding to play the eccentric: Her choice of clothing (the white dress), her oblique notes, her so-called seclusion are apparently all conscious poses assumed so as to confuse curious neighbors and local busybodies. *The Belle of Amherst* proposes that if Dickinson is regarded as the town oddity, the incomprehensible—if fascinating—"Myth" that Mabel Loomis Todd and others surmised, it is a perception of Dickinson's own creation and perpetuated for her own amusement. "I enjoy the game," Luce's Dickinson tells us (18).[4] In Luce's version, Dickinson knowingly performs as the town "curiosity," concocting stories and playing roles for her own entertainment as much as for her neighbors'. Luce's Dickinson is the town show.

Although contemporary times offer tantalizing opportunities to examine renditions of Emily Dickinson and explore how she lives in twenty-first-century popular culture, my interest is the relationship of Emily Dickinson to the popular culture and popular entertainments of her own time.

In chapter one, I explore the phenomenon of exhibition as practiced, specifically in the public arena of P. T. Barnum's American Museum and in the traveling circus, and consider possible affiliations between the theatrics of these forms of popular entertainment in the nineteenth century and the theatrics of Dickinson's verse. These popular entertainments of the century and Dickinson's verse performed similar culture work: With their shared tropes and in their respective venues, each tested and mimicked a nation's anxieties about itself, regarding such issues as the comprehension of race, the clarification of gender roles and rights, the attribution or denial of citizenship, and the mysteries of the monstrous, dangerous, and different.

Chapters two and three examine Dickinson's personal sheet music collection and the relevance of nineteenth-century popular music—as practiced both on the stage and in the home—to Dickinson's writing.

In chapter two, I explore Dickinson's awareness of music and musicians that were tied to the reform movements of her day. Her collection includes music performed by the Hutchinson Family Singers, one of the most famous of the family singing groups of the nineteenth century. Musical voices in the causes of emancipation, women's rights, and peace, the Hutchinsons performed widely at abolitionist meetings and other political assemblies. Dickinson's sheet music collection itself, evidence that she played popular songs on the piano, and evidence that she attended at least a few concerts and heard a number of bands and singers perform (including the Hutchinson Family Singers) all attest to the prominence of popular music in Dickinson's life. I posit that popular music was an influence on Dickinson's metrical forms and, more significantly, that the social commentaries and public concerns dramatized in popular music were relevant to Dickinson's writing. The Hutchinson Family Singers and their songs were living illustrations for Dickinson of how to engage a world of social struggle in lyric.

Chapter three addresses the prominence of blackface performance in nineteenth-century America and its presence in Dickinson's writing. While the voices of minstrel entertainers were heard loudly in nineteenth-century America, the experience of attending a performance was complicated by one's understanding of what exactly one was seeing and hearing. Scholars and historians such as Dale Cockrell, Robert C. Toll, and Eric Lott hold conflicting views regarding the meanings of blackface performance, although most scholars assert that this form of popular entertainment combines performance and social critique. Dickinson's sheet music collection contains several pieces of music that were part of the blackface minstrel repertoire. In many of Dickinson's poems, the tropes of the minstrel show are repeatedly at play: singing, dancing, musical instruments connected to the minstrel stage, masquerade, riddles, satire, and social critique. A number of Dickinson's poems have a figure who evokes the minstrel performer or exhibits the mischievous spirit of the minstrel player; these tropes draw together a cache of cultural narratives from folklore, folksong, myth, and history.

Dickinson's education in the meanings of captivity, terror, and trauma derived from many corners and forces, including the popular fiction of the day, the kind of stories that she could (and did) read in the pages of the *Atlantic,* one of the many publications that came into the Dickinson household. In chapter four, I address the role that contemporary popular fiction had in the national discourse on captivity and confinement, with especial attention to Harriet Prescott Spofford's 1860 short story "Circumstance," a story that had extraordinary allure for Dickinson. In examining the two writers' mutual attention to the terrors and mysteries of captivity, one can see that the crisis detailed in Spofford's story was replayed many times in Dickinson's verse: a person encounters a demon (a goblin, a ghost) and she sings in response. In so many of Dickinson's poems, one can sense the shadow of Spofford and of other writers who ponder women's desperate efforts to live, the spectral presences that inhabit families and homes, the ghosts of national history. With their share of assailed, stranded, and frightened individuals, Dickinson's poems also conceive an American woman's narrative that, as in Spofford's tale, bespeaks both threat and allure.

In chapter five, I argue that an examination of specific vital objects associated with Dickinson—such as the 1846/1847 daguerreotype (and other photographic images that are speculated to be of Dickinson) and the white dress—illuminates the longtime and ongoing process of composing the Emily Dickinson persona. The creation of an Emily Dickinson persona revolves around the central matter of how we "see" her and thus how we "compose" her. The daguerreotype, thus, is a fitting object and trope for this process. Nineteenth-century perspectives of early photography often emphasized mystery and magic: Commentators fostered the view that the new visual technology could conjure a "living presence" and could reveal obscured or intangible parts of a person. The mythologizing effect of various portraits of Dickinson (or of women who might be Dickinson) and of her white dress mirrors the history of Dickinson studies, a history that has itself combined facts and fantasies and has presented an Emily Dickinson (or many Emily Dickinsons) who remains elusively and complexly perceived.

This condition of uncertainty—which is also common in the poems—undermines trust in empirical evidence and puts forward the jostling alliance between what is known and what is unknown. In her poems, Dickinson's faith in different angles of vision, in indirection and obliquity, in shadows and parts, conveys these perplexities of seeing and knowing.

The epigraph for this introduction, "Ne'er saw I such a wondrous scene — ," comes from the poem "There is a morn by men unseen" (F13), in which Dickinson's speaker revels in the magic of dance and song. As discussed in each of the chapters, tropes of performance have shifting, twisting significances, the singing and dancing that infuse Dickinson's verse presenting invitations to contemplate matters that are difficult to apprehend. In this poem, the speaker explicitly informs us of what she has not seen and "may never name." The vision described—"maids" (and later "People") dancing, singing, and frolicking upon a "mystic green"—can readily be understood in religious terms, the "unseen" world a paradisal afterlife. Since the speaker may "never name" (or know) such an idyllic heaven, the scene of delights also reveals her expected deprivation, even if, in the fourth stanza, the speaker states that she awaits a new "morn," "fantastic bells," "other dells," and a "different dawn."

While the poem seems to invoke faith in or hope for a merry eternal life, confidence in the existence of such a heaven does not comply with the religious doubt and critique that Dickinson expressed so frequently in her writing or with the spiritual concerns sometimes expressed by others about her (at Mount Holyoke Female Seminary, she was apparently considered a lost cause, declared a "No-hoper" by Mary Lyon [Sewall 2: 360–61]). Recognition that Dickinson was not a pious person or a believer in orthodox Christianity expands the possibilities of what "unseen" realms are being conjured. Dickinson often mixes images of otherworlds with the present world, and she has many poems that combine references to biblical stories with current times and earthbound situations, for example, "A transport one cannot contain" (F212), "I've known a heaven like a tent" (F257), "I took my power in my hand" (F660), "It makes no difference abroad" (F686), and "Title divine is mine!" (F194). The word "unseen" might hint at something hidden, disguised, ignored, or not recognized.

As with other Dickinson poems, what might initially seem light-hearted can quickly shift into other registers. The scene portrayed in "There is a morn by men unseen" is one of holiday "gambol[s]," but images of so-called holidays and of play can be peculiar and disturbing in her poems. In one well-known poem, a speaker observes school children who "strove / At Recess" (F479), their play evidently requiring labor and diligence; in another poem, a wry speaker tells us that "We" would "play on Graves" if there were only more "Room" and if the ground were less sloped (F599); in another, a group of revelers ends up in "Jail / For a Souvenir" (F1220); in another, the feeling of "Terror" is described as unleashed on a "Gay, Ghastly, Holiday" (F341). Toward the end of "There is a morn by men unseen," the speaker mentions "far — fantastic bells." Bells, too, in Dickinson's writing can signal varied states. Bells are rung in recognition of war battle victories, but those with a "paler luck," like the speaker, hear "fewer Bells" (F704). In the poems, some bells are connected to disorder and rowdiness (F355, F1220, F1618) and to loss and pain: "The mixing Bells and Palls — // Makes Lacerating Tune — " (F722). In one alternative phrase in "One joy of so much anguish," the "Bells of Day" ring in accompaniment to the painful "Dirks" of birdsong (F1450). In her poems, as in life, there are bells of celebration and bells of mourning, church bells and clock bells, sleigh bells, bells rung at carnivals, fairs, and circuses, and bells played by musicians on other stages of popular entertainment. Perhaps the poem resonates with all of these dimensions. The poem projects into a possible fun-filled future, but in 1858 (the date of the poem) the nation is in turmoil. Despite the lighthearted scenes of music and pleasure, the unseen future is likely one of a more solemn and unsettled kind.

My observations about "There is a morn by men unseen" return me to another poem and my contention that what can be read as a charming and gentle (even if dramatic) depiction of a natural landscape can also be read as something far more menacing. While it might be comfortable to read the poem "Like mighty foot lights burned the red" as a tribute to the seasons, the poem recalls other Dickinson poems in which catastrophes are conveyed through natural imagery: soldiers in battle "dropped like Flakes" and "dropped like stars — / Like Petals from a Rose — " (F545); in "The name of it is 'autumn,'" the earth itself bleeds and "Scarlet Rain" falls on women's "Bonnets" (F465). In the introduction to *The Dickinsons of Amherst*, Benfey emphasizes that Dickinson lived in an historical moment and in a community and in a family: "She did not live in some cloistered haven of social ignorance, perpetual renunciation, and repressed sexuality. She lived, instead, in a grown-up and recognizably modern world of passion and flawed marriages, abortion and adultery, financial difficulties and debt" (6).

How to understand Emily Dickinson? How does one commune with her creative spirit? She has often been positioned in a small domestic space, or even insistently perceived there, lauded for bread-baking and quaint ways, placed in a bedroom or in a white dress, locked into a 2¾ inch by 3¼ inch daguerreotype frame. Even if one perceives Dickinson as a recluse attached to her home, this need not simplify our views or understanding of her. Private spaces are not simple. Notwithstanding Victorian ideals of the domestic sphere of comfort, love, and piety, there is a long history of the home as the site of all manner of surreptitious, illicit, and unholy doings. While not ignoring the home as a private theatrical space of performance and entertainment, recognizing the appeal to Dickinson of many forms of popular culture allows us to situate her and examine her in the context of the "recognizably modern world," which in her lifetime experienced national and social upheavals and transformations.

The wondrous scenes envisioned through the productions of popular culture represent and critique that world, too, displaying a nation's struggles and anxieties through its many forms of entertainment and exhibitions, putting forward seemingly endless variations of the enchanting and the anomalous: singers, dancers, and revelers as well as demons, ghosts, and monsters. Studying some of the day's popular theatricals, especially those forms that Dickinson herself was most drawn to or participated in, does not explain her, although recognizing her enjoyment in and engagement with a number of different forms of popular culture helps us to see her differently and, I think, more fully. Dickinson's alignment with the tropes and narratives of popular culture turns a light on provocative shimmering blends of fact and fiction, revealing and dramatizing what is difficult to see, know, and tell.

CHAPTER ONE

EMILY DICKINSON'S AMERICAN MUSEUM

Is it an animal? Is it human?
❦ Newspaper advertisement for the exhibit "What Is It?" in London, 1846

Only when there is an Other can you know who you are.
❦ Stuart Hall

She is a sister of Mr. Dickinson, & seems to be the climax of all the family oddity.
❦ Mabel Loomis Todd in a letter to her parents, 1881

There is always one thing to be grateful for — that one is one's self
& not somebody else.
❦ Emily Dickinson to Thomas Wentworth Higginson

An advertisement promoting P. T. Barnum's American Museum describes some of the "living curiosities" that could be viewed in 1860 for a mere twenty-five cents: "the celebrated AZTEC CHILDREN," a "Man-Monkey," and two "WHITE NEGROES." This advertisement for what was arguably the most famous of popular family entertainments in the nineteenth century suggests that Barnum's American Museum, filled with wonders and oddities (over 850,000 of them if one can believe the ad), specialized in exhibiting icons of cultural Otherness ("Living Curiosities"). The particular kinds of curiosity or Otherness announced by this advertisement emphasize racial paradox, the allure of the exotic, and the puzzlement of human categorization. Other attractions focused on all manner of physical variation, some of which specifically questioned gender definition (such as bearded ladies) and others that generally tested the limits of possibility for bodies, both human and animal (such as dwarfs, giants, and alleged mixed-species animals).[1]

From his earliest days as a showman, Phineas Taylor Barnum was interested in marketing wonder and transgression. A visitor to his American Museum could witness strange and improbable scenes: an armless woman serving tea, a "Two-Headed Girl" singing harmonies, and a "negro turning white" (Barnum, *Struggles* 544). One of his most enduring exhibits, entitled "What Is It?" presented a biological puzzle: Is it human or animal?[2] Although many attractions straddled categories or were labeled "nondescripts" to entice visitors with their ambiguity, the overt, even spectacular, transgression of many of those exhibited provided opportunity for shaping definitions and reinforcing norms. Barnum's American Museum specialized in the riddle, offering almost endless variation of the same questions, while suggesting that such questions were mysterious, illusory, tricky: What is a white person? What is a "Negro"? A human being? What is alien? What is normal and ordinary?

Emily Dickinson ponders the same sorts of questions in her poetry, which one might think of as a poetry of exhibition. Her poetic performances as man, bride, corpse, queen, child, and many others demonstrate that, as with the "attractions" in Barnum's shows—whose bodies often exceed the parameters of the "normal"—she is not restricted by apparent physical boundaries. Dickinson's assumption of multiple personae suggests that she can be anything or anyone, whether female or male, human or animal, mortal or divine. The ostensible ease with which Dickinson acts such a varied repertoire intimates that every pose—every identity—is surprisingly familiar for Dickinson, even if also marked as extravagant or alien. While Dickinson's impersonations can exude dramatic grandeur—to play the queen, the giant, the god—her unrestrained posing sometimes slips into the realms of the haunted or monstrous. Dickinson's speakers are, for instance, sometimes "mad." As one gazes into the cosmorama of the poems, one views scenes of the majestic and the marginal, of the ecstatic and the agonized. Here the speaker is a Goliath ("A Giant — eye to eye with you" [F301]); here she is a vanishing point ("It would have starved a Gnat — / To live so small as I — " [F444]); here, a titled proprietor ("who am the Prince of Mines" [F597]); here, a person suffering physical impairment ("Before I got my eye put out" [F336]). In her poetry, Dickinson rehearses the spectacle of a permeable identity and practices a continuous interrogation of self through the performance of roles that seem genuinely to express her own self while manifesting identities that are, on the surface at least, other than her. Is it fair to say that Dickinson imagines who she is by imagining who she is not? Is it fair to say that Dickinson places herself on exhibition in her poems?

By exploring the phenomenon of exhibition, as practiced in particular in the public arena of P. T. Barnum's American Museum and the traveling circus, one begins to notice potential affiliations between the theatrics of popular entertainment in nineteenth-century America and the theatrics of Dickinson's verse. The kinds of exhibition developed by Barnum operated to create a clear, observable image of the Other— a sensational Other that was somehow fixed even in its ambiguity, demeaned as it was applauded. Even the few brief examples cited illustrate how dramatically these popular forms of spectacle are racially inflected, and how they were directly employed to theatricalize issues that emanated from the intense social struggles of the day, such as the designation and comprehension of race, the clarification of gender roles and rights, and the attribution or denial of citizenship. The poetry of Emily Dickinson sets forth the same drama as it produces and projects the kinds of tensions seen in Barnum's shows. Dickinson, like Barnum, muses on the puzzle of identity as she traverses the borders of the comprehensible, although Dickinson's attention to the transgressive body—and her identification with it—suggests that the line separating the normative from the alien is more permeable for her than it would appear to be for Barnum.

While Barnum's American Museum was the most famous of the dime museums, these entertainment venues flourished throughout the country in the nineteenth century. Andrea Stulman Dennett discusses the dime museum as the most prevalent form of recreation in nineteenth-century America, identifying eight dime museums in Boston alone. The most significant was Moses Kimball's Boston Museum and Gallery of Fine Arts, which opened in June 1841, six months before Barnum's American Museum, and which exhibited attractions similar to those promoted by Barnum in New York, although Kimball's eventually became known for its theatrical productions. Ostensibly an educational and wholesome form of family entertainment, dime museums were hugely popular through the second half of the nineteenth century, their eclectic exhibits and live performances ensuring the capacity to puzzle and amaze those who entered their halls.

It is a curiosity in itself how frequently those exhibited on a Barnum stage were either non-Western people or U.S. people of color. The slave woman Joice Heth enacted one of Barnum's riddles—a visual enigma that affirmed an intimate link between the nation and race while undermining that connection. In July 1835 at the age of twenty-five, Barnum first heard about Joice Heth, purported to be a 161-year-old slave and former nursemaid to the infant George Washington. Upon hearing of a business opportunity involving Heth, who was already on exhibit in Philadelphia as "one of the greatest natural curiosities ever witnessed," Barnum went to that city to see her and to make inquiries of R. W. Lindsay, her current manager (Barnum, *Life* 148). Apparently satisfied by a 1727 bill of sale for a fifty-four-year-old Joice Heth and by Lindsay's story placing her at the birth scene of Washington, Barnum "determined if possible to purchase [her]," which he did for one thousand dollars (Barnum, *Life* 149–51).[3]

One of the anomalous (and captivating) elements of Joice Heth's story, of course, is that an African woman—a slave woman—is tied closely to the familiar origins of the new American republic. As the woman so strangely honored on the exhibition stage as the one who raised George Washington, she not only assumes the status of true patriot, but also, in effect, gains eminence as the mother of the father of the country. In addition, the marvel of her ostensible age seems a physical rendering of the fame that immortalizes her in her close association with Washington. In his 1855 autobiography, Barnum describes his first impressions of Joice Heth's appearance: she is immobile, paralyzed in her "lower limbs," permanently bent, blind, toothless, and seemingly helpless.[4] What is the significance of associating a woman of this description with the celebrated figure of American patriotism? Exalted and trivialized at the same moment, Heth appears as different from

General George Washington as she could possibly be: black, female, enslaved, disabled, and impossibly old. An incarnation of the devalued and dismissed, Joice Heth exemplifies, in composite form, everything undesirable in nineteenth-century America, as scholar Rosemarie Garland Thomson asserts (59). In calling her "the quintessential American freak" (59), Thomson emphasizes Heth's exclusion from American cultural norms. The extremeness of Heth's persona emphasizes how different she is from "America," even if "America" is dependent on her.

The mystery of Joice Heth intensified when she appeared in Boston in 1835. An anonymous letter appeared in a local newspaper asserting that Heth was a hoax, a "humbug," a mechanical contraption: "A curiously constructed automaton, made up of whalebone, india-rubber, and numberless springs" (Barnum, *Life* 157). The letter succeeded in drumming up business, as people returned with renewed curiosity to the exhibit to determine her constitution. Intended as a publicity ploy, the charge that "Joice Heth is not a human being" (Barnum, *Life* 157) did impart some truth; perceived and presented as a money-making opportunity, a slave, a machine, or a puzzle, Heth was not thought of as a human being at all. Comprehended as alien, her very humanness was questioned from the moment she was placed on exhibition. Made famous by her juncture with the consummate American, she herself was fabricated into something foreign and aberrant.[5]

Barnum's "What Is It?" exhibit became another famed icon of cultural Otherness. Although several incarnations of the character appeared over several decades, the exhibit always posed a racial query—a racial image—that was tied inextricably to the question of humanness. Barnum distanced himself from the first attraction labeled "What Is It?" at a show that was quickly closed in London in 1846 because it caused such protest, but it became a standard act after 1860 at Barnum's museum (and later in his circus).[6]

Many scholars point to William Henry Johnson as the person who assumed the role of "What Is It?" for Barnum in 1860.[7] Johnson would continuously play the part for more than sixty years, embodying a character described in a caption of an 1860s Currier and Ives lithograph as a combination of "ORANG OUTANG" and human, "captured in a savage state in Central Africa"; by the turn of the century the character had transformed into "Zip," a more clownish version.[8] Johnson, born around 1840, was probably a black man from New Jersey. A very short man with microcephaly, he appeared with his small head shaved except for a topknot, grinning, grunting, never speaking, wearing a fur suit; whether he was mentally impaired or not is a matter of disagreement.[9]

The "What Is It?" exhibit seems to have been designed to denote "blackness" although the advertised controversy over the character did not concern race; rather, the debate hovered over determination of his species. Grounded in the claim that he was "discovered" in Africa, the presentation of "What Is It?" suggested that he—like his place of origin—must be a mystery, a savage and subhuman entity. Despite scholar James Cook's argument that "What Is It?" was a "racially undefined persona" (148), the designation of him as African remained constant even when the specific locale shifted (Lindfors, "'Hottentot Venus'" 96, and "Barnum" 22). The American Museum pamphlet describing the figure also details the "peculiar" shapes and placements of features, cited to confirm the ambiguity of his species: the pamphlet likens virtually every part of his body to those of an "Orang Outang" (head and skull, arms, legs); only the "lower part of the face" (excluding the jaw and teeth) and the heel of the foot are identified as "native African" (Lindfors, "Barnum" 21–22). In effect, "What Is It?" fashions a spectacle out of a black American man. He is identified as a native of Africa and advertised as a deviant possessing the anatomical structure of a wild animal. The anonymous author offers a bold proclamation regarding "What Is It?": "He has been examined by some of the most scientific men we have, and pronounced by them to be a CONNECTING LINK BETWEEN THE WILD NATIVE AFRICAN AND THE BRUTE CREATION" (quoted in Lindfors, "Barnum" 22, and Saxon, *Barnum* 98–99).

Perhaps it is inevitable that figures that allegedly blur the distinction between human and animal and that are purported to be "missing links" would appear during a period of growing interest in theories of evolution alongside the 1859 publication of Darwin's *Origin of Species*.[10] The fascination with "man-monkeys" also invokes the pro-slavery arguments of men such as Josiah Clark Nott, who, in his efforts to classify blacks and whites as separate species, professes that the anatomy of the Negro, especially the African, is closer to an ape's than a human's (223–24). Other nineteenth-century ethnologists validated views of black people as beasts. In his study of the "Families" that comprise the Ethiopian race, Samuel George Morton, for example, describes some Africans as the lowliest of animals, unclean, unclothed, "savage and degraded," living in "mud hovels, bushes, caves and clefts in the rock" (90–91). The trope of "Africa" served as a sufficiently distant shorthand for referring to the alien, the unclassifiable, the not-wholly-human—in short, the freakish—and all of this became a metaphor for black people in America.

Another category of so-called living curiosity in Barnum's museum consisted of people with physical disability—people without arms or legs, for example—or people with extreme body variation, "giants" such as Anna Swan, the Giantess of Nova Scotia, and little people, such as General Tom Thumb, Commodore Nutt, and the Lilliputian King.[11] Barnum also exhibited conjoined twins such as Chang and Eng, who appeared for six weeks in 1860 and were celebrated as the original Siamese twins, and Millie-Christine, the Two-Headed Nightingale, slaves who sang in harmony and danced ("Sketch of the Life"; Kunhardt et al. 144–47; McNamara, "Congress of Wonders" 224; Fitzgerald 521). Bearded women and girls, including a very young Annie Jones billed as "the Infant Esau," so-called living skeletons, and tattooed men appeared alongside groups of Native Americans, who would demonstrate war dances and scalping techniques (Barnum, *Struggles* 543–44; Bogdan; Harris; Kunhardt et al.; Saxon, *Barnum* 100–104). In 1884 Barnum realized a longtime dream of assembling a "Congress of Nations" for which he procured male and female "specimens" of "all the uncivilized races in existence," or, in other words, persons identified as non-Western or non-white: Zulus, Australian aborigines, Sioux Indians, Polynesians, Hindus, Burmese, Chinese (Adams 175–85; Kunhardt et al. 296).[12]

In the Lecture Room of the American Museum, physical anomaly and non-white racial identity were similarly exoticized. Since physical

variation was perceived as oddity, non-white people and physically disabled people of any race or ethnicity were juxtaposed and equated,
and together they came "visually" to "signify absolute alienness," to
cite Thomson's language (17). In Barnum's museum show and later in
his circus, the identity of many performers was fixed in abnormality.
Even if the ascribed identity was not quite human, even if the identity
was pronounced indeterminate, even if the identity was fabricated—
or perhaps because of these things—it was imperative to designate
race, ethnicity, or gender in some way, as a corollary or as an explanation. According to Homi Bhabha, this "process of *ambivalence*" is
the process of creating the Other (18). The production of ambiguity
and judgments of anomaly, repeatedly reinforced by Barnum, allowed
visitors to the American Museum to entertain a fantasy of Otherness
from which they could dissociate themselves. Referring to the English, Stuart Hall proposes that the purpose of such fantasy is to define
the norm of oneself: "They have to know who they are *not* in order to
know who they are" (16). One could say that Barnum made a career
of producing visual images of the "alien." One could also say that Barnum's multitude of examples reveals more than a fascination with the
extraordinary. Even if his process of designation relied on ambiguity
and even if an identity could be labeled only "nondescript," it was important to name—and apparently display—the allegedly undesirable
and abnormal.

DICKINSON'S AMERICAN MUSEUM

Like the performers that Barnum exhibited, the "body" that Emily
Dickinson imagines in her poems could be called transgressive. A
phenomenon of transformation, a liminal site of possibility, a scene of
fragmentation and fusion, Dickinson's metamorphosing poetic body
exceeds every boundary.

Numerous scholars have examined or remarked on the conspicuous
array of personae that appears in the poems.[13] Dickinson's speakers
don all variety of female costumes (bride, schoolgirl, maid, housewife,

madwoman, nun, and more), and they sometimes identify as male—a boy or man, an "earl," "prince," or "czar."[14] A speaker acts the soldier, appearing on a battlefield, surrounded by "Piles of solid Moan" (F704). Elsewhere she deliberates a "Woman — white" (F307) as well as "The Ethiop within" (F415). As suggested above, she (or he) often wears a crown or assumes a royal station, for instance, as queen. In addition, her religious guise comes in many styles: a "Wayward Nun" (F745), the "Empress of Calvary" (F194), a skeptic, a heretic. The speaker "wear[s] the 'Thorns' till Sunset," temporarily crucified (F267); in a poem that tabulates the causes of grief, the speaker contemplates "the fashions — of the Cross" (F550). Disillusioned with a paternal deity, Dickinson's speakers themselves assume the status of creator and authority, visionary and sacrifice.[15] Even animal personae appear regularly: the speaker names herself "a Sparrow" (F121), "Rhinoceros / Or Mouse" (F736), a "fainting Bee" (F205), not to mention the scores of poems in which the speaker identifies with animals—leopard, deer, antelope, worm, spider, bird, and butterfly. Hundreds of birds populate the poems.[16] Like a ventriloquist's, Dickinson's voice seems ubiquitous—it issues from a sparrow; it rises from beyond the grave. Joyce Carol Oates considers that "after a point, it was not possible for Dickinson to speak except by way of a persona" (818). In a letter to Thomas Wentworth Higginson in June 1869, Dickinson muses, "It is difficult not to be fictitious" (Letter 330).[17] Perhaps one can only be amused by Dickinson's comment, reported by Higginson in a letter to his sisters after meeting Dickinson for the second time in 1873: "There is always one thing to be grateful for — that one is one's self & not somebody else" (Leyda 2: 213).[18]

The determination and eclecticism of such imposture inevitably tenders the question: What does the "body" signify for Dickinson? Despite her apparent claim to Higginson, the poems depict the difficulties in enunciating and classifying a self: Dickinson not only crosses identities, but also consolidates them. That is, while the poems document a dispersal of self, they also create an endlessly conjugated identity: the speakers are feminine and masculine, human and animal, gigantic and petite, alive and dead, mortal and infinite, wounded and preternatural. Through her skills as an impersonator or contortionist,

Dickinson creates an unclassifiable hybrid creature. If, through her poems, she evokes incongruity, if she is unrestrained by the boundaries of the body, if she eludes classification, if she becomes a riddle, then she is not so different from the extraordinary exhibits of the nineteenth-century dime museum.

Dickinson creates a fantasy of power and dominance as well as one of diminution, debasement, and death. She enacts roles that are distinct from the actual Dickinson, such roles as a man or a bride, and that are often illustrative of the normative, the privileged, or the powerful. Conversely, she simulates an excess of roles that emphasize the speaker's depreciated state. The speaker is so tiny at times, the smallest in the house, no larger than a bird or a daisy. "Crumbs — fit such little mouths — ," one speaker modestly assents (F195), and others exhibit all manner of impairment—helplessness, blindness, madness.[19] These roles avow the poet's kinship with the disempowered. Moreover, her repertoire of conventional female roles—schoolgirl, bride, wife— forcefully demonstrates not security within heterosexist norms, but rather the unorthodoxy of Emily Dickinson. The combination of roles that, on the one hand, brandish fictitious status and authority and, on the other hand, portray a diminished presence underscores Dickinson's teetering pose.

In short, all points signal the Other for Dickinson. The ongoing relationship in the poems between the powerful and the marginal is less a contrast of dual fantasies and more a reinforcement of the speakers' (and Dickinson's) subordinate status. Hall's keen point that "the Other is not outside, but also inside the Self, the identity" (16) speaks acutely to the elasticity of Dickinson's poetic identities as well as to the unusual directness with which she assumes personae that connote marginality. One might perceive Dickinson as continuously testing and representing the extent of her and her personae's dispossession.

The spectacle and conundrum, the drama and wonder, the transgression and Otherness rehearsed in Dickinson's poems find a popularized representation in the mélange of Barnum's American Museum. Consider the poems: the myriad animals, giants, little people, ghosts, monsters, captives, corpses, and disabled figures that inhabit them.

Consider, too, the gender ambiguity, the haunted chambers, the voices from the dead, the titles of high station, the battle scenes, the weaponry, the religious drama, the tableaux of wonders and miracles, the riddles so characteristic of Dickinson's verse: the poems comprise Dickinson's own American Museum. Note that Barnum's museum included an assemblage of sensational novelties: snakes, collections of insects and butterflies, an aviary, menageries, "living curiosities," mind-readers, mesmerists, ventriloquists, magicians, impersonators, escape artists, gender-ambiguous people, contortionists, knife-throwers, "chambers of horrors," waxworks, trick mirrors, a rifle and pistol gallery, war enactments, "moral theater," and plays based on biblical narratives. By 1863 it was possible to create the illusion of spectral figures on the stage, so ghosts appeared in a number of plays produced at Barnum's Lecture Room (Saxon, *Barnum* 105).[20] One can easily see parallels between the content of Dickinson's poems and the acts performed on Barnum's stages. One might even think of the individual poems as attractions, tableaux, or enactments, each occupying a separate platform, the entire collection of 1,789 poems (Franklin's count) resembling a museum of wonders and curiosities.

The popular entertainment of the nineteenth century—exemplified by Barnum's American Museum—and Dickinson's verse performed similar culture work. With their shared store of tropes and in their respective venues, each sponsored exhibitions that tested and mimicked a nation's anxieties about itself: the prolific display of attractions and poems that confront mysteries of the monstrous, dangerous, and different also ponder the ostensible boundaries of the normative. In other words, in nineteenth-century America, what counted as normal and what as aberrant? What was human and what was savage? Both Dickinson and Barnum persistently addressed the apparent conundrums of identity as well as invigorated transgressive possibilities for bodies.

While it is ultimately unimportant whether Dickinson visited Barnum's museum (or similar sorts of entertainment venues) or patronized the dime museum's incarnations as the traveling circus and menagerie, circuses did stop in Amherst during the spring and summer. In fact, some of the biggest circuses and menageries of the time passed through Amherst: Rockwood and Stone's Mammoth Circus in 1845, Welch and Mann's Mammoth National Circus in 1846, Van Amburgh's Menagerie in 1846, Raymond and Waring's Menagerie in 1847, Welch's National Circus in 1852, the Circus of Niblo and Sloat in 1860, Lent's Great National Circus in 1861, G. F. Bailey & Co.'s Great Quadruple Combination! in 1866, the Great North American Circus in 1873, Maginley's Circus in 1874, Van Amburgh and Company's Great Golden Menagerie in 1868 and in 1877, and Frost's Roman Circus and Royal Colosseum in 1877.[21] At least one traveling menagerie appeared in South Hadley when Dickinson was a student at Mount Holyoke Female Seminary. Writing to her brother, Austin, in October 1847, Dickinson reports that a traveling menagerie was in town and that "the whole company stopped in front of the Seminary & played for about a quarter of an hour" (Letter 16). Barnum himself delivered public lectures throughout the Connecticut Valley in mid-December 1852, events that apparently excited much interest, as an extra train was scheduled to carry Amherst residents to Belchertown to hear Barnum, and his appearance in Northampton drew one of the largest crowds that had ever gathered in the town hall (Lombardo, *Hedge Away* 27–28).

The circuses and menageries that moved about the countryside in the spring and summer transported grand assemblages of exotic animals—elephants, lions, tigers, leopards, zebras, monkeys—as well as trained horses and dogs, acrobats, jugglers, rope-walkers, equestrian daredevils, contortionists, and clowns. One of the main attractions of George Bailey & Co.'s Great Quadruple Combination! was a "Colossal HIPPOPOTAMUS! The Great Antediluvian Wonder and 'Behemoth' of Holy Writ," as advertisements for the show proclaimed. Maginley's Circus and Menagerie exhibited a trained rhinoceros. Van Amburgh's Great Golden Menagerie claimed to offer "the Largest, Most Varied and Comprehensive Collection of Rare and Curious Beasts and Birds in America."[22] In the 1850s, Spalding and Rogers's North American Circus blazoned its "moving musical palace" the Apollonicon as "the greatest Musical Invention of the Age." A combination of pipe organ and parade wagon, the Apollonicon was pulled by a team of forty

ornately adorned horses and produced the music of "a vast reposi-
tory of over One Thousand distinct Musical Instruments, having more
power, compass and precision than a band of Fifty Musicians."[23] In
addition to these headlining attractions, most circuses had sideshows,
that is, entertainments and exhibitions in small canvas tents near the
"big show." The sideshow included the kinds of curiosities that dime
museum proprietors such as Barnum displayed—people with bodies of extraordinary physical variation, "missing links," collections of
snakes, "monstrous" animals, and novelty acts such as sword-swallow-
ers. Blackface minstrel entertainers also performed in the sideshow;
Carl Wittke is among those who have noted that "there was scarcely a
circus, a street fair or a patent medicine show which did not carry one
or more blackface performers among its entertainers" (64–65).[24]

We know that Dickinson loved the novelty and excitement that
accompanied the circus. When George F. Bailey and Co.'s Great Quadruple Combination! was in town in 1866, Dickinson wrote to Mrs.
J. G. Holland: "Friday I tasted life. It was a vast morsel. A circus passed
the house — still I feel the red in my mind though the drums are out"
(Letter 318). In a letter to cousin Frances Norcross a few years later,
Dickinson mentions watching the cavalcade of the Great North American Circus into the early morning hours as it made its way through the
streets of Amherst on its way out of town (Letter 390). The extravagance
of the grand procession as it came into town (and, later, the chance for
last glimpses of its extraordinary sights as it departed) undoubtedly
drew many townspeople to windows and streets. The arrival of Raymond and Waring's Menagerie at ten o'clock on a Wednesday morning
in August 1847 was heralded by a "Gorgeous ROMAN CHARIOT literally covered with Gold!! and drawn by Ten Magnificent Black Horses!"
An advertisement in the *Hampshire and Franklin Express* declared that
"The Chariot will be followed by THIRTY CARRIAGES, Containing VARI-
OUS ANIMALS IN THIS EXHIBITION, drawn by ONE HUNDRED HORSES!"
("Raymond and Waring's"). Similarly, Lent's Great National Circus
paraded through Amherst with a "Golden Dragon Band Chariot Drawn
by a LONG LINE OF CREAM-COLORED STEEDS" in its Grand Expositive

Procession ("Lent's"). The entrance of Van Amburgh and Co.'s Great Golden Menagerie into town offered the promise of thrilling sights and sounds: as described on an 1868 broadside, the Great Golden Chariot led the way, "drawn by Ten Splendid Horses, richly and elegantly harnessed, and gaily plumed and caparisoned," and carrying "PROF. KOPP'S GOLDEN OPERA BAND, who will render a choice selection of Musical Gems from the most celebrated masters, interspersed with the most popular and favorite airs of the day." The chariot was followed by the Great Golden Car of Egypt, "a magnificent mass of golden splendor—modeled after ancient Egyptian designs, and constructed on a scale of magnificence hitherto unprecedented." Riding atop was "AN AFRICAN LION, LOOSE! Entirely unchained and free from any restraint whatever, except the alert and watchful eye of his keeper." This was followed by a series of dens and cages drawn by "ONE HUNDRED AND FIFTY-EIGHT HORSES, the finest and most symmetrical the world can produce or that money can purchase, and forming by no means the least attractive feature of the GRAND HOLIDAY CORTEGE!" (Van Amburgh).[25] Recalling that "every one went to and gloried in the circus" in Amherst, Mac-Gregor Jenkins projects Dickinson's particular pleasure in it:

> The circus traveled, at that time, over the road, and its arrival and departure were moments of delirious delight to every boy in town. But no boy, haunting the circus field from the moment of its arrival to the midnight hour of its departure, was more thrilled by it than Miss Emily. It passed her father's door either going or coming, and there was a delightful uncertainty about it. On circus night she sat up all night lest she miss it, peering from her darkened window and listening intently to hear the first sound of its approach. I like to think of her watching the creaking vans file by in the gray of dawn. The closed and silent wagons, with men and women and beasts in them, going slowly through the village streets, while a little woman in white sat at an upper chamber window and gloated in the suggested romance of the road and this nomad life, a romance enhanced by the morning twilight and the stillness of a country village as it slept. (131–32)

In a letter of July 1, 1853, to her brother, Dickinson makes reference to a hippodrome and museum in Boston that Dickinson seems to have expected her father to have visited (or at least heard about) on his recent visit to Boston. Dickinson intimates disappointment that her father did not report on these entertainments ("and he came home so stern that none of us dared to ask him"), although she also remarks that she would not discuss the hippodrome in front of her grandmother: "besides Grandmother was here, and you certainly dont think I'd allude to a *Hippodrome* in the presence of that lady! I'd as soon think of popping fire crackers in the presence of Peter the Great!" (Letter 130). Dickinson specifically says she wants a report on the hippodrome from Austin when he gets home. In the July letter, Dickinson does not specify, but the hippodrome must refer to Franconi's Colossal Hippodrome, which arrived with much fanfare on June 27 and had a twelve-day run at the Public Garden in Boston. The newspapers were full of stories about the great spectacles of the hippodrome—its "Restoration of the Festivals, Games, and Amusements! Of the Ancient Greeks and Romans"—as the show travelled throughout Massachusetts. On June 8, 1853, the newspaper *National Aegis* announced the arrival of the hippodrome in Worcester that morning:

The bills promise a great outside display of chariots driven by Amazonians in full costume, richly dressed cavalcades in which

Figure 1. Broadside for Van Amburgh & Co's Great Golden Menagerie, the Great Moral Exhibition of the Age, in Worcester, Massachusetts, 1868. Courtesy of the American Antiquarian Society.

31

Figure 2. Broadside for the North American Circus, in Springfield, Massachusetts, 1850. The advertisement appeared in the *Daily Republican* (Springfield), on May 27, 1850. Wood engravings by Thomas W. Strong. Courtesy of the American Antiquarian Society.

all the pirncipal [sic] horsemen and horsewomen appear: a train of camels, elephants, ostriches, and a wilderness of monkeys also make up a part of the pageant. The most prominent feature, however, will be the "Car of the Muses," containing some seventeen life size Golden Statues, which we are told are modeled with most exquisite art. ("The Hippodrome": 2)

Many other news stories reported on the sensational sights and excitement of the show, such as this account in Boston's *Daily Evening Transcript,* which notes the appearance of 140 performers and 80 horses: "Franconi's beautiful horses will exhibit their fleetness and agility in chariot races, tournaments and steeple chases; assisted by elephants, ostriches, gladiators, gymnasts, and jugglers" ([Franconi's Hippodrome] May 2, 1853). Worcester's *National Aegis* reprinted a story from the *Hartford Times* that recounts the thrill of the horse races and the "bold and fearless" female riders, "their long hair streaming behind them" ("The Hippodrome" June 8, 1853: 3). The papers also reported on "unfortunate accidents" in the chariot races and horse races, many involving women riders (although a story in the *Boston Post* and a report in the *San Francisco Evening Journal* on September 8, 1853, claimed that the deaths of the young women at the hippodrome shows were faked) ([Hippodrome, Boston] September 8, 1853).[26] With its collection of exotic animals, its fearless Amazonian women, its tales of daring, danger, injury, and tragedy, the hippodrome was another type of spectacular show of which Dickinson was well aware.

Considering Dickinson's fascination with the circus and other spectacular shows, it is not surprising that she would directly refer to traveling shows, menageries, circuses, and theatricals—or intimate these types of entertainments—in several poems. Although references to popular entertainment might initially seem out-of-keeping with a less worldly view of Dickinson, the trope of the circus or theatrical— the "show"—registers her attentiveness to earthly wonders and to the otherworldly. In addition, to the extent that a circus or traveling show conjures another reality—something fantastical, enigmatic, elusive— it stands as a fitting conceit for Dickinson's concerns with transcendent states and spiritualized spaces.

In a poem from about early 1861, for instance, Dickinson relies on circus imagery to express the power of "transport." Mingling the worldly and the otherworldly, Dickinson contemplates bizarre and exciting scenes.

> A transport one cannot contain
> May yet, a transport be —
> Though God forbid it lift the lid,
> Unto it's Extasy!
>
> A Diagram — of Rapture!
> A sixpence at a show —
> With Holy Ghosts in Cages!
> The *Universe* would go!
>
> (F212)

Perhaps the most startling image in the poem is the one of "Holy Ghosts in Cages." Depicted as if they were wild animals or carnival attractions similar to the "nondescript" creatures that Barnum and other showmen exhibited in chains or cages, Dickinson's Holy Ghosts mix the sacred and the secular: the line correlates the rapturous speech and feeling provoked by the presence of divine spirit with the speaker's euphoria (and perhaps more generally with a poet's paeans). One can appreciate the relevance to a poet of stories that commend ecstatic fulfillment and the extraordinary ability to speak languages as on the day of Pentecost (Acts 2:1–6). In biblical accounts, the Holy Ghost materializes in recognizable forms, such as a dove or flames; Dickinson's representation is even more earthly. In her poem, spirit is made mundane (even if spectacular) through its rendering as a carnival attraction as well as through its imagined plurality. The peculiar image of Holy Ghosts oddly enough elicits the same sort of queries as do the "curiosities" in dime museums and circuses: Are they dangerous or helpless? Wild or tamed? Aberrant or ordinary?

The nineteenth-century circus itself augmented the spectacle of its processions with depictions of biblical narratives. The side panels of circus cages and wagons would sometimes be decorated with painted illustrations of some of the more astonishing Bible stories, such as Jonah and the whale or Daniel in the lions' den. Advertising itself as "the Great Moral Exhibition of the Age," Van Amburgh's Golden Menagerie, for example, paraded "vans, dens and cages" decorated with "Illustrations of Holy Writ" painted on their side panels. Such a promenade recalls the production of the medieval mystery plays in which stories of the Old and New Testaments were dramatized atop a series of pageant wagons— one specific story performed on each wagon—that moved to assigned locations around a town throughout the day (or over several days). The performance of the mystery plays—such as the Corpus Christi plays— drew large crowds for communal celebration as well as for religious instruction, the occasion marked by the pomp of the pageant wagons, festival, and high mirth (Kolve 134, 268–69, 270). Noting that "a carnival atmosphere reigned on days when mysteries and *soties* were produced," Bakhtin describes the importance during medieval times of pageants, theatrical processions, fairs, and parish feasts with their "open-air amusements, with the participation of giants, dwarfs, monsters, and trained animals" (5). One can see that the array of spectacle and living wonders, animal acts, and acrobatic entertainments connected with the mystery plays of the thirteenth and fourteenth centuries foreshadowed the nineteenth-century circus, as Marian Murray proposes (60–69). The decorated wagons of a nineteenth-century circus procession, which Dickinson would have seen from the window or from the street, rendered stories from scripture on their painted panels. While the combination of religious drama and community amusements is clearly not novel to the nineteenth century, and the overlay of religious iconography would have had business purposes (dressing the circus as moral entertainment would likely draw larger crowds), the mixing of circus fantasticalness with stories of religious faith still raises a provocative question: What unexpected wonders might the circus reveal? In addition to the painted panels, circuses promoted a moral and educative purpose by including quotations from scripture on circus broadsides: George F. Bailey and Co.'s Circus, for instance, quoted passages from the book of Job in its advertisements for its "Great Antediluvian Wonder"—the hippopotamus: verses such as "He is chief of the ways of God" (Job 40:19) and "Upon Earth there is not his like" (Job 41:33) promoted the great hippo as the revelation of a prophecy and more generally exalted in the revelation of scripture made possible through the circus.

Through its reference to Holy Ghosts and words such as "transport," "Extasy" and "Rapture" in her "A transport one cannot contain," Dickinson too insinuates that something astonishing is revealed through the circus. A corollary to the questions of human identity so persistent in Barnum's exhibitions, the poem stretches the query to comprehension of the divine: Are these caged Holy Ghosts dangerous or helpless? Are they wild or constrained? What sort of "transport" is both caged and uncontainable? Possibly, Dickinson laughs at the affiliation of the circus with biblical narratives, relishing in the apparent joke that ricochets between sacred texts and a world that celebrates the variousness of earthbound creatures and human ingenuity. The poem, however, conveys an excited wonder through its vocabulary of "Extasy" and "Rapture" and through its four exclamation points, as if the speaker (and Dickinson) were bedazzled by the circus marvels before her and enjoying the ironic display that would pretend to capture the divine (such as through painted illustrations on a circus wagon) in order to reveal it.

About eleven years later, Dickinson assigns the status of performer to her "Neighbor."

> The Show is not the Show
> But they that go —
> Menagerie to me
> My Neighbor be —
> Fair Play —
> Both went to see —
>
> (F1270)

According to this poem, no distinction exists between the museum attractions and the person viewing them. In her study of the dime museum, Dennett notes that the arrangement of displays at Barnum's museum (and at other dime museums) ensured that the patrons would necessarily observe each other while viewing the exhibits (5). Dennett may be correct in proposing that the museum exhibits "affirmed the common person's worth and restored his dignity" (5), although the encouragement to watch or even study those in attendance turns the museumgoers themselves into curiosities. In her poem Dickinson seems to share Dennett's observation. Compressing the elaborate narratives and extraordinary spectacles of the museum exhibition into six restrained lines, Dickinson alludes to the most remarkable and dramatic roles for herself and her neighbors. As oddities, puzzles, or marvels, "they that go" step into transgressive space where the self and carnivalized Other merge. The word "Menagerie" in line three more directly names them all as exotic or wild animals, collected and kept for exhibition, an image reminiscent, too, of the caged Holy Ghosts in "A transport one cannot contain." The conjugation of viewer and viewed implies also a conflation of worlds: The circus world permeates the ordinary world, scenes of wonder blend with the everyday, the mysteries of the carnival stage recur everywhere.[27]

In an 1862 poem that deliberates the creation of the exotic,

Dickinson also imagines the experience of the alien, in this case represented by a leopard.

> Civilization — spurns — the Leopard!
> Was the Leopard — bold?
> Deserts — never rebuked her Satin —
> Ethiop — her Gold —
> Tawny — her Customs —
> She was Conscious —
> Spotted — her Dun Gown —
> This was the Leopard's nature — Signor —
> Need — a keeper — frown?
>
> Pity — the Pard — that left her Asia!
> Memories — of Palm —
> Cannot be stifled — with Narcotic —
> Nor suppressed — with Balm —
>   (F276)

Here, the leopard models the quintessential Other, characterized by its dark color (noted three times—"Tawny," "Spotted," "Dun") and by its origins in Africa and Asia, a homeland both expanded and conflated in a way reminiscent of the simultaneous expansion and conflation of races by some nineteenth-century historians and ethnologists.[28] Perceived by civilization as wild, dangerous, inferior, different, the creature needs to be controlled, held in the custody of a "keeper." The poem presents opposing perspectives: that of a "civilization" that "spurns" the leopard and that of an Africa (or "Ethiop") that esteems her. "Civilization" ignores the leopard's richness—her variety of "Gold" and "Satin"; Africa appreciates her fineness. "Civilization" regards the leopard as subordinate; Africa values the "Leopard's nature." The information that the leopard "left her Asia" implies that she was taken, perhaps captured, perhaps stolen. And her current circumstance is similarly suspect: Is she held in captivity? Caged in a zoo? Marketed in a show? She seems appreciated by so-called civilization only in a commodified form. The representation of the leopard resonates both with the ostensible "freaks" exhibited in Barnum's shows and with African slaves in America, the latter an association Daneen Wardrop makes in her discussion of this poem ("'That Minute Domingo'" 80–81).[29]

The figure of the leopard also bespeaks the spectral presence of Dickinson. The speaker, for instance, identifies with the leopard. Her query "Was the Leopard — bold?" suggests she knows from personal experience that a female may suffer for her boldness, an intimation supported by another poem of about the same time in which the speaker, "twice as bold," "Was all the one that fell" (F660). In addition, the leopard, specifically female, possibly invokes the grim condition of white women in nineteenth-century America. Consider the many ways in which white women of the nineteenth century were "spurned," so to speak, by the legal and judicial system; deprived of economic and educational opportunity and divested of civil rights, women were proclaimed "civilly dead" in the 1848 "Declaration of Sentiments" authored by several women, including Elizabeth Cady Stanton. The human attributes of Dickinson's leopard gradually emerge through the poem, and the final lines emphasize the leopard's consciousness of her extreme divestiture: "Memories — of Palm — / Cannot be stifled — with Narcotic — / Nor suppressed — with Balm— ." She will always know her loss. With her anthropomorphized leopard, Dickinson inverts the presentation of Barnum's circus freaks: the animalized human is here a humanized animal. So carefully contrived as foreign, savage, captive, Dickinson's animal-human hybrid becomes a literalizing translation of the promotional narratives and stagings that proposed that certain museum and circus performers—such as "What Is It?"—resembled wild animals in appearance and behavior. A representation of the carnival attraction, of the African slave, and of the nineteenth-century white woman, Dickinson's leopard compresses multiple exoticized Others.

In contrast to the representation of the "Tawny" leopard, another poem of about 1862 ("The Malay took the pearl") sets forth whiteness as a sign of racial Otherness. Curiously, one might conjecture that whiteness emerges as a primary object of scrutiny in Barnum's museum: The many acts that presented people of color and non-Western people as impaired or stigmatized argued for the desirability and normality of whiteness. However, what of the many acts that presented whiteness itself as the enfreaking quality? In 1864, for example, Barnum introduced the so-called Circassian Beauties, women said to be the purest examples of the Caucasian race, the whitest whites.[30] Apparently willing to engage in slave-trafficking, Barnum sent his assistant John Greenwood Jr. to Constantinople to locate and purchase the women, renowned for their beauty, although Barnum does not acknowledge any actual transaction (*Struggles* 578–81).[31] Barnum promoted the Circassian Beauties as ideals of white womanhood, but also as Circassian slaves who had been freed from Turkish harems. Hence, the display generated tension between images of the emancipated and of the captive: the women were both free and commodified, both admired and enfreaked, both white and Other.[32] As models of Victorian white womanhood, the Circassian Beauties stood for purity, chastity, delicacy; the women, however, were also dressed and posed to accentuate the erotic and exotic (Frost, "Circassian Beauty" 257), and their characteristic bushy hair made these white women seem foreign, even wild and "primitive." Linda Frost contends that the Circassian Beauties' hair "would have resonated for contemporary audiences with images of African and tribal women circulating in the culture" ("Circassian Beauty" 259).

Barnum also presented persons he termed "White Negroes," described as albino children with black parents; as albino families, the most renowned being the Lucasies, billed as being of "black Madagascar lineage" (Kunhardt et al. 113); and as a "Leopard Girl."[33] In 1850, he advertised a weed purported to turn black skin white. While promoting the weed as the solution to the problem of slavery in the country (he suggested that as black skin disappeared so would slavery), Barnum exhibited the black man said to have discovered the weed; local New York papers regularly reported on changes in the man's skin color (M. R. Werner 204), such as in the *New-York Daily Tribune* "business notices" on August 13, 1850: "His arms are quite white already, and his hands show the dark skin now peeling off. He has a rare cosmetic to cure slavery." In this world characterized by excess, relentless promotion, hoaxes, and outright lies, black was conceived as alien and so was white.

In Dickinson's "Malay" poem, whiteness and blackness, conjoined and compressed, both bear the sign of troublesome difference.

> The Malay — took the Pearl —
> Not — I — the Earl —
> I — feared the Sea — too much
> Unsanctified — to touch —
>
> Praying that I might be
> Worthy — the Destiny —
> The Swarthy fellow swam —
> And bore my Jewel — Home —
>
> Home to the Hut! What lot
> Had I — the Jewel — got —
> Borne on a Dusky Breast —
> I had not deemed a Vest
> Of Amber — fit —
>
> The Negro never knew
> I — wooed it — too —
> To gain, or be undone —
> Alike to Him — One —
>
> (F451)

Two of the key figures in this script of longing and fear are racially marked—the "Dusky" Malay and the white "Pearl." A racial designation in the nineteenth century, the Malay was ranked as inferior, associated with the African by some ethnologists (Jeffries 9; Hannaford 207–8). Samuel George Morton's account of the Malay "Family," brown-skinned people who established themselves throughout Southeast Asia, depicts them as people to be feared and distrusted: "They possess an active and enterprising spirit, but in their temper are fero-

cious and vindictive. Caprice and treachery are among their characteristic vices; and their habitual piracies on the vessels of all nations,
are often conducted under the mask of peace and friendship" (56–57).
Morton's sources testify that the Malay are "remorseless cannibals"
who eat their victims alive (57).

Dickinson's poem encompasses these views of the Malay. The Malay
in the poem is certainly active and enterprising, managing to carry the
"Jewel" far away from the speaker, who can only lament the loss and
disdain the culprit. The Malay's apparent obliviousness ("The Negro
never knew / I — wooed it — too — ") and alleged indifference ("To
gain, or be undone — / Alike to Him — One — ") could certainly
make him seem capricious or treacherous. Described as "Swarthy"
and "Dusky," this character and his hut are coded as barbarous—both
distant, foreign, different, primitive. The insinuation of force and theft
mark "The Negro" as dangerous.

While the second figure in this drama, the Pearl, is notably inert—
hidden, taken, carried—it implicitly offers something precious. The
Pearl may be inanimate, but it inspires extreme passions. Commodify-
ing the image of the loved one as a pearl arguably objectifies the body,
although its commodified form is such that anyone would appreciate
its high value. One might think of the "pearl of great price" (Matthew
13:45–56), equated with a heavenly kingdom, or recall the "orient pearl"
that Shakespeare's Antony sends to Cleopatra with his own promises
of "kingdoms" (1.5.40–47). Dickinson, too, provides other images of
valuable pearls in her poems, pearls whose attainment would require
great sacrifice or courage, if attaining them were even possible.[34]

Does the whiteness of the Pearl add to its value? Its sharp contrast
to the color of the Malay, insistently dark, suggests that the Pearl's
white color is significant.[35] Does the contrast imply that the Pearl
stands in opposition to the Malay? Curiously, the presentation of the
Pearl is as ambiguous and disturbing as that of the Malay. The Pearl is
courted; the Pearl is captive. Whether "Jewel" or "Destiny," adornment
or merchandise, the Pearl is and remains an object of exchange. In addition, although the Earl, like the Malay, covets the Pearl, it represents
something intimidating, even incomprehensible, to him. An emblem

of fear and fascination, the white Pearl, much like the Malay, stymies the speaker.

A few scholars have correlated the Earl-Pearl-Malay triangle of the poem with a love tangle involving Dickinson, suggesting that the black Malay stands for the man who blocks Dickinson's access to a beloved woman.[36] One can accept postulations that identify either Austin Dickinson or John Anthon as Dickinson's rival (John Cody 185–258; Farr, *Passion* 147; Patterson, *Riddle* 260–61), although perhaps the more vexed query concerns the depiction of the perceived sexual rival as a racial Other. Here again, as in nineteenth-century popular entertainments, the image of the racial Other insinuates something ambiguous and dangerous, a puzzle verging on the alien or inhuman, a test of the borders of the "normal" and comprehensible. The racial naming in "The Malay took the pearl" perhaps observes a comparably uncontained difference, not just Emily's difference from Austin, as Farr suggests (*Passion* 149), but also the "foreignness" of homoeroticism next to a heterosexual norm. In other words, the ungoverned racial Otherness of the Malay expresses the unnamed sexual Otherness of Dickinson's love for a woman.

If the poem discloses feelings that would be considered inappropriate at best, perhaps it is not surprising that the speaker's assertion of desire is matched by a confession of paralyzing fear: "I — feared the Sea — too much." While pearls are among the "small round objects" strewn throughout Dickinson's poems that scholar Paula Bennett connects with an assertive female sexuality (*Emily Dickinson* 172–73, 180), pearls are found in lakes, rivers, and seas; the variety and vastness of these bodies of water resonate metaphorically: the surface and depths of the feminine, the navigations of emotion, an engulfing or submerged sexuality, the vast and unfathomable divine, the unconscious, mystery, eternity. Suggesting that the Pearl stands for the "wholeness" Dickinson was seeking, Theodora Ward notes that the sea in this poem acknowledges the "depths she feared" (63). In her analysis of the poem, Farr associates the sea with various states of wonder and danger regarding the much-loved Susan (*Passion* 149–50). Importantly, the Malay will swim, but the Earl will not. The Earl may understand well the dangers of diving for the Pearl and swimming with it—the risk, for example, of being lost at sea or devoured by it. Perhaps cannibalism does make an appearance in the poem after all, in the apparent anxiety of being swallowed alive by the sea or in the circumstance of being consumed by desire. More broadly, the innuendo of alleged perversions hovers in the poem.

In "The Malay took the pearl," as elsewhere, Dickinson focuses on bodies that are not fully seen or valued, on bodies that are represented as excessive, on bodies that are labeled "different": non-white bodies, female bodies, bodies perceived as foreign, aberrant, transgressive. This poem creates a permeable line between white and black, between self and Other. Reminiscent of the intermingling of blackness and whiteness in Barnum's shows, in this poem "The Negro" and the white are conjoined not only in the narrative of adulation and pursuit, but also as mutual signs of a troublesome difference. In addition, the conflation of the racial and the sexual places both in the realm of the ambiguous, the uncomprehended, the threatening.

Dickinson's attention to these issues brings the drama of her poems close to a Barnum stage. Both Dickinson and Barnum participate in the cultural phenomenon of exhibition, displaying ostensibly transgressive bodies in order to grapple with the conundrums of human categorization that preoccupied nineteenth-century America. In attending to an astonishing variety of bodies through their respective theatrics, they each mime the nation's fascination with race, gender, and apparent puzzles of human identity. Both Barnum and Dickinson would seem to concur with Hall's observation that "only when there is an Other can you know who you are" (16), although they connect differently to his insight: Barnum aims to elucidate the "self" by exhibiting and viewing the Other; Dickinson imagines the "self" by acting the Other.

Naming and displaying "living curiosities" may have made Barnum the celebrated man of "a million wonders" (Saxon, *Barnum* 93), but they also performed culture work that must have seemed vital to many: containing fear of the foreign, guarding against difference, defining the norms of America. In line with Thomson's powerful argument that freak shows "symbolically contained the potential threat" of difference

(66), such manufactured Africans as Joice Heth or "What Is It?" stood for the quintessentially alien and embodied potential threat, although they were presented as utterly tamed and even helpless. Moreover, these acts, among others, represented a fantasy for the use of white Americans, that is, that one could apprehend "whiteness" by viewing "blackness." The capacity to define and identify blackness and whiteness related fundamentally to the most basic aspects of daily life: judgments regarding the normal, the human, the acceptable, the frightening, the barbaric, the dangerous, the terrifying, the mystifying, the desired. However, one can also credit Barnum's seemingly endless supply of human variation with promoting public debate concerning difference and normality. If Barnum participated in defining a nation's norms, his assembly of spectacular bodies helped to question as well as to shape those definitions. He invited the patrons of his American Museum to know what they were by seeing what they were not, but he extended, inevitably, the corollary invitation—to ponder that distinction and perhaps reconsider it.

While Dickinson, like Barnum, contemplates the mysteries and possibilities of human identity, unlike Barnum, she aligns herself with the image of the museum or circus curiosity. In naming and displaying a self, Dickinson points to stigmatized figures or diminished presences not only to express what has been culturally demeaned or unarticulated but also to explore her affiliation with the alien and fantastical. Like the riddles posed by Barnum's attractions, the composite portrait summoned by Dickinson's poems confounds easy classification, as does the historical Emily Dickinson, who swerves wide of the normative boundaries of nineteenth-century America, who was called "the climax of all the family oddity" by Mabel Loomis Todd (Leyda 2: 357). As both showman and curiosity, Dickinson uses the tropes common to popular entertainment—the circus, Africa, the exotic, the nondescript—to announce her personae (and implicitly herself) as well as to propose the convergence of self and carnivalized Other: Dickinson displays the anomaly of Victorian womanhood, the foreignness of homoerotic sexuality, the ambiguous status of whiteness, and her own elusive and incongruous poetic body.

CHAPTER TWO

DICKINSON, POPULAR MUSIC,
AND THE HUTCHINSON
FAMILY SINGERS

Emily with her dog, & Lantern! Often at the piano playing weird
& beautiful melodies, all from her own inspiration.
❦ Kate Anthon to Martha Dickinson Bianchi, October 8, 1917

How natural for music, as well as poetry, to be on
the side of humanity and the captive.
❦ "The Hutchinson Singers" in the *Liberator,* December 30, 1842

Music pervades Emily Dickinson's poetry—in the rhythm and meter of the poems, in her numerous references to melody and tune, and in the recurring images of musical instruments, including violins, trumpets, and flutes. The poems reverberate with singing and whistling, with the ringing of bells, and the distant tatting of drums. Dickinson expresses confidence in the revelatory and oratorical powers of music, her verse a "Translation — / Of all tunes I knew — and more — ," as she writes in poem F378. In another poem she asserts the integral presence of music and proposes a macabre proof for those who doubt: "Split the Lark — And you'll find the Music — " (F905).

While Dickinson's poems have long been related to the form of the Protestant hymn, I consider here the relevance of nineteenth-century popular music—as practiced both on the stage and in the home—to Dickinson's writing. Dickinson's interest in music was given a chance to develop when, as a child, she had instruction in both singing and playing the piano. In a letter to her brother, Austin, in the autumn of 1844, Dickinson notes that she attends Mr. Woodman's "singing school" and speculates that Austin, too, will want to attend when he returns from

Williston Seminary (Letter 4). The arrival of a piano—a Brazilian rose-wood pianoforte made by Hallet and Davis—that her father purchased for her when she was fourteen appears to have been a happy event of her youth: On September 25, 1845, Dickinson wrote to her good friend Abiah Root, "I am taking lessons and am getting along very well, and now I have a piano, I am very happy" (Letter 8).[1] About seven weeks earlier, Dickinson had first mentioned her piano in a letter to Abiah—inviting her to come practice on it—and announced that she was taking music lessons from her Aunt Selby (Letter 7).[2] Years later, Dickinson still refers to her piano, such as in an 1848 letter to Abiah in which Dickinson reports playing and singing "a few tunes" for her father on Thanksgiving evening (Letter 20), and implicitly in a letter, also to Abiah, in January 1852 in which Dickinson writes, "I thought to return to you so soon as tea was done, but father asked for some music, and I could not deny him" (Franklin, "Emily Dickinson to Abiah Root" 31). In the letter of April 25, 1862, to Thomas Wentworth Higginson, Dickinson offers a brief and demure assessment of her skill on the piano (Letter 261).[3] While Thomas Johnson states that "No reliable account of her play-ing has been preserved" (Note to Letter 7), some friends and relatives have noted Dickinson's abilities to compose and perform: Kate Anthon recalls that Dickinson improvised "weird & beautiful melodies" (Leyda 1: 367); Dickinson's niece Martha Dickinson Bianchi suggests that Dick-inson was a clever and proficient performer who played frequently in the evenings; MacGregor Jenkins, a childhood friend of Martha ("Mattie") and her brother Ned, similarly describes Dickinson as an enthusiastic pianist who would "thunder out a composition of her own which she laughingly but appropriately called 'The Devil'" (Jenkins 36).[4] During her seven years at Amherst Academy and one year at Mount Holyoke Female Seminary, instruction in music was a regular part of the cur-riculum (Lowenberg xix–xx; Cooley 11, 23; Sewall, *Life* 2: 365; Habeggar 195; Edmonds 35). In a letter to Abiah Root, Dickinson recounts her daily schedule at Mount Holyoke, indicating that most of the afternoon was devoted to music instruction and practice: "from 1½ until 2 I sing in Seminary Hall. From 2¾ until 3¾. I practice upon the Piano" (Letter 18).[5] In 1873, Dickinson praised the charismatic Russian pianist Anton

Rubinstein following a concert of his in Boston attended by her cousin Frances Norcross. Dickinson reportedly stopped playing the piano herself after hearing a pianist, perhaps Rubinstein, perform, "convinced that she could never master the art"—if one accepts the account of neighbor Clara Bellinger Green given fifty-one years after the conversation in which Dickinson apparently told her this (Leyda 2: 272–73).[6]

Dickinson attended few public music performances in her lifetime. In a letter of September 8, 1846, Dickinson writes to friend Abiah that she visited the Chinese Museum in Boston, and there heard a Chinese musician perform: "The Musician played upon two of his instruments & accompanied them with his voice" (Letter 13). In the same letter, Dickinson reports having attended two concerts: one, a performance of "secular music and songs" given by the Teachers' Class of the Boston Academy (on August 27), and the other, Haydn's *The Creation* (on September 3) (Leyda 1: 112). Dickinson seemed to enjoy a concert in Amherst of the Germania Serenade Band that she attended with her sister, Vinnie, and their cousin John Graves in April 1853 (Letter 118). A couple of years earlier, in 1850 and 1851, the celebrated Swedish singer Jenny Lind had traveled to New York, Philadelphia, Boston, Cincinnati, New Orleans, St. Louis, and several other cities on an American concert tour sponsored by P. T. Barnum.[7] Austin Dickinson attended one of Jenny Lind's concerts in Boston in June 1851; Emily herself saw Jenny Lind on July 3, 1851, in Northampton at a concert held in the "old church," as reported by the *Hampshire Gazette* on July 8 (Leyda 1: 205).[8] Dickinson described the event and stormy evening in a letter to Austin three days after the concert: "how Jennie came out like a child and sang and sang again, how boquets fell in showers, and the roof was rent with applause—how it thundered outside, and inside with the thunder of God and of men—judge ye which was the loudest—how we all loved Jennie Lind, but not accustomed oft to her manner of singing did'nt fancy *that* so well as we did *her*" (Letter 46).[9] George Boziwick reports that members of the Dickinson family attended performances of singers such as Henriette Sontag and Catherine Hayes, who were "celebrated" even if "eclipsed" by Lind's fame (138).

It also appears likely that Emily Dickinson heard the popular singing group the Hutchinson Family while attending Mt. Holyoke Female Seminary. Although Mary Lyon, the founder and principal of the school, would not allow students to attend a concert by the Hutchinson Family in South Hadley one evening, she permitted a performance by the Hutchinsons at the school the following morning. Amelia D. Jones, Mt. Holyoke class of 1849, records this episode with the Hutchinson Family as taking place during the 1847–1848 school year, describing it within a context of events that occurred during the third term that year (between May 11 and August 2, 1848). When Mary Lyon would not permit several students to attend a concert by the Hutchinsons at the town meeting house, some of the students were disappointed with her decision:

> A few said it was inconsistent in Miss Lyon to urge us to cultivate vocal music and then not let us hear any but our own. The Hutchinsons showed their good will by giving a serenade that night, yet the malcontents continued to grumble a little. Early the next morning, the young ladies on duty near the parlor passed the word that Mr. Hutchinson was calling on Miss Lyon and was probably giving her a piece of his mind for her disrespect to his family. Then even the murmurers took her part, for all knew that her judgments were right, and no one wished her to suffer reproach for our sakes. By the time she bade us good morning in the hall, ill humor had subsided and every heart was loyal.
>
> After devotions, Miss Lyon told us of her pleasant interview with Mr. Hutchinson in which he had kindly offered to give us a concert. Upon this a door was opened, the singers filed in, took their places on the platform, and for an hour entertained us in the happiest manner. All agreed that this was better than an evening out, and no face expressed more pleasure than Miss Lyon's. ("Memorabilia of Mary Lyon" 90–91)

While it is usual to associate the form of many of Dickinson's poems with the hymn measure and to identify the hymn-tune as a critical influence on Dickinson's verse, my interest here is in Dickinson's connections to particular types of popular music of the nineteenth century and in the relevance of popular music to Dickinson's verse.[10] While the correspondence of the metrical structures of the Protestant hymn to the meters of many of Dickinson's poems has been noted as evidence of the hymn's formative influence on Dickinson, the Protestant hymn is not the only kind of music written in these meters. The "hymn meter" (or common meter) and the variety of meters typical of the eighteenth-century and nineteenth-century hymn are the meters for much popular music.[11] Such nineteenth-century favorites as Stephen Collins Foster's "Old Folks at Home" and his "My Old Kentucky Home," Walter Kittredge's "Tenting on the Old Camp Ground," and the traditional "Auld Lang Syne" are all, for example, written in common meter (that is, in quatrains with a stress pattern of 4-3-4-3). "Old Dan Tucker," "Dandy Jim From Caroline," and "Home, Sweet Home" are written in long measure (quatrains with a 4-4-4-4 stress pattern).[12]

Dickinson's personal album of sheet music reveals that she had an avid interest in popular music.[13] While the Dickinson family library contained such songbooks as *The Psalms, Hymns, and Spiritual Songs of the Rev. Isaac Watts* (1834 edition) and Lowell Mason's *The Boston Academy's Collection of Church Music,* her personal collection includes many marches, polkas, and quicksteps in addition to songs such as "Yankee Doodle," "Bonnie Doon," and "The Girl I Left Behind Me."[14] The family library also had an 1865 edition of Thomas Moore's *Irish Melodies;* Dickinson's personal collection includes copies of individual songs from that much-loved anthology: Moore's "Believe Me, If All Those Endearing Young Charms," "The Admired Canadian Boat Song," "Araby's Daughter," and "The Last Rose of Summer."[15] She possessed the sheet music to songs composed by the celebrated English songwriter and performer Henry Russell,[16] and a copy of Henry Bishop's and John Howard Payne's phenomenally successful "Home, Sweet Home," a song that in the early 1850s became linked to Jenny Lind, identified as her trademark piece, and, starting in Washington, D.C.— the sixth city on her American tour—performed at every concert (Davis 117; Barnum, *Life* 342). Dickinson's collection includes selections from Michael William Balfe's 1843 opera *The Bohemian Girl,* including "I Dreamt I Dwelt in Marble Halls" and "Then You'll Remember Me," songs that gained wide attention as individual pieces.[17] In addition, Dickinson owned the music to some of the biggest hits of nineteenth-century blackface minstrelsy: "Lucy Neal," "Dandy Jim," "Lovely Fan" (later known as "Buffalo Gals [Won't You Come Out Tonight?]"), "The Blue Juniata," "Who's That Knocking at the Door," "Old Dan Tucker," and "The Jolly Raftsman."[18] Other songs in Dickinson's album, such as folk dances like "Fisher's Hornpipe" and "Durang's Hornpipe," became part of the minstrel dance repertoire in the 1840s and 1850s (Winter 233). In addition to the songs written and performed by Dan Emmett and William Whitlock (both of the original Virginia Minstrels), by Cool White (of the Virginia Serenaders) and others, another in her collection—Marshall Pike and L. V. H. Crosby's "Oh Give Me a Home If in a Foreign Land"—was performed by the Harmoneon Family, also a blackface minstrel group.[19]

Attention to these particular facts of Dickinson's life and interests steers us to a little-used vantage point from which to peer at her poems. Her own musical experience reveals that Dickinson pursued an interest in popular music, and she was aware of musicians and the music tied to the reform movements of her day as well as curious about songs that were part of the repertoire of minstrel entertainment. These two observations prompt a consideration of the influence of nineteenth-century popular music on Dickinson's writing, and in particular for this study, the association of the Hutchinson Family Singers with her poems. The association of Dickinson and her verse with popular musical entertainments of the nineteenth century suggests not only that popular music provided an influence on her forms but also that the social commentaries and public concerns dramatized in popular music were relevant to Dickinson's writing.

The presence of the Hutchinson Family Singers in Dickinson's musical experience—that is, the likelihood that she heard them perform at Mount Holyoke while a student there and the presence of four Hutchinson Family songs in her sheet music collection—is particularly interesting because of the Hutchinsons' prominent place in the social reform movements of the time. The Hutchinsons also performed in Amherst, Massachusetts, at least twice (in the later 1840s and in 1859) and likely more often.[20] Abolitionists and temperance advocates from Milford, New Hampshire, the members of the Hutchinson Family Singers—brothers John, Judson, Asa, and sister, Abby—first performed publicly in 1841, then under the name the Aeolian Vocalists. Renamed the Hutchinson Family Singers in 1842, the original quartet enjoyed their most flourishing celebrity through the 1840s, although the Hutchinson Family Singers in various configurations continued to perform throughout the rest of the nineteenth century.[21] Songs such as their "There's a Good Time Coming" and "Get off the Track" unmistakably declared the Hutchinsons' anti-war and emancipation views. Over three days in January 1843, the quartet sang at their first abolitionist meeting at Boston's Faneuil Hall in the company of William Lloyd Garrison, Wendell Phillips, Nathaniel P. Rogers, and Frederick Douglass. Their performance there of several songs including "The Negro's Lament" and "The Old Granite State"—the latter with the addition of "a series of stanzas" that brother Jesse Hutchinson reputedly composed "on the spot, while Phillips was speaking, embodying the leading arguments"—launched their career as social reformers.[22] First acquainted with Frederick Douglass in Lynn, Massachusetts, in 1841, the Hutchinsons appeared at many political assemblies with Douglass in America; during an eleven-month concert tour in 1845 and 1846, the Hutchinsons appeared together with Douglass many times in England and Ireland (Hutchinson, *Story* 1: 142, 145, 154, 156–57; Jordan 120–30; Foner, 117, 122; Hamm, *Yesterdays* 146–47, 149). In his *North Star* review of two recent Hutchinson Family concerts in Rochester, New York, in October 1848, Douglass describes the effect of the Hutchinsons' singing in a racially charged setting:

When we entered Minerva Hall, there was evidently some ill feeling towards the colored part of the audience, but as the glorious harmony proceeded, caste stood abashed—the iron heart of prejudice, pride and scorn, seemed to melt away, and the general expression of the audience, among white and black, confessed the truth of a common origin and a common brotherhood. We all looked and felt alike.

Singers "for freedom, for temperance, for peace, for moral and social reform," as Douglass wrote ("Introduction" xv),[23] the Hutchinsons sang for presidents in the White House (Tyler in 1844, Lincoln in 1862), for Union soldiers at army camps and hospitals during the war, and at labor meetings.[24] Champions of women's rights, the re-configured Hutchinson family groups of the 1850s started to appear in support of women's suffrage, sharing the stage with many of the day's prominent women's rights advocates: In 1853, for example, the Hutchinson Family (a grouping consisting of John, wife, Fanny, and "brothers") performed at the Methodist Church in Fall River, Massachusetts, on a program with Lucy Stone, who became a persuasive voice in enlisting their continuing service in the cause (Hutchinson, *Story* 1: 314, 316).[25] As popular as the Hutchinson Family Singers were, some critics thought that the Hutchinsons should restrict themselves to singing and stay clear of politics; some critics considered the Hutchinsons too "black" in their songs and interests and objected to the presence of the "colored population" in their audiences (Douglass, "Hutchinson Family"; Hutchinson, *Story* 1: 223–25; Gac 213–15; Jordan 143, 237; Roberts 357, 360–61).[26]

Although they were not blackface performers themselves, perhaps it is not surprising that the Hutchinson Family became associated with blackface minstrel groups, both as an early model—in the structure of the group and the harmonized singing style—and as a topic for parody in minstrel shows. Musicologist Dale Cockrell postulates that the Hutchinsons "provided the germinal concept for the development of the minstrel show" (152–53); in addition, they were viewed as a model for blackface performers who wanted to make themselves more widely appealing to northern audiences (Gac 202). Early blackface minstrel groups advertised themselves as singing in the "style" of the Hutchinson Singers, and minstrel groups were compared by reviewers to the Hutchinsons (Cockrell 152–53; Nathan 158).[27] Gac argues that even when the actual songs of blackface minstrel performers "continued

Figure 3. Engraved title page of "The Old Granite State." This lithograph by G. and W. Endicott of the original foursome of the Hutchinson Family Singers became a widely seen image of the group. This piece is in Emily Dickinson's "bound volume of miscellaneous sheet music," EDR 469, Houghton Library, Harvard University.

the racial characterizations of the 'rollicking minstrel show,'" images on sheet music covers in the mid-1840s increasingly resembled the "four well-dressed Hutchinsons, presenting a hint of propriety" (202).

The Hutchinsons performed many types of song—dramatic and sentimental ballads and comic numbers as well as political and protest songs. Acclaimed and denounced in the press wherever they appeared, the Hutchinsons were described variously as bona fide American singers, as fierce patriots committed to the political causes of liberty and equality, and as rabble-rousers who misused their notoriety and musicianship. While more than one reviewer offered the opinion that politics had ruined the Hutchinsons and railed against them for "foisting their Abolition songs upon audiences" ([Hutchinsons] March 27, 1845), Walt Whitman singled out the Hutchinson Family Singers as exemplary American Democrats in a review of December 5, 1846

(191–92), and Harriet Martineau described the Hutchinsons as "genuine Yankees" in her review of a London concert in February 1846. In his account of the Hutchinsons, printed in the *Daily Atlas* on June 25, 1846, William Howitt wrote that "the Hutchinson Family are exactly what Americans—the children of a young, bold republic—ought to be." A decade later they were still being lauded in the press as "the most popular singers in America" (*Bangor Daily Whig & Courier* January 1, 1855).[28]

The evidence suggests that Dickinson was interested in *them*. The Hutchinson songs that she owned were ones distinctively associated with this particular singing group: a song about the Hutchinson family, a song with which they opened or closed virtually every concert, three of their signature tunes, songs that directly addressed the incendiary issues of the times—war, slavery, emancipation—and which they performed in concert and at political gatherings. These songs are "The Old Granite State," "There's a Good Time Coming," "The Grave of Bonaparte," and "The Little Maid."[29] "The Old Granite State," one of the Hutchinsons' hallmark songs, either welcomed the audience or bid them farewell at nearly every concert. This was the practice of "the various tribes of the Hutchinsons for nearly fifty years," as Brink notes (66).[30] The Boston publisher Oliver Ditson issued the sheet music in late 1843 with a lithograph of the quartet by G. and W. Endicott on the cover that became a widely seen image of them. This was the version of the song that Dickinson owned. Dickinson also acquired the political "There's a Good Time Coming" (music by the Hutchinsons, words by Charles Mackay), another of the Hutchinson Family signature songs, published by Oliver Ditson in 1846. A third Hutchinson Family song appears to be one of the first pieces that Dickinson learned to play on the piano: In a letter to her good friend Abiah Root in August 1845, Dickinson specifically mentions practicing "The Grave of Bonaparte" on the piano, describing the song as "beautiful" (Letter 7). Composed by Lyman Heath (music) and Henry S. Washburn (lyrics), this song was one of the earliest performed by the group—while they were still known as the Aeolian Vocalists—and it became a standard in their repertoire (Hutchinson, *Story* 1: 296; Jordan 36–37). Heath was a friend of the Hutchinsons and sometimes performed with them in concert in the early 1840s (Cockrell, *Excelsior* xxix). Oliver Ditson published "The Grave of Bonaparte" (in 1843) and marketed it as one of the "songs of the Hutchinson Family" (Jordan 59–60).[31] The fourth Hutchinson Family song in Dickinson's collection is the ditty "The Little Maid," composed by Judson Hutchinson and published by Oliver Ditson in 1846.

These songs could have provided models and influences for Dickinson as examples of accentual verse and, just as important, as illustrations of musical meter or isochronism, which is a pattern of beats organized in equal measures of time.[32] The musical meter of each of the four Hutchinson songs is 2/4 time, two beats per musical bar, that is known as a ballad meter. The stress pattern of the lyrics of "The Old Granite State" is half meter (or trimeters: 3-3-3-3); the lyrics of "There's a Good Time Coming" are primarily common meter (4-3-4-3); those of "The Grave of Bonaparte" are long meter (or tetrameter: 4-4-4-4); "The Little Maid" is half meter. Many of Dickinson's poems match these metrical patterns. With meters as common to popular songs as to hymns, hundreds of Dickinson's poems (virtually all of them) have either four or three stresses per line.[33] I am not claiming that Dickinson wrote poems directly to the melody of "The Old Granite State" (or to any of the other Hutchinson songs or any particular song); I am proposing that the meter and rhythm of popular songs she owned and played, such as "The Old Granite State," would likely have found their way into her writing.[34]

In addition, some of Dickinson's most distinctive images and narratives resonate with these few songs by the Hutchinson Family. One notes the prominent references to graves, liberty, captivity, diminutiveness, desolation, yearning, and betrayal in these songs. "The Little Maid" tells a tale of determined wooing and unexpected deceit; the seemingly simple tune opens up a torrent of heartbreak. The smallness of the maid—the miniature dimensions of everything about her (bonnet, finger, ring, waist, blood, eyes, hat, hand, and so forth)—marks her as an elfin figure or as a child. Not only is the story of "the little maid" familiar to readers of Dickinson's verse, but she also echoes a tiny female figure who appears in many Dickinson poems: Dickinson summons "the smallest in the house" or the "little girl" locked in the closet, the petite unobserved figure, or in some poems, the "little maid" (F832, F200).[35] Repeated in nearly every line of the Hutchinsons' song, the word "little" is one frequently used by Dickinson. The little girl has been identified as a key persona by several scholars who propose varied but similarly paradoxical readings of its significance. In her examination of "strategies of reticence" in Dickinson's verse, Joanne Dobson argues that the little girl persona allows Dickinson, as it does other Victorian women writers, to express anger and defiance safely, although the child persona also suffers mistreatment, is "silenced, frowned at, shut out" (65–66, 68). Also noting contrary implications, Paula Bennett asserts that Dickinson "uses her smallness and insignificance ironically as a source of power" (*My Life* 49) even as she suggests that the little girl persona reflects Dickinson's sense of herself in the late 1850s and early 1860s as "abandoned, wounded, helpless, childlike" (48). Suzanne Juhasz posits that the "voice of the little girl" in Dickinson's verse offers duplicity, paradox, or the skills of legerdemain: "It can sound like one thing and reveal something else" ("Big Tease" 34; also see Mossberg 63–64, 147–55; Todd 1–93; and Wolff 178–200).

In the Hutchinsons' "There's a Good Time Coming," the confluence of tones—whereby the anguished meets the upbeat—is reminiscent of many Dickinson poems in its irony and texture. That the sunny times ahead remain always "a little" in the future in "There's a Good Time Coming" brings to mind the many Dickinson poems in which bliss or contentment is always just out of reach (as in "A pit but heaven over it" [F508], "'Heaven' is what I cannot reach!" [F310], "The nearest dream recedes unrealized" [F304], and "Victory comes late" [F195]). The four verses of the ballad "There's a Good Time Coming" imagine some future time of peace and liberty. Some have heard this song as a burst of cheer, as "perfectionist propaganda" (Moseley 719), or as a statement of "genuine faith in the inevitable progress of mankind" (Jordan and Kessler 18)—a mood created by a quick syncopated tempo and by the thought that "there's a good time coming." Others have emphasized the revolutionary prospect of the lyrics: "There's a Good Time Coming" was included in both William Wells Brown's *The Anti-Slavery Harp* (1848) and George W. Clarke's *The Harp of Freedom* (1856), both compilations of anti-slavery songs. Hamm notes that the song became a "symbol of [the Hutchinsons'] anti-slavery activity" (Hamm, Liner notes 6). The ostensible promise offered in the song is tempered by the repeated caution that we must "wait a little longer," a warning that occurs so often—twelve times in the song, three times in each verse—that it shapes the prominent mood of the song. While the lyrics imagine an end to many forms of violence, they also speak the cold possibility that "we may not live to see the day," news we are handed early in the song. Rather than a vision of a harmonious nation, the song expresses faith in certain tactics and virtues that may repair a splintered one: a belief that intelligence can quell the horrors of the time, that sound words—"the pen"—can vanquish slavery and the corruptions of religion, that a humble spirit can put an end to "slaughter." In short, the present moment that prompts the song is one of chaos, and though the song posits faith in good sense and good people, the "good time" never arrives. As the song tunefully reminds us, we must "wait a little longer." Just as in Dickinson's poem of 1863 in which she writes, "I many times thought Peace had come / When Peace was far away — " (F737), "a good time" may be not just out of reach but a long way off, the song's vision of a nation and world divested of "hateful rivalries of creed" and free of war largely fanciful.

Jesse Hutchinson's lyrics for "The Old Granite State," set to the melody of "The Old Church Yard," a hymn associated with the New England Millerites,[36] converted a song about the imminent coming of the Lord into one announcing the arrival of these singers from the mountains of New Hampshire. That "The Old Granite State" originated as a song that identified and characterized the Hutchinson family seems key, as Dickinson's possession of this piece of music suggests that she was indeed interested in this particular family of singers. The verses name all fifteen members of the family (thirteen children plus parents Jesse and Mary) as well as describe them as a "good old-fashioned" family, comprised of respectful children and supportive "aged parents." The song honors the bedrock of family, explicitly this family of musicians with their "wild mountain singing," and, by implication, the nation, since "we are all real Yankees." Therefore, when Jesse started to add abolitionist verses to "The Old Granite State" in 1843 and continued to amend the song with political verses over the years, the Hutchinson Family Singers' politics were being presented as the natural and respectable outgrowth of this solid American family. The version of the song in Dickinson's collection contains ten verses, verses seven and eight explicitly pronouncing the cause of emancipation, such as in the first part of verse eight: "Yes we're friends of emancipation / And we'el sing the proclimation / Till it echoes through our nation / From the 'Old Granite State.'"[37] In addition, composers other than Jesse Hutchinson rewrote "The Old Granite State," supplying it with a variety of anti-slavery lyrics: *The Harp Of Freedom* includes four songs that are rewritten versions of the "The Old Granite State," one of them even carrying the notation that the song was "to be sung at the close of anti-slavery meetings and conventions," following the Hutchinsons' own practice with their song. "The Old Granite State" was even pressed into service as a campaign song for Abraham Lincoln (Clarke).[38]

"The Grave of Bonaparte," too, presents its own curious mix of images and tone: Written just after a mission in 1840 to retrieve the remains of Bonaparte from St. Helena Island and return them to the banks of the Seine for burial, the song, full of tempests and dead soldiers, offers an Emperor Bonaparte who is more emblematic than historical. Similar in attitude to "There's a Good Time Coming," "The Grave of Bonaparte" evokes war's endless pit of dying and makes clear that any triumphs or glories of war are ephemeral at best. The song holds much in common with many of Dickinson's verses: the depiction of desolate battlefields and burying grounds, the mingling of victory and defeat, and the invocation of the dead through the natural world are seen in such Dickinson poems as "Success is counted sweetest" (F112), "They dropped like flakes" (F545), "My portion is defeat today" (F704), "The name of it is 'autumn'" (F465), "Whole gulfs of red and fleets of red" (F468), and "Victory comes late" (F195).

Why is it relevant that Dickinson knew of the Hutchinsons and had selections of their key repertoire in her personal album of sheet music? Perhaps, simply, Dickinson liked their songs. However, the presence of these Hutchinson Family songs suggests something more: that Dickinson was curious about—or perhaps felt kinship with—those who risk censure and safety in their creative expression. More than once, Dickinson sought out and associated herself with people such as Thomas Wentworth Higginson and Samuel Bowles who were passionately devoted to social causes that were at the heart of American life and the nation's struggles for freedom and justice. Interestingly, the Hutchinsons were also personally acquainted with Higginson, appearing with him at political meetings and conventions and, over the years, becoming friends (Hutchinson, *Story* 1: 492; 2: 30, 372), and possibly with the gregarious Bowles, with Cockrell's note in *Excelsior* suggesting that the newspaper editor who talked about "slavery concerts" with the singers after a performance in Hartford in 1844 may have been Samuel Bowles (258). Her interest in the Hutchinsons fortifies a view of Dickinson as aware of public events in the nation: like them, she "sang" about freedom and captivity, courage and vision.

Did the presence of the Hutchinson Family Singers in her life help Dickinson forge her poetic voice? The many points of contact are suggestive. The symmetry of the Hutchinsons' music—their four-part harmonized singing style as well as the repetitive structures of some songs, for example—would have been a familiar musical style for people of the church tradition in nineteenth-century America. At least some of their songs were performed in a style recognized and accepted by white protestant Americans, and this familiarity may have enhanced the singers' credibility with audiences. In noting the Hutchinsons' musical affiliation with the "hymns and anthems of the New England churches," Hamm describes the frequently heard (and sung) church music of composers such as Lowell Mason and George Webb: "The most widely sung pieces in such collections [of sacred music], the music the Hutchinsons—and millions of other American families—sang at home and in church, were simple, symmetrical, diatonic tunes harmonized with the most basic chords. This was the music that established the musical vocabulary and largely defined the musical taste and tolerance of most white, Protestant Americans in the North, East, and Midwest" (*Yesterdays* 159). The Hutchinsons' singing style also included elements outside the hymn style, such as a "call and response" pattern (evident in "The Old Granite State" and "Get off the Track") and solo voices, such that their music can be understood to bridge the hymn style and a more popular style of nineteenth-century music.[39] Dickinson's use of meters that call to mind hymn meters also crosses into more popular and secular forms of expression through her tropes, ideas, and irregularities of verse form. The Hutchinsons and their songs were potential models for her meters, and, more than that, living illustrations for Dickinson of how to engage a world of struggle in lyric. Throughout their careers—in the original quartet of the 1840s and the various re-configured Hutchinson Family groups through the rest of the nineteenth century—the Hutchinsons signified resolve, strength, emancipation, and justice. Their voices were the vehicle for many courageous stands. A voice of courage breaks forth so importantly in Dickinson's verse, often a singing voice that declares, defiantly and triumphantly, its right to be heard. In one poem of about 1865, the speaker boldly announces, "Bind me — I still can sing — " (F1005). In another poem of the same year, a brave bird sings from its "Heart" and produces a startling blood-soaked "Tune": "Sang from the Heart, Sire, / Dipped my Beak in it, / If the Tune drip too much / Have a tint too Red // Pardon the Cochineal — " (F1083). In an earlier poem, the speaker asserts that she "shall keep singing!" and confides that she "shall bring a fuller tune" (F270).[40]

As noted earlier, the Hutchinson Family Singers have been associated with the rise of the blackface minstrel troupe. While several of the Hutchinsons' songs were claimed by others for the minstrel repertoire, one of the blackface minstrel pieces in Dickinson's album has important connections to the Hutchinson Family. In 1844 Jesse Hutchinson wrote new lyrics to Dan Emmett's "Old Dan Tucker," metamorphosing one of the most popular blackface minstrel numbers into the most provocative of their political songs, "Get off the Track."[41] The eleven verses of the song depict emancipation as a "majestic" railroad car traveling throughout America, picking up speed. The song cajoles politicians, ministers, and others who may want to block the train's progress to "get out of the way" or to "jump on board" while, as stated in verse seven, "All true friends of Emancipation, / Haste to Freedom's Rail Road Station" (Jordan and Kessler 335–37). One can appreciate the audacity in converting the popular blackface minstrel number into a rousing cry for emancipation. It is a song that evoked strong reactions whenever the Hutchinsons performed it. In his account of a performance of "Get off the Track" at the Boston Anti-Slavery Society meeting in May 1844, Nathaniel P. Rogers "exults" over "these matchless anti-slavery songsters":

> Their outburst at the convention, in Jesse's celebrated "Get off the track," is absolutely indescribable in any words that can be penned. It represents the moral railroad in characters of living light and song, with all its terrible enginery and speed and danger. And when they came to the chorus-cry that gives name to the song—when they cried to the heedless pro-slavery multitude that were stupidly lingering on the track, and the engine "Liberator" coming hard upon them, under full steam and all speed, the Liberty Bell loud ringing, and they standing like deaf men right in its whirlwind path,—the way they cried "Get off the track," in defiance of all time and rule, was magnificent and sublime. They forgot their harmony, and shouted one after another, or all in confused outcry, like an alarmed multitude of spectators, about to witness a terrible railroad catastrophe. . . . It was the cry of the people, into which their over-wrought and illimitable music had *degenerated,* and it was glorious to witness them alighting down again from their wild flight into the current of song, like so many swans upon the river from which they had soared, a moment, wildly into the air. The multitude who had heard them will bear me witness that they transcended the very province of mere music—which is, after all, like eloquence or like poetry, but one of the subordinate departments of humanity. It was exaggerated, sublimated, transcendent song. God be thanked that the

Hutchinsons are in the anti-slavery movement—for their sakes as well as for ours! (Hutchinson, *Story* 1: 117–18)

The response was not always so ecstatic. In an editorial in the *Brooklyn Daily Eagle* on December 5, 1846, Walt Whitman records that the song provoked jeers when the Hutchinsons sang it in concert the evening before (191–92).[42] Some newspapers in New York and Boston and elsewhere took issue with the song, denouncing its "trashy words" and urging the Hutchinsons to stop performing it.[43] Finson notes that the performance of "Get off the Track" sometimes provoked theater riots (122–24).[44]

Dickinson apparently did not own "Get off the Track," but she did have the music to the tune that the Hutchinsons used: "Old Dan Tucker," published in 1843 by Chas. H. Keith and marketed as part of "Old Dan Emmit's [*sic*] Original Banjo Melodies." Dickinson's first-edition copy of the music identifies the version "as sung by the Virginia Minstrels" (and the sheet music cover lists the names "Emmit" [*sic*], Brower, Whitlock, and Pelham, the original members of the Virginia Minstrels).[45]

As both an enormously popular blackface number and a song re-born as an anthem of emancipation, "Old Dan Tucker" is a fascinating piece of music to find in Dickinson's collection.[46] First, consider the character and story of Old Dan Tucker: A first-rate mischief-maker, Old Dan Tucker comes to town periodically, and when he does, one would best "get out de way." Part fun-loving ("He use to ride our darby ram"), part disruptive ("I hear de noise an saw de fight"), Old Dan Tucker instigates trouble: his antics agitate and cause problems, in particular for Old Dan Tucker's friend, the slave who narrates the tale. The appearance of Old Dan Tucker forecasts disorder, although his crimes remain on the moderate side: the narrator reports that Old Dan Tucker was a "hardened sinner," who "nebber said his grace at dinner"; he recounts that "Old Dan Tucker an I got drunk / He fell in de fire and kick up a chunk." Some scholars describe Old Dan Tucker in various unflattering ways: Cockrell sees Old Dan Tucker as "stupid, horrendously ugly, with no refinement at all (in fact he has animal characteristics), and is violent, drunk, and oversexed" (*Demons of Disorder* 156); Finson calls him "a primitive backwoodsman" even while acknowledging his "awesome abilities" (178). Despite being "endowed with comical magic," Old Dan Tucker, according to Ronald L. Davis, remains "a vagabond, laughed at and scorned by his people" (217).[47] In Dickinson's 1843 version of the song, however, Old Dan Tucker materializes as something more mystical and powerful: a conjured figure of rebellion. The narrator's relationship to Old Dan Tucker is mostly helpful and pleasing to the narrator; they are friends, and the narrator clearly enjoys the commotion that comes with Old Dan Tucker's company. At points in the song these two characters virtually converge, such as in verse six: "I went to town to buy some goods / I lost myself in a piece of woods / De night was dark I had to suffer / It froze the heel of Daniel Tucker." In another verse, the narrator breaks "Massa's" pump so "Dar was work for ole Dan Tucker." In the opening lines of the song, the narrator comes to town on the same night as Old Dan Tucker. One wonders if Old Dan Tucker inspires the narrator to break the master's pump. Is it the mutinous spirit of "Old Dan Tucker" that prompts the slave to stay out all night in the woods? Eric Lott gleans an innocent joviality in the song, which, he writes, "conveys the inspired abandon of childhood" (*Love and Theft* 144). While I appreciate Lott's sense of the exhilaration unleashed by Old Dan Tucker, the spirit that is conjured seems rather than the carefree exuberance of children, to be one of sabotage and revenge. Old Dan Tucker embodies an energizingly subversive possibility: he encourages an ongoing disruption of the normal order of daily life, without apparently endangering himself in any significant way. What could be more appealing or useful for someone who might want to defy an authority or combat an oppressive situation? That the melody of "Old Dan Tucker" was enlisted in the cause of emancipation, not only by the Hutchinsons with their "Get off the Track" but also by other writers of anti-slavery songs, would seem to make plain the rebellious energy as well as the threat of tumult lurking in the song.[48]

This is a spirit that Dickinson appreciated and cultivated. Many of her poems shine with a gleam of mischief and with outsized (even joyful) defiance. The speaker of one poem announces that "A Glee possesseth me" (F381); in another the speaker imagines breaking out "in wilder song" (F176). A plucky upstart recognizes that her power may be limited, but declares that she is "twice as bold" (F660). In a poem of about 1869, the speaker prefers "my little Gipsey being" and "little sunburnt bosom" to a more refined demeanor (F131), while another young woman celebrates the revelry of "maids" who "Employ their holiday" and, each morning, "wait thy far — fantastic bells" (F13). A playful narrator, who says that she and the Bee "live by the quaffing," cheerily dangles the question, "Do we 'get drunk'?" (F244). The children Dickinson describes "storm the Earth And stun the Air" (F1553). They "caper when they wake" (F127) and freely "play upon the green" (F79). Dickinson honors "The sacred stealth of Boy and Girl" (as well as their "happy guilt") (F1583). Some Dickinson poems exactly fit the long meter (the 4–4–4–4 stress pattern) of "Old Dan Tucker"—such as "Split the lark and you'll find the music" (F905) and "I met a king this afternoon!" (F183)—but perhaps of more interest is the consideration that the spirit of Old Dan Tucker lives in some poems, her "Little Tippler" an enraptured "reeling" version of the drinking, devilish, larger-than-life agitator, her barefoot "czar petite," a youthful rendering of a trickster king. Dickinson's ubiquitous "little beggar" belies a pride and confidence; her skeptic taunts man and God; her impounded bird can "Look down upon Captivity — / And laugh" (F445). Dickinson herself exhibited some of these same qualities. People who knew her have commented on her talent for mischief. In *Emily Dickinson Face to Face,* Dickinson's niece Martha Dickinson Bianchi writes that "it is this element of drollery in her, the elfin, mischievous strain, that is hardest for those who never knew her to reconcile with her solemn side" (*Face to Face* 63). Jenkins comments on her "pure mischief" and states that "there was much of it in her" (36). Dickinson is the brilliant friend that Samuel Bowles called "rascal" (or, perhaps more precisely, "you damned rascal"), a term that some in her family also thought aptly described her (Bianchi, *Face to Face* 63).[49] Some possibly thought Dickinson to be a "hardened sinner"—or at least unsaved or unsaveable (a member of the class of "no-hope," as Mary Lyon, Dickinson's

principal at Mount Holyoke Female Seminary, would categorize her).
At the age of nineteen, Dickinson declared herself "one of the linger-
ing *bad* ones" (Letter 36). Like Old Dan Tucker, Dickinson exhibits
many paradoxical profiles in her writing: she dons masks of boldness as
well as masks of inconsequence; she depicts desperation and revelry;
she embodies pauperism and greatness.

Dickinson owned numerous songs that are tied to the web of American social and political movements of the nineteenth century. Each of
the songs that I have specifically cited has a rich history as do others
in Dickinson's collection. The composers and performers were part of
American political and social history, and the songs accrued meanings
and redirected purposes, with sometimes one arrangement of a song
appearing in ironic counterpoint to other versions of it: the Hutchinsons' "The Old Granite State" and "There's a Good Time Coming"
were featured songs at political assemblies; "The Old Granite State,"
itself a rewriting of "The Old Church Yard," was transposed numerous
times into abolitionist songs. Some of the minstrel pieces in Dickinson's collection had reincarnations as abolitionist tunes: in addition
to "Old Dan Tucker," the songs "Lucy Neal" and "Dandy Jim" were
pressed into use as anti-slavery songs (see Clark, *The Harp of Freedom,*
33, 205, 303, 321; and Brown, *The Anti-Slavery Harp* 37–38). Irish and
Scottish melodies such as Thomas Moore's and G. Kiallmark's "Araby's
Daughter," Robert Burns's "Bonnie Doon," Peter K. Moran's "Kinloch
of Kinloch," and William R. Dempster and Mrs. Price Blackwood's
"The Irish Emigrant's Lament" (all of these in Dickinson's collection)
were called upon for the abolitionist cause.[50] In addition to the outright
minstrel numbers, some songs in Dickinson's personal album were
featured on the minstrel stage, frequently in parodic form. "The Old
Granite State" was a particular favorite for blackface minstrel show
parody as were the Hutchinson Family Singers as a group; songs from
Balfe's *The Bohemian Girl,* too, became a special focus of minstrel
show burlesque.[51] Some songs in her album, such as "Yankee Doodle,"
"Old Dan Tucker," and "The Old Granite State," were re-written as political campaign songs for Lincoln (Hutchinson, *Songster*); the melodies of "Yankee Doodle," "Old Dan Tucker," "Araby's Daughter," "Auld

Lang Syne," and "Home, Sweet Home" were borrowed by American temperance movement proponents;[52] the traditional Irish melody that became known as "The Girl I Left Behind Me" was an oft-heard song during the Civil War (Cornelius 86–88; Silber 308, 327). Sam Dennison has discussed the common mid-nineteenth-century practice of setting abolitionist lyrics to music from the hymnody, minstrel repertoire, and other popular music sources (158–61; also see Southern 142 and Roberts 351). As noted above, anti-slavery song anthologies such as *The Anti-Slavery Harp, The Harp of Freedom,* and *The Liberty Minstrel* illustrate the marriage of anti-slavery words to various well-known melodies. While Dickinson's album offers many examples of songs used for that practice, Dickinson's collection of sheet music also evinces an extensive interwoven history of church songs, blackface minstrelsy, popular music, and the music of social reform in the nineteenth century. Dickinson traveled along that weave, whether intentionally or not, consciously or not, collecting music that participated importantly in nineteenth-century American social history. Some of the music in her possession was reshaped into political anthems; some of it sounded loudly in the most momentous of American cultural and social movements; some of it delivered inspiration and some threat. While the makeover of a song may have facilitated the expression of daring ideas, the imposition of a new arrangement still, however, carried a song's earlier forms, so that, for example, the most ardent "emancipation" verses of "The Old Granite State" live alongside the many initial verses that pay tribute to plain respectable American folk—and every version of the song resonates with the cadence of the hymn. A number of anti-slavery songs were born and made memorable, even if complicated, by their union with blackface minstrel melodies or with other popular airs.

In addition to owning numerous pieces of sheet music that represented merged genres and purposes, Dickinson mirrored these kinds of conjoinings and transformations in her own verse, latching the secular and the sacred, mixing the idiom of protest, rebellion, and acquiescence, collapsing the distance between exuberance and anguish, whimsy and pain. Whether deliberate or not, Dickinson in her verse mimics the phenomenon witnessed repeatedly in the songbooks, on the theatrical stages, at the political rally, at the anti-slavery convention, and at one's own piano in the home: that the popular, the political, and the religious were tightly wrapped around each other and held each other's musical forms and histories. In any number of poems, Dickinson combines genres, as it were, merging the religious, political, and pastoral. In many poems, the language of scripture merges with the image of insurgence, as in "I took my power in my hand," in which the speaker, comparing herself to David (1 Samuel), goes "against the World" (F660), and in "Who never lost are unprepared" in which references to "Revolution" and "*Bullets*" sit alongside "Angels" (F136). While Shira Wolosky observes that in Dickinson's verse, "militant imagery appears in religious contexts, reflecting the rhetoric of her age" (*Emily Dickinson* 54), Faith Barrett connects the militant to the natural, referring to the "strangely seamless blending of landscape and carnage" in Dickinson's Civil War poems ("Addresses" 79).[53] The natural world, so often her site for religious appraisal or parody, can be her medium for expressing social upheaval, as in "The name of it is 'autumn'" (F465), "Did you ever stand in a cavern's mouth" (F619), or "They dropped like flakes" (F545). Her poems twist and turn much like the malleable forms of popular songs, accruing meanings, too, as the lenses with which we view them re-focus.

So much of the drama and wonder of the times played out on the home "stage." When a fourteen-year-old Emily Dickinson sat at home on West Street (now North Pleasant Street) practicing "The Grave of Bonaparte," "Lancer's Quickstep," "There's a Good Time Coming," or "Oh, Susanna," she was, in effect, recreating in her home at least an echo of the public popular concert, the dance hall, the political assembly, and the minstrel show. If Emily Dickinson played "The Old Granite State" on her piano, what does that suggest about her and her musical and political interests? If she played "Old Dan Tucker" or "Dandy Jim," what does that suggest? Her collection of sheet music intimates that she enjoyed dance tunes, the melodies of popular entertainment, and the music associated with public social movements. Dickinson may very well have also practiced and performed psalms and hymn tunes on her piano—the Dickinson family owned several songbooks of church music; her personal album of sheet music, however, does not contain any pieces of church music. The specific songs she mentions in her letters, the concerts she attended, and the sheet music in her album all reveal more secular interests as well as perhaps something roguish in her temperament and personality. In addition to the many types of dance music (the quicksteps, waltzes, polkas, hornpipes, and minstrel numbers), the presence of pieces of Irish music, such as several songs from Thomas Moore's *Irish Melodies,* contributes to the sense that Dickinson was drawn to lively popular music. Hamm explains that American audiences in the early decades of the nineteenth century heard Irish music, such as Moore's, as "wild" and "irregular" rather than as refined; its novelty, earnest emotion, and unrestrained spirit were part of its popularity (Hamm, *Yesterdays* 50).

Dickinson's album evinces her interest in the musical voices of the abolitionist movement and of other social struggles. While the Hutchinson Family Singers sang for social justice, they were not universally beloved and admired. They were feared and even hated by some, and some regarded their music as dangerous. The Hutchinson Family Singers were indisputably an important political force in the nineteenth century, their music often rousing a crowd (or calming an unruly one) and characterizing a cause. Demonstrating the effective engagement with political and social controversy, the Hutchinsons and their music are perhaps the most dramatic example from Dickinson's collection of the musical presence in American social reform and in American cultural history. That the music she collected was of significance socially and politically suggests that Dickinson herself was interested in these events, issues, and debates. Like the Hutchinsons, Dickinson "sang" for humanity and for liberty. The popular lyricists and the poet both describe an American consciousness riven by battles between the forces of captivity and those of freedom. A thousand times the Hutchinson Family lifted their harmonized voices in the cause of human rights and justice, proclaiming that "equal liberty is our motto" and "we cannot be enslaved." In a multitude of ways, Dickinson too recognized the forms and shapes of bondage and expressed faith in the necessity of freedom. At the close of one poem Dickinson declares, "Captivity is Consciousness — / So's Liberty — ," the condensed equations of these lines entwining the fact of subjection with a vision of autonomy: captivity is consciousness, and liberty is consciousness (F649). In the poem, the speaker correlates the individual with the national community, the traumas and tensions experienced by the speaker reflected in the experience of the country: while claiming a hard-won liberty for her "Soul" (and implicitly her mind and imagination), her testimony of torture and confinement will inevitably bring to mind the anguish of enslavement and the promise of emancipation.

CHAPTER THREE

DICKINSON AND MINSTRELSY

I fear I am your little friend no longer, but Mrs. Jim Crow.
❦ Emily Dickinson to Samuel Bowles, early August 1860

My business is to *sing*.
❦ Emily Dickinson to Dr. Josiah and Elizabeth Holland, circa summer 1862

The music of minstrelsy was widely heard, performed, and distributed in nineteenth-century America. Blackface performance was a common part of many holiday traditions and many forms of mass entertainment: pageants and parades, Christmas and New Year theatricals, traveling circuses and menageries, dime museum attractions, and minstrel shows. As noted in chapter two, Dickinson's collection of sheet music contains several pieces of music that were popular in the blackface minstrel repertoire. Perhaps then it is not so surprising that Dickinson's poems contain references—some direct, some oblique—to blackface performance. Dickinson's poems are full of musical references: to song and dance and to a variety of musical instruments, notably for this discussion, the instruments associated with the minstrel troupe. Members of the Virginia Minstrels, generally recognized as the first blackface minstrel troupe, which first began performing in 1843, played the violin, tambourine, banjo, and castanets, instruments that became standard in blackface minstrel shows.[1] The many minstrel troupes that formed, especially in the 1840s and 1850s (but also through the rest of the century), incorporated into their performances such additional instruments as drums, cymbals, bugle, bells, flute, accordion, triangle, mandolin, and trumpet (Winans 141–45; Nathan 147; Gura and Bollman 17–30; Rice). References to all of these instruments occur in Dickinson's verse.

Given the prominence of the blackface performer in nineteenth-century culture, perhaps it is not so strange that the tropes of blackface minstrelsy are present or a minstrel figure appears in several of Dickinson's poems. The beginnings of blackface minstrelsy pre-date the Virginia Minstrels, and are often connected to Thomas Dartmouth Rice's creation (or appropriation) of the character and song "Jim Crow," probably first performed by him around 1830, although the date (and place) are in contention. Before the development of the minstrel show with its program of song, dance, short plays, novelty acts, and comic sketches, blackface performers appeared on stage between acts of plays or as afterpieces, in circuses and menageries, such as at P. T. Barnum's American Museum and other places of entertainment. From its inception, the American Museum's Lecture Room included minstrel shows, and T. D. Rice himself appeared there regularly in the late 1840s (Kunhardt et al. 74; Adams 91; Reiss 20, 66, 187). In Dickinson's sheet music collection, the cover illustrations of three minstrel pieces—"Old Dan Tucker," "The Jolly Raftsman," and "Who's Dat Knocking at the Door"—display racial caricatures or blackface entertainers. Curiously, in a letter of around August 1860 to Samuel Bowles, Dickinson refers to herself as "Mrs. Jim Crow," an overt reference to that widely seen image of blackface performance made famous by Rice. Stephanie Dunson has addressed the nineteenth-century phenomenon whereby the increased publication of sheet music, in combination with the widening appeal of the piano as an instrument of the middle class, brought the possibility of blackface minstrel performance into the home (246). In short, Dickinson was unquestionably familiar with blackface minstrel music and the cultural production of images associated with this entertainment, both the blackface performer and the caricature of the slave who is featured in so many minstrel songs as well as in sheet music illustrations.

Dickinson's allusions to the minstrel player and the minstrel show place her in cultural conversations and contemporary debates regarding race, gender, war, and politics. In her engagement with the music and imagery of minstrelsy, Dickinson enters a territory different in kind from the mix of reform, controversy, and irony represented by musicians like the Hutchinson Family, for minstrelsy presents a puzzle: What exactly is one seeing and hearing in a blackface minstrel performance? When the images of the minstrel performer or the components of the minstrel show appear in Dickinson's poems, the complex and ironic signification of blackface minstrelsy allows for little straightforward clarity.

What does it mean when Dickinson drops a blackface minstrel figure into the scene of a poem? What does it mean, for example, that a minstrel is present at the center of an apocalyptic drama in a poem written in 1863? In this poem, as the world erupts into fire and Christ makes his slow way toward Calvary, a black bird plays a banjo:

> It makes no difference abroad —
> The Seasons — fit — the same —
> The Mornings blossom into Noons —
> And split their Pods of Flame —
>
> Wild flowers — kindle in the Woods —
> The Brooks slam — all the Day —
> No Black bird bates His Banjo —
> For passing Calvary —
>
> Auto da Fe — and Judgment —
> Are nothing to the Bee —
> His separation from His Rose —
> To Him — sums Misery —
>
> (F686)

It is an ordinary day—a morning passes into noon—but a terrible day. The shock of the poem is in the unfurling of such fiery devastation in the midst of such ordinariness, its unfolding out of the calm of brightness and beauty. The minstrel figure, an image of surreal entertainment in the center of incineration, appears in the exact middle of the poem. As the procession passes, a "Black bird" strums vigorously, perhaps indifferently, on his banjo, seemingly there to serenade the onlookers at an execution. Line seven suggests that there may be a whole troupe of musicians present—since "No Black bird bates His Banjo"—constituting a chorus of witnesses and commentators. Does the minstrel here play an executioner's song? Are we to see the crucifixion of Christ as another one of Dickinson's "Shows"?

The summoning of the blackface minstrel places the scene of the crucifixion in America, the composition date of 1863 pertinent to an image of a world on fire. The images in the poem present a natural world that is assaulted and assaulting, unveiling the alarming underside of a normal day, leaving one gasping in a nightmare: "Noons" burst into flame, a violent cacophony hurtles out of the countryside, the drama of sacrifice advances. "Misery" has the final word. In the poem Dickinson reveals an obscene destruction, pressing the apocalyptic onto the loveliness and commonness of wildflowers and sunshine. Pronouncements of violence and judgment converge in this nexus of Civil War, crucifixion, apocalypse, trials, and execution. Out of this cauldron of horror rises a minstrel player, his presence demonstrating the place of spectacle and theatrics, but less a figure of entertainment than a marker of America. This banjo-playing bystander is the distinctively American sign of the poem.[2] As if the many forms of pain referenced in the poem were not unsettling enough, this figure, bearing its own puzzling meld of racial caricature, entertainment, social satire, and "cultural robbery" (Lott, *Love and Theft* 8), contributes to the shock of the scene.[3]

Dickinson's minstrel in "It makes no difference abroad" strums his banjo, not only accompanying the spectacle of fire and sacrifice, but also seeming to conjure a bridge into another world. The minstrel surfaces in this scene of suffering, the grandness of the stage and events pushing us into a mythic realm of violence and dying. Dickinson's poem invokes the drama of Orpheus, the poet and musician whose skill was so extraordinary that he could charm the gods, entrance the rocks and trees, tame wild beasts, and bewitch the birds. In the Greek myth, Orpheus does the unthinkable and willingly travels past the Taenarian Gate into the underworld, where, because he plays upon his lyre so beautifully for the gods, his request to retrieve his beloved wife Eurydice is granted. All pain and punishment in the underworld are suspended when Orpheus plays, his music a mixture of love, and love's twin, grief. Orpheus's effort to leave the realm of the dead with his beloved is not, of course, successful. However, seemingly all parts of the natural world hear his music and all are enchanted by its power.[4] The echo of the tale of Orpheus in Dickinson's poem prompts some new possibilities. Does her musician reside in a kind of underworld? Or might he be playing songs of grief and sorrow in this startling land-scape? Does he play in an effort to relieve suffering and even stay the pain of sacrifice? It seems that, in Dickinson's poem, the realms of the living and of the dead coincide, the apparent underworld and the natural world occupying the same sphere.

In the last lines of a different poem, "The Bible is an antique vol-ume " (F1577), Dickinson proposes that there is a more alluring "Tale" than the one told in scripture, and she specifically names Orpheus as her gifted singer and orator:

> Had but the Tale a warbling Teller —
> All the Boys would come —
> Orpheu's Sermon captivated —
> It did not condemn —

Clearly, music holds special powers for Dickinson. The music of Orpheus, the "warbling Teller," is sacred here, capable of beauty, se-duction, magic. Her American Orpheus—the minstrel—might even seem to orchestrate the movement of the scene: in "It makes no differ-ence abroad," her "warbling Teller" is, in fact, central to the poem (as noted, the minstrel figure enters in the middle of the middle stanza). However, in the Greek myth, all of nature is animated by the music of Orpheus, and now nature seems indifferent to human experience: "Auto da Fe — and Judgment — / Are nothing to the Bee — ." Instead, nature is occupied with its own pain: "His separation from His Rose — / To Him — sums Misery — ." The potency of music has an effect in Dickinson's poem different from the charms unloosed by Orpheus in the myth. While William Sherwood sees the "racket and jangle" depicted in F686 as "the projections of her own discordant spirit upon the natural world" (126), the innuendo of myth pitches the drama beyond Dickinson herself and suggests that she trusts in Orphic powers to transform the state of things, since all are affected by the condition of the world and that condition is terrible and frightening. Unlike the "meek members of the Resurrection" (F124), those present in the world Dickinson describes in "It makes no difference abroad" are touched by morning and are touched by Noon. Hovering in mythic realms and fantastical settings, her minstrel comprehends America, bearing a memory of the nation's complex narrative of violation and judgment and keeping alive the possibility of a transformed and enchanted place.

Interestingly, the illustration by Bouve and Sharp lithographers on the cover of Dickinson's sheet music for "Old Dan Tucker" conveys this same quality of enchantment, that is, a folkloric atmosphere that calls forth a world in which people and animals interact in unexpected ways (one might well think of the gifts of Orpheus as well as the adventures of Odysseus or the tales of Davy Crockett).[5] As portrayed on the sheet music cover, the music of the minstrel troupe pervades and animates the natural world and, thus, would seem to emphasize the fantastical elements of the song. In the odd scenes of apparently idyllic plantation life on the cover, the figures meant to depict slaves handle the instruments of the blackface minstrel troupe (the banjo, fiddle, tambourine, and bones). In the illustration, a banjo player has entranced a rooster; another seems to have enraptured several small animals who sit by the water's edge; a fiddler delights a dancing couple; a man enlists the neck of a banjo to curl the tail of a bull; and a man rides a banjo to escape the open mouth of an alligator. In the illustration, the banjo is an instrument of bravura and allure—it is associated with the fantastical, with scenes of "impossibilia," as Finson says (179), bringing together human and natural worlds in magical ways. In its history, the banjo is also associated with slave music and dancing. It is among the "most common plantation instruments" alongside the fiddle and percussion instruments such as the tambourine and castanets (Southern 137–38, 171–72).[6] The banjo and tambourine are also among the instruments prominent in the parades and celebrations of the black festivals in New England in the eighteenth and early nineteenth centuries (Southern 52–53; Crawford 110–11; Piersen 103, 117, 121–22). In the poem "It makes no difference abroad," the banjo evokes all of these resonances and associations with the slave plantation, the minstrel show, festival, folk life, enthrallment, danger, and chance.

In another poem of around 1884, a blackface minstrel figure hovers in the first line in the image of the jaybird playing castanets, also called "bones" by minstrel players. The poem is full of music and voices and images of blackness.

> The Jay his Castanet has struck
> Put on your Bells for Winter
> The Tippet that ignores his voice
> Is impudent to nature
> Of Swarthy Days he is the close
> His Lotus is a chestnut
> The Cricket drops a sable line
> No more from your's at present
> (F1670)

Dickinson's poem resonates playfully with a slew of cultural images and narratives that propel the poem into a plane of myth and folklore, marked by epic journeys, coded tales, and the power of enchantment. For example, Dickinson's castanet-playing jaybird invokes a long line of jaybirds that appear in African American folklore and folksongs, and in blackface minstrel songs. In T. D. Rice's "Clare the Kitchen" (1832), "A jay bird sot on a hickory limb, / He wink'd at me and I wink'd at him" (Damon no. 16). These same lines—or similar ones—appear in other popular songs and verse, such as "Jaybird," "Jawbone," and Dan Emmett's 1840 "Jim Crack Corn" (see Talley 14–15; Toll 49; Scarborough 191). Thomas W. Talley's compilation in *Negro Folk Rhymes* illustrates the preponderance of animal lore in African American folksong and folk rhyme, including lore regarding the jaybird: Talley cites "Jaybird," "Jaybird Died with the Whooping Cough," "Animal

Fair," and "The Town [Bird] and the Country Bird" among his many examples (14–15, 36, 159, 166–67, 254, 312–13). Just as African American folklore is full of animal lore, so is early minstrel music. Toll notes, for example, that "early minstrel songs often included verses about raccoons, possums, jaybirds, alligators, frogs, chickens, hounds, and other animals, whose exploits were both 'nonsensical' (in that they lacked social meanings) and quite pointed" (48). "Old Dan Tucker" illustrates this pattern well: many versions of that song are full of "nonsensical" and "pointed" animal lore, including a verse that compares Old Dan Tucker to a jaybird (*Dandy Jim*).[7] Verse five of Emmett's "High Daddy" includes the lines "The black man is a very curious thing, / I met High Daddy in the morning; / His jay-bird heel can shuffle cut and wing" (Nathan 400). These lines apparently refer to a minstrel dance called the "jaybird wing," which, Nathan states, "if identical with a frontier dance of practically the same name," was considered "indecent" for a woman to dance or even observe (91).[8] Animals in these songs and verses are often impudent, more brazen than Br'er Rabbit in "Jaybird," saucy like the winking jaybird in "Clare the Kitchen."

In Dickinson's poem, the jay's admonition to "Put on your Bells for Winter" exhorts one perhaps to don bells for community revels, as for a carnival or charivari. The invocation of bells also connotes something more solemn, a respectful bow in acknowledgment of the dying of one season and the onset of another, although the references to food, music, and pleasure more strongly suggest merry-making, the jingling and clanging of bells announcing the arrival of winter or of wintertime holidays. Bakhtin describes the widespread and "indispensable" presence of bells in all manner of holiday festivals and community rituals throughout the centuries from ancient times (214–15). The history of Christmas season festivities in America reveals a surprising wealth of trouble and controversy, the season of "Christmas misrule," as Nissenbaum calls it, characterized by disorder, drinking, licentiousness, vandalism, and violence, generally perpetrated by roving groups of boys and young men, sometimes called callithumpian bands or cowbellions, so called because of the "rough music" they produced with drums and other makeshift percussion instruments, horns, bells, and loud voices. In response to the threat of public disorder, seventeenth-century New England Puritans discouraged the celebration of Christmas, even passing a law in 1659 that prohibited any observations of the day (and levying a fine against any violators) and that stood for twenty-two years (Nissenbaum 3–4). In Boston in the latter half of the eighteenth century, the upsurge in Christmas season misrule included the straightforwardly coercive tactics of groups of masked young men, known as the Anticks, who entered the homes of Bostonians demanding money in return for the dramatic "performance" they imposed on whomever was present (Nissenbaum 42–45). Into the nineteenth century, when Santa Claus appeared as a domesticating icon of Christmas, the day and season could still be marked by excessive public rowdiness. Among many instances, Nissenbaum cites a New York *Tribune* report that the 1852 New Year was accompanied by "a Saturnalia of discord, by Callithumpian and Cowbellian bands, by musketry and fire-crackers, by bacchanal songs and noisy revels" (98). Whether the occasion for revelry or rioting, or public or private religious devotions, Christmas was not recognized as a legal holiday in Massachusetts until 1856 (Nissenbaum 309–10).[9] During Dickinson's year at Mt. Holyoke Female Seminary, Christmas was seen mostly as a problem by Mary Lyon, and there was no holiday break on that day, as was apparently true for all the schools and colleges in New England (Johnson and Ward 1: 60–61). Mary Lyon preferred Christmas Eve to be a day of "fasting and prayer" (Habegger 201; McLean 32–35). The Dickinson family did celebrate Christmas, as evidenced by the many letters in which Dickinson acknowledges Christmas gifts or refers to hanging up her "stocking on the bedpost as usual," although Dickinson's comment in a letter of December 1874 that her father had "frowned upon Santa Claus — and all such prowling gentlemen" (Letter 425) hints that the character of Santa Claus could be viewed as troublesome and unwelcome in one's home.[10] In another poem, not overtly centered on Christmas season celebrations, Dickinson presents a portrait of the "Popular Heart," largely comprised of images of street mayhem and debauchery and including the ringing of bells: "The Popular Heart is a Cannon first

— / Subsequent a Drum — / Bells for an Auxiliary / And an Afterward of Rum — " (F1220). The noisy revelers end up in "Ditches" and with "a Trip to Jail / For a Souvenir."

Striking his castanet, the jay is not necessarily assembling a callithumpian band for wintertime revels, but his voice is commanding as he declares the correct rituals for the season. The jay's choice of instrument, the castanets, aligns him (alongside the banjo-playing black bird in "It makes no difference abroad") with a blackface minstrel tradition. The images of blackness in the poem reinforce this connection. With its common reference to complexion, the word "Swarthy" seems an unusual modifier for "Days"—are these days dark, overcast, blackish? As seen in another poem, the word "Swarthy" carries a racial charge for Dickinson. The only other poem in which she uses the word is "The Malay took the pearl" (F451). In that poem, she describes as "Swarthy" the Malay, a racial designation associated by nineteenth-century ethnologists with Africa. The Swarthy Malay is also named "The Negro" in the poem. Placed in this context, the phrase "Swarthy Days" conducts a racial meaning, the phrase beckoning images of Africa or a place that recalls Africa, such as perhaps a plantation. Possibly the word "Swarthy" connotes blackface costuming, as nineteenth-century American festivities connected with Christmas and New Year's were frequently marked by masqueraders, including revelers with blackened faces (Cockrell, *Demons of Disorder* 32–33; Nissenbaum 100–102, 125–27). The word "sable," with its ceremonial associations with mourning or pageantry, also has (perhaps inadvertent) ties to the minstrel show, in that "sable" was a common part of the name of many nineteenth-century blackface troupes.[11] In line seven, the cricket who "drops a sable line" apparently delivers a ritualistic nighttime song that, in the last line of the poem, recites a common closing to a letter ("No more from your's"). A cricket's chirping calls are often identified in musical terms, such as the courting song and the calling song, and in other Dickinson poems, crickets are notable for their voices and noises: her crickets speak, pray, laugh, tick, and sing.[12] In her discussion of "Further in summer than the birds" (F895), Virginia Jackson posits that while the "birdsong" represents for Dickinson "a lyricism unattainable by the human poet," the cricket is a more extreme version of supra-human articulation: "The cricket's song is even 'further' removed from the capacity of human expression than is the nightingale's or skylark's or bluebird's" (74). In "The jay his castanet has struck," the jay and the cricket both speak musically, one rousing and one quiet, the jay's clear voice calling forth other voices in the poem's medley of fable and myth, the cricket offering a polite (if temporary) good-bye.

This poem points toward extraordinary realms, just as in "It makes no difference abroad," with the presence of the minstrel touching the epic contours of myth. The reference to the "Lotus" in line six calls to mind the episode in Book Nine of *The Odyssey* in which Odysseus and his crew find refuge from the exhausting trials of a long journey in the land of the lotus-eaters. Dickinson's image also summons a poem by Alfred Tennyson, a writer she much admired: In Tennyson's 1842 poem "The Lotos-Eaters," it is music that sweeps one into the restful realm of sleep and dreams. The bells in the first lines of "The jay his castanet has struck" may also invoke the stanzas in Tennyson's "In Memoriam" that describe the bells that "ring in" and "ring out."[13] In Dickinson's poem, the "honeyed" fruit of drowsiness and dreams is a chestnut as well as a cas-tanet (which is etymologically related to the word "chestnut"), food and music the twin sources of nourishment, contentment, and dreams. The jay who plays his castanet is well regarded, even noble; he seems much like the jay that Dickinson describes in another poem as "A Neighbor and a Warrior too" (F1596), a valorous citizen deserving of "Immortal-ity." The music conjured in the poem—its instruments, bells, chirpings, and voices—bridges many spheres: the dreamworld, the natural world, mythic narratives, the coded worlds of African American experience and folk culture, the spaces enlivened by popular entertainments, and the social rituals of winter carnival. An homage both to remembrance and to repression, the poem channels a variety of stories and voices that drift in and out of the consciousness of the poem. The poem's many undula-tions and echoes compose a fantastical scene, one less cataclysmic and more elliptical, characterized by the anticipation of tumult and change and by the lulling pleasures of enchantment.

Another minstrel figure appears in the second stanza of a much earlier (about 1860) poem, "If I could bribe them by a rose" (F176). It is a curious poem full of fanciful musings and extravagant pledges, narrated by a speaker who yearns to discover what will persuade a nameless "they" to grant her dearest wish:

If I could bribe them by a Rose
I'd bring them every flower that grows
From Amherst to Cashmere!
I would not stop for night, or storm —
Or frost, or death, or anyone —
My business were so dear!

If they w'd linger for a Bird
My Tamborin were soonest heard
Among the April Woods!
Unwearied, all the summer long,
Only to break in wilder song
When Winter shook the boughs!

What if they hear me!
Who shall say
That such an importunity
May not at last avail?
That, weary of this Beggar's face —
They may not finally say, Yes —
To drive her from the Hall?

In the first two stanzas, the speaker sounds obsessed, nearly delirious with desperation, on the edge of frenzy. Imagining herself with supernaturally heroic abilities, she boasts that she would be unstoppable as she gathers "every flower that grows" in the world; in the second stanza, she imagines herself possessed, playing her tambourine (or "Tamborin") tirelessly all spring and summer before bursting into "wilder song" in the winter. What is this wilder song? A song of passion, of madness, of fury? Is it the wild winter song associated with

Christmas season misrule? Her tambourine playing is so unrelenting that, by the third stanza, this frenetic speaker-musician anticipates that she may be able to erode the resistance of those who can grant her what she seeks. Curiously, the conditional mode of the poem conveys that, despite her furious playing, she is not heard, although she clearly hopes—expects—that if she persists, her music will win her that "Yes." The tambourine is the speaker's primary tool of "importunity." Shaking her tambourine, this gleeful "Beggar" is full of tall-talk and brazen behavior. She cultivates such unruliness one wonders that she would so urgently need anyone's approval. Rather, she is very much the Antick, whose begging takes the form of clamoring and whose intrusion into the home (or "Hall") continues until the "gift" of money (or affirmation) is offered: "That, weary of this Beggar's face — / They may not finally say, Yes — / To drive her from the Hall?"

The tambourine associates her with the blackface minstrel player as well as with others: slaves on plantations, black revelers in holiday parades, roaming entertainers, country folk, and common people. The Biblical Miriam, sister of Moses, played the tambourine and danced with other women in celebration after the miraculous salvation of the Israelites from the Egyptians at the Red Sea (Exodus 15:20). The tambourine is an instrument marking the victories and celebrations of ordinary people and oppressed people. Dickinson's speaker shakes and strikes her tambourine in the woods, apparently alone, her music announcing her turbulent emotional state, the tambourine an emblem of her solitary voice, her song, nonetheless, sounding through every season. Beth Maclay Doriani specifically discusses Miriam as a model of the poet-prophet for Dickinson, noting that images of dancing and singing in her poems affiliate Dickinson with "the prophetic tradition associated with women" (3, 200–201). For Doriani, this tradition is one in which women, such as Miriam, "functioned specifically as divinely chosen leaders and speakers" who "often spoke their messages through poetic song" (22). In the poem, the player's music seems to have possessed her, yet with less evident consequence of spiritual guidance and with more hope placed in the eloquence of her misrule. The intended audience for Dickinson's tambourine player is apparently not

spellbound, impressed, honored, or delighted by her playing and singing, but still the speaker believes in the potency of her music: "What
if they hear me!" she wonders with conspiratorial glee. What if they
hear her? If the tambourine-playing beggar is connected to the divinely
prophetic, she seems to be a voice-as-yet-unheard, her link to the prophetic tradition Doriani cites made through her connection to the ignored (or disbelieved) seer, and through her zealous anticipation of a
miracle. In this poem, as others, Dickinson's minstrel provides a con-
duit to realms marvelous and unappreciated. What if they hear her?
The same question could be asked of the nineteenth-century minstrel
performer. What attitudes, desires, resistance, or defiance might one
hear in the songs of this lively entertainment?

MINSTRELSY AND MRS. JIM CROW

By the late 1840s, the minstrel show was well established, its evolution
characterized by the growing variety of entertainments included in its
programs: musical numbers, dance, comic skits, jokes and riddles,
mock oratory, and short plays.[14] Generally recognized as "the chief
American popular entertainment of the nineteenth century" (Bean, et
al. xiii), the blackface minstrel show offered a stage for satires and parodies of high culture (such as opera and Shakespeare's plays) as well
as of popular culture (such as musical performers like the Hutchinson Family or Jenny Lind). Like the musical acts of minstrel troupes,
the minstrel show was built on the premise of masquerade: impersonations of characters or real people for comic or satiric effect; carica-
tured or sentimental portrayals of race and gender (which relied on
blackface make-up, flamboyant or exaggerated costumes, and cross-
dressing); and burlesques of preachers, politicians, and reformers and
their views on topics such as women's rights, temperance, and current
scientific or technological developments. Mahar describes the minstrel show as a kind of musical theater (1–8, 332); Winans characterizes it as "theatrical music" or as a "musical event" (141). Many scholars
of the minstrel show propose that its prominent style was burlesque.[15]

In exploring the popular phenomenon known as the minstrel show, many scholars emphasize two key qualities: that the minstrel show was a performance, and that it depicted social conflicts of the nineteenth century and presented social satire. For example, in his *Behind the Burnt Cork Mask,* Mahar argues that the minstrel show was theatrical entertainment that satirized American life (41, 353). Although he posits that "the primary purpose of the genre was burlesque," not reform, he suggests that the minstrel show addressed a miscellany of concerns, fears, threats, and injustices of American society of the nineteenth century (353). Primarily attentive to minstrelsy's role in the evolution of racial caricatures and stereotypes, and stressing the exploitation and manipulation of African Americans and African American culture in minstrelsy, Toll examines this "national institution" through the materials of the nineteenth-century entertainment industry and identifies blackface minstrels as "professional entertainers" (40, 51). While recognizing the minstrel show as popular theatrical entertainment, Lott argues minstrelsy's role in nineteenth-century class formation, that is, he demonstrates how transgressions of blackface performance mediated and directed the establishment of a self-consciously white working class: minstrelsy's "languages of race so invoked ideas about class as to provide displaced maps or representations of 'working-classness'" (*Love and Theft* 68). Cockrell, too, sees performance as the key to the blackface show, and, like Lott, credits minstrelsy with serious class critique and class satire (*Demons of Disorder* 152–53, 161–62, 169). Unlike others, Mahar does not think that class critique was a defining issue of the minstrel show, although Mahar, too, concludes that minstrelsy addressed "the unfairness of privilege" and the "exclusivity of class" (353) through the burlesque of American elitism and the ridiculing of people of all classes: "Minstrelsy did not define the contents of the shows on the basis of class because all classes were its patrons as well as its targets, the term *targets* meaning the array of hypocrites, parvenus, and confidence men of all classes and social stations" (348). In short, historians of minstrelsy emphasize that the minstrel show was a performance and they address the social and cultural critique displayed in this form of popular culture.

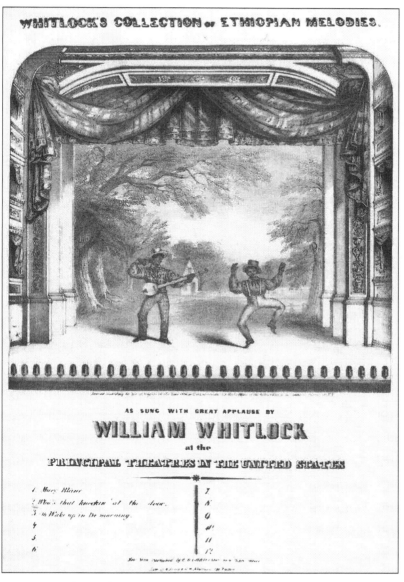

Figure 4. The title page for "Who's That Knocking at the Door," Whitlock's Collection of Ethiopian Melodies. This piece is in Emily Dickinson's "bound volume of miscellaneous sheet music," EDR 469, Houghton Library, Harvard University.

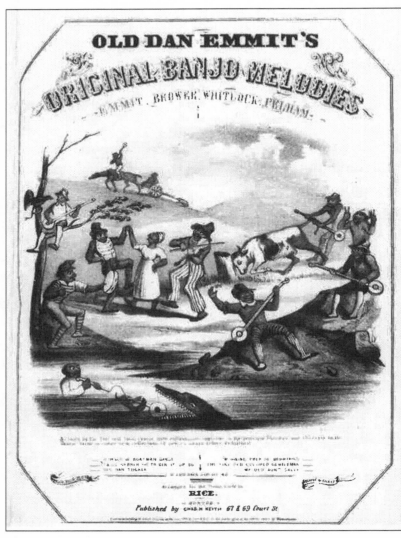

Figure 5. The title page for "The Original Old Dan Tucker," Old Dan Emmit's Original Banjo Melodies. This piece is in Emily Dickinson's "bound volume of miscellaneous sheet music," EDR 469, Houghton Library, Harvard University.

Figure 6. The title page for "The Jolly Raftsman," Second Series: Old Dan Emmit's Original Banjo Melodies. This piece is in Emily Dickinson's "bound volume of miscellaneous sheet music," EDR 469, Houghton Library, Harvard University.

The origins of minstrelsy are found in dance as well as song. Made famous by his performance of "Jim Crow" and credited with creating its stage presentation, T. D. Rice reputedly copied "Jim Crow" from an older black stablehand (or slave or "negro-stage-driver") whom Rice observed singing and dancing an unusual shuffle and jump step around 1830.[16] One of the members of the original Virginia Minstrels, Frank Brower was primarily a dancer (Nathan 113). Many other dancers found fame on the minstrel stage, one of the most renowned being William Henry Lane, probably a free-born black man, performing under the name Juba, who in his act imitated numerous blackface dancers (such as Brower and John Diamond) before performing an "imitation of himself."[17] Diamond performed as a duo with William Whitlock early in his career and, like Juba, appeared in P. T. Barnum's shows in the early 1840s (Winter 226–27; Nathan 62, 64; Lott, *Love and Theft* 112–16; Rice 40, 42). Three pieces of minstrel music in Dickinson's personal album have cover illustrations that display dancing figures, the cover to Whitlock's "Who's That Knocking at the Door" apparently depicting Whitlock himself playing his banjo while John Diamond (or possibly another dancer who entertained under the name Frank Diamond) jumps or hops in his accompanying dance (Nathan 64). The type of music Dickinson gathered in her sheet music collection suggests that dance appealed to her, as her collection contains many pieces of lively dance music—a number of quicksteps, waltzes, polkas, hornpipes, and jigs. A fundamental part of the minstrel show, all of these types of dance, as well as ballet, were included in minstrel performance, parody, and burlesque (Cockrell, *Demons of Disorder* 87–88; Lott, *Love and Theft* 112–17; Nathan 70–97; Winans 160; Mahar 40; Dizikes 106).

In several of Dickinson's poems, a dance—most frequently unspecified, but sometimes a jig or waltz or ballet—is mentioned.[18] In a poem from about 1862, Dickinson's speaker imagines herself on stage performing a comic ballet.

> I cannot dance opon my Toes —
> No Man instructed me —

But oftentimes, among my mind,
A Glee possesseth me,

That had I Ballet Knowledge —
Would put itself abroad
In Pirouette to blanch a Troupe —
Or lay a Prima, mad,

And though I had no Gown of Gauze —
No Ringlet, to my Hair,
Nor hopped for Audiences — like Birds,
One Claw opon the Air,

Nor tossed my shape in Eider Balls,
Nor rolled on wheels of snow
Till I was out of sight, in sound,
The House encore me so —

Nor any know I know the Art
I mention — easy — Here —
Nor any Placard boast me —
It's full as Opera —

(F381)

Although the speaker protests her skill in the classical art of ballet, her accumulated denials construct a vivid portrayal of her performing the dance, or rather some antic parody of it. Her startling performance renders the poem as a comic skit: in declaring what she has not done (not "hopped" or "tossed" or "rolled") and what she does not have ("no Gown of Gauze," "No Ringlet, to my Hair"), she brings to life the image of herself as the most unconventional of ballerinas, a dancing bird, graceful but untutored and most definitely un-balletlike, hopping before an audience, "One Claw opon the Air."

Many scholars have discussed this poem, noting its attention to artistic performance and the techniques of the artist as well as addressing the contrast between the speaker's (or Dickinson's) ostensibly modest acknowledgment of her lack of training and the revelation of her complete confidence in her skill and originality as an artist. Perceiving the dance or ballet as Dickinson's metaphor for writing, several scholars have addressed the mood of irony, parody, or satire in the poem.[19]

Recognition of Dickinson's knowledge of popular music adds a plausible dimension to her satire beyond the ironic tension between renunciation and self-promotion or the witty demurrals that display not her amateurism, but her impatience with conventional technique and presentation. In other words, someone so clearly informed about the popular music and popular culture of her time might well parody not only the conventions and status of ballet and other classical arts but also the parodic performances of those arts as presented on the minstrel show stage. There are several examples of words and imagery in "I cannot dance upon my toes" that hold specific meanings in the world of blackface performance or that evoke blackface minstrelsy. For example, the "Glee" that "possesseth" the speaker denotes high spirits as well as song, as some critics have noted: Anderson connects "glee" musically to "collegiate singing groups" (23) and Small references popular song and glee clubs (35). The word "glee" refers, more specifically, to a song arranged in parts, a popular style not only for collegiate singing groups but also for musical troupes like the Hutchinson Family and minstrel troupes. Minstrel songs were commonly referred to as "Ethiopian glee." In unraveling the syntactic riddles of the poem, critics have arrived at varying understandings of the last line ("It's full as Opera — "), quite reasonably understanding Dickinson to correlate the fullness of opera with her ability to write, the poems themselves, her mind, and her inner life (see Mossberg 158; Miller, "Sound" 206; Anderson 23; Juhasz, "Big Tease" 57). This poem does exult in the fullness of the speaker's imagination; however, in terms of both syntax and semantics, it is also the speaker's "Glee" that can be identified as the referent for "full as Opera," the fifteen intervening lines (lines 5 through 19) describing the fantasy of the speaker's performance had she "Ballet Knowledge." Thick with allusion, the word "glee" joins her song (and a bewitching song at that) to joyfulness, the comparison of her "glee" to opera not only underscoring the vitality of song but also stressing the theatrical spectacle animated by the speaker's imagination. While the word "Opera" immediately calls to mind European opera, the poem itself does not depict the opulence of high opera, rather stressing the comic and parodic, and thus pointing again toward that other opera so popular in nineteenth-century America, the Ethiopian Opera, that is, the minstrel show. Some minstrel entertainers called themselves members of opera troupes or opera companies (such as Palmo's Burlesque Opera Company and Kunkel's Nightingale Opera Troupe [Hamm, *Yesterdays* 134, 139]), and, particularly in large cities of the Northeast, such as New York, Boston, or Philadelphia, minstrel troupes sometimes had their own theaters, called Ethiopian Opera Houses.[20]

Similar to the word "Opera," the word "Troupe" offers double meanings, connoting both a dance ensemble and a minstrel troupe. The speaker's expectation that her pirouettes would "blanch a Troupe" suggests, most readily, the altering effect that her bizarre or extraordinary dance would have on the rest of the dance company—they would turn pale from amazement. The word "blanch" is curious, suggesting more than a face turning ashen. The word "blanch" emphasizes the removal of all color or a process of whitening. Dickinson's image is especially potent if the troupe being blanched were a blackface minstrel troupe, their whitening somehow magical as if the transformative effect of her dance were beyond a merely physical reaction, the burnt cork makeup vaporized right off the performers' faces. The reference in line eight to the "Prima" also compresses the "high" and the popular, suggesting not only the prima ballerina or the prima donna of an opera company, but also the female impersonator in a minstrel show, who was called the "prima donna." By 1860 the minstrel show prima donna was a well-established major role (Toll 139–45, 144; Bean 248–51). The extraordinary success of the minstrel show prima donna Francis Leon, who acted, sang, and danced, including ballet, generated so many copycat impersonators that Leon became known onstage as "The Only Leon" (Bean 251; Toll 142–44; Garber 276–77). Testing an audience's understanding and perception of the genuine and "real," Francis Leon, a serious and refined female impersonator, played a woman convincingly and stated that his ballet dancing was "the real thing, not a burlesque" (Toll 144).[21]

Significantly, such impersonation is central to the speaker's activity in the poem. The speaker, who claims that she cannot dance, impersonates a ballet dancer, a comedic dancer, a minstrel dancer. One could view her also as a female impersonator, burlesquing conventional ideas of the female and feminine with her visions of a gown of gauze, ringlets, and a tutu. The speaker concocts a caricature of a ballet dancer: a hopping creature, one "Claw" held high, she is both graceful and clumsy, at the least an unusual figure of feminine artistry. But the rendering is more than unusual. It is fantastical, the dancer exposed as a gigantic bird, performing its series of little jumps and its pirouettes, sufficiently outrageous to "lay a Prima, mad." The dance steps also conjure an entertainer on the minstrel stage. Historians of minstrelsy describe the variety of movements that comprise the minstrel dance, including kicks and spins, slides, posturings, and hops and jumps. As described by Nathan, the placement and movements of arms and hands were also critical in the minstrel dance: "Arms and hands formed a most expressive part of the dancer's performance. According to its character, they were intense or relaxed, held over the head or extended in front, with the fingers usually spread wide apart" (75). Other descriptions and the illustrations in Nathan's study often note one arm or hand posed in the air (70–97). In Dickinson's poem, the dancer, likened to a bird hopping with one "Claw" held in the air, mimics the gestures of the minstrel dance, even the famous "Jim Crow," whose chorus ends with the line, "Eb'ry time I weel about, I jump Jim Crow" (Damon no. 15; also see Toll 43–44; Nevin 608–10).

The poem dramatizes the speaker's (or Dickinson's) fantastical imagination, not only its prankish conflation of classical arts and popular entertainments, but also the power of her "Art." The speaker herself is bewitched by her song, her mirth, her imagination. Projecting a scene of both the classical ballet and the minstrel parody of it—and perhaps even a parody of the parody—the speaker is entranced by her vision. It, like her glee, "possesseth" her. When the speaker asserts in the final stanza that "Nor any know I know the Art," one wonders at her presumption and at her certainty that her knowledge remains undetected. One also contemplates what unseen gifts she might identify as "the Art." The ambiguity of the line invites a variety of understandings: her "Art" is "her ability to write," as proposed by Mossberg (158), or it is the song, as Small suggests (35–36), or it is the ballet of which she does indeed have "expert" knowledge (Anderson 22–23). All of these readings account for what the speaker practices in the poem, but her tone of intrigue suggests some additional expressive skill, something mysterious and illusory, perhaps something disguised or so unexpected that it is, in effect, invisible: "Nor any know I know the Art." The poem proposes many possible names for her undetected "Art": the speaker's (or Dickinson's) virtuosities of performance and parody, her gifts of imagination, her talent for impersonation, or her powers of bewitchment.

Initially an image that purportedly conveys her strangeness, the pirouette rolls forward as the prominent metaphor for the many turns of the poem. Within the poem, multiple meanings of "Glee," "Opera," "Troupe," "House" and "Prima" are set spinning. Images of the classical arts and the popular arts whirl around each other and turn into each other. This mixing of the "high" and the "low" as it were carries an implicit class consciousness, suggesting the speaker's own divided or mischievous sensibility; she courts the classical arts but identifies with the popular forms. Notions of gender are wheeled around, the regalia and postures of the prima ballerina parodied and replaced with the playful (or earnest) performance of the prima female impersonator. In the burlesque presented in the poem, the speaker names the ballet but her dance seems more suited to the minstrel show stage.

Once again, one has to ponder what the minstrel figure connotes for Dickinson. If in other poems the minstrel is a witness, a reveler, a trickster, an enchanter, an oracle, and a voice resonating with many cultural narratives, in this poem the minstrel's inventiveness unfolds, revealing her talent for both parody and artistry. As in other poems, the minstrel figure draws together a cache of cultural narratives; this time the allusions spin madly around cultural conceptions of white and black, male and female, art and entertainment. Propelled by her "Glee," the speaker courts a persona that transgresses norms of gender and that plays with a culture's complicated responses to race.

Dickinson's familiarity with a popular icon of minstrel misrule is evident in a letter to Samuel Bowles in early August 1860. Dickinson figuratively puts on a minstrel mask, referring to herself as "Mrs. Jim Crow" (Letter 223). Separated from its immediate context, the letter is enigmatic for a contemporary reader (perhaps for any reader other than Bowles), although it appears to be an apology for some offense. Ironically, the letter's cryptic private references draw on very public iconography, suggesting that the tensions that prompt an apology from Dickinson seem to have involved current political matters.

Dear Mr Bowles.
I am much ashamed. I misbehaved tonight. I would like to sit in the dust. I fear I am your little friend no more, but Mrs. Jim Crow.
    I am sorry I smiled at women.
    Indeed, I revere holy ones, like Mrs Fry and Miss Nightingale. I will never be giddy again. Pray forgive me now: Respect little Bob o' Lincoln again!
    My friends are a very few. I can count them on my fingers — and besides, have fingers to spare.
    I am gay to see you — because you come so scarcely, else I had been graver.
        Good night, God will forgive me — Will you please to *try*?
                                                    Emily.

If the August 1860 dating of the letter is accurate,[22] Bowles was in Amherst as usual to report on Commencement Week activities for the *Springfield Republican*. This year Governor Nathaniel Banks was also present in Amherst for commencement and was staying at the Homestead as the guest of Edward Dickinson (Leyda 2: 13). Habegger suggests that the letter implies a disagreement between Dickinson and Bowles over women's role in public affairs: "It looks as if Samuel had brought out his belief that women should become more prominent in public life and Emily had scoffed at the notion" (391). In agreement with Habegger, Domhnall Mitchell reads the letter as one in which Dickinson "apologized to Bowles for having poked fun at women who were socially active" (101). Habegger's and Mitchell's views seem valid, as Dickinson writes "I am sorry I smiled at women" and implicitly distinguishes between the "holy" ones and those women perhaps perceived as more worldly and, thus, less respectable. However, the women Dickinson names—Miss Nightingale and Mrs. Fry—were engaged in work of the most honorable public service: Florence Nightingale attended the wounded on the battlefield during the Crimean War and, in 1860, established the Nightingale School for Nurses in London; Elizabeth Fry (if this is the Mrs. Fry Dickinson means) advocated tirelessly for prison reform in Britain and throughout Europe and worked to improve treatment of the mentally ill. The contentious issue between Bowles and Dickinson does not seem to have been women's social activism or public service, as Habegger and Mitchell suggest, but rather some judgment of worthy purpose or respectability.

The immediate political context—heightened by the presence of Bowles and Governor Banks in the Dickinson home—reinforces a reading of the letter that centers on political matters. By August 1860 Abraham Lincoln's election was seeming more certain, even as his candidacy provoked threats of secession from the Southern states and the level of protest and alarm rose dramatically in the South as did instances of violence against blacks, abolitionists, and people who had the misfortune of being strangers or looking suspicious (Nevins 306–7). In the letter, the phrase "Bob o'Lincoln" seems a clear reference to the presidential candidate, an identification fortified by the title of one of the Lincoln campaign songbooks, *The Bobolink Minstrel: or, Republican Songster for 1860,* compiled by George W. Bungay.[23] In "The Bobolink's Campaign Song," the bobolink laments that his "song of freedom" is unheard in the South as he chants for Lincoln's election and urges others to "repeat the song of bobolinks": "I'll vote for honest cousin Lincoln, / To take the Presidential throne."[24] Bowles, who along with Banks was instrumental in organizing the Republican Party in Massachusetts in the mid-1850s, staunchly supported Lincoln after his nomination as did the *Springfield Republican* (Merriam 1: 139–45, 265–66, 349; Weisner 51). Writing from Chicago, the site of the Republican Convention, on May 18, 1860, Bowles reports to his wife Mary that "the excitement is tremendous" over the nomination of Lincoln, and that everyone (other than the supporters of William H. Seward) "feels that it is a right result, and that the Republicans will succeed with him" (Merriam 1: 303). The following week, Bowles wrote in the *Springfield Republican* that "Lincoln is a man of the most incorruptible integrity—firm as a rock against duplicity, dishonesty, and all dishonorable conduct, public and private" (quoted in Weisner 27).[25] The context of an intense presidential campaign in the summer of 1860 suggests that the women at whom Dickinson "smiled" may have been involved in the unholy business of political campaigning. In support of Lincoln in 1860, women involved themselves in ways that may have seemed amusing or even ridiculous: women formed political committees and participated in political rallies, they rode in parades dressed as states of the Union, sang campaign songs, and put their domestic skills to political use in decorating campaign headquarters, preparing food for rallies, and sewing political banners (Rozinek). The August 1860 letter is private and elusive in its meaning, and the cause of Dickinson's apology left to conjecture, although the contentious topic of women's proper role in the public or political sphere might well have touched off a sparring of wits and perhaps inclined Dickinson to step back or to mask herself afterwards.

Habegger posits that with the "self-blackening" allusion to "Mrs. Jim Crow," Dickinson is "exaggerating her unacceptableness" and showing "humble and needy self-denigration" (391–92). He adds, "And so she puts on blackface, presenting herself as a pariah and scapegrace in order to get back into master's good graces" (392). While Dickinson's appeal to Bowles is conciliatory—"God will forgive me — Will you please to *try?*"—the suggestion that Dickinson assumes the mask of the unacceptable or costumes herself as a pariah does not follow. In nineteenth-century America, the minstrel image of Jim Crow was not unacceptable and was not anything like a pariah. On the contrary, the reception for "Jim Crow" was wildly enthusiastic, and the song and character achieved widespread popularity not only in America but also abroad. Evolving out of his fame in America, the character Jim Crow was introduced in London with sensational success in 1836 by T. D. Rice and, thereafter, appeared in English entertainment for decades. Jim Crow became a regular figure in Christmastime pantomimes and Punch and Judy shows, and the name "Jim Crow" became associated with British clowns (Rehin, "Harlequin" 687; Rehin, "Blackface" 21–22; Lott, "Blackface" 10). The character Jim Crow paraded with the "masquerading mummers" in Christmas day parades in New York in the 1860s.[26] The merchandising of Jim Crow was also very profitable, with a "dancing 'Jim Crow' toy" introduced in 1864 reportedly earning a "fortune" ("Home and Foreign Gossip").

As with just about everything concerning minstrelsy, the Jim Crow character is overrun with conflicting views. It is difficult for a twenty-first-century reader or audience to fathom the significance of a blackface performer to a nineteenth-century audience, although many fine historians and musicologists have determined a variety of purposes and imports. An archetypal "demon of disorder" in Cockrell's view, Jim Crow was a folkloric character in the tall-tale tradition, performed not with the purpose of demeaning but with the purpose of "adopting the visage of the Other in an effort to reconfigure a hard world" (Cockrell, *Demons of Disorder* 82). Seeing Jim Crow as "a kind of superman," Finson agrees that Jim Crow acts out a "carnivalesque masquerade" (163–65). Scholars such as Cockrell, Finson, Nathan, and Toll argue that Jim Crow bursts forth as a trickster, a surprisingly powerful, outsized character, influential, clever, and outspoken.[27] However, with his tattered appearance and stereotyped dialect, Jim Crow can easily be read as an offensive caricature of a black man, the unrealistic narrative of the song and the widespread performance by Rice (and many others) evidence of the disrespect that white people held for black people. The rhapsodic reception and the free appropriation of the character into a variety of entertainment venues (such as circuses, parades, pantomimes, and plays) could enhance the sense that the scorn ran very deep. Professing this view, Dennison asserts that songs like "Jim Crow" are meant to ridicule and to show a "depth of contempt" for black people, and scoffs at the idea that Jim Crow is some kind of heroic figure along the lines of Davy Crockett (67–68). Dennison shares a disdain for blackface minstrels with Frederick Douglass, who refers to them, in his October 1848 *North Star* review of the Hutchinson Family (who were not blackface performers), as "the filthy scum of white society, who have stolen from us a complexion denied to them by nature, in which to make money, and pander to the corrupt taste of their white fellow-citizens." Douglass sarcastically calls songs like "Jim Crow" "specimens of American musical genius."

The likelihood that Jim Crow meant different things to different audiences seems eminently sensible, even inevitable: if some regarded Jim Crow as evidence of racial inferiority, and some saw him as a cultural sign of white people's hatred for black people, others could read him as a subversive, witty, attractive, and powerful character. Countering those historians and activists who reject any worthiness in Jim Crow and concluding that many spectators (and performers) found Jim Crow to be empowering, Cockrell ponders, "Could it be that 'Jim Crow' and kindred songs functioned, during this period, for black people much as they did for common white people, as songs of subversion, about dancing and the body and laughter, and of how the performance of joy and pleasure can remake a less than perfect world?" (*Demons of Disorder* 84). Could it be that Jim Crow represented the thrill of subversion and the euphoria of victory over oppressive forces and not hatred for blacks?[28] To return, then, to Dickinson's letter to Bowles, one is left to puzzle over the contrary possible tenors of "Mrs. Jim Crow." Is Dickinson showing contempt for slaves or free blacks? Does she adopt the mask of Jim Crow to make plain the extent of her shame? If her apology is sincere and she truly fears that she has lost Bowles' friendship, would she invoke this popular symbol of audaciousness? Perhaps, rather than sincerely apologizing in the letter, she continues a game of wits and mischief, much in the spirit of Jim Crow.

A picaro and a politician, Jim Crow is characterized in dozens of verses (mostly composed by unknown writers) that swing from the silly to the degrading to the heroic and glorifying.[29] A loquacious fellow, Jim Crow recounts his adventures as he freely wanders the country, drinking hard, singing and dancing, playing his fiddle, and courting women. Jim Crow loves women and women love him: "I went down to the ribber, / I dident mean to stay; / But dare de galls dey charm me so, / I cudent get away." Many verses focus on Jim Crow's political insights and aspirations: Jim Crow will run for political office; he will debate in Congress; he consults with the President; he remarks on the easy life of politicians ("dey only hab to eat dinners, / And spend pe peoples money"). In several verses Jim Crow entertains visions of insurrection and emancipation: "Should dey get to fighting, / Perhaps de bracks will rise, / For deir wish for freedom / Is shining in deir eyes." Jim Crow is quick to add, "I am for freedom, / An for union altogeder, / Although I am a brack man, / De white is called my broder." With the numerous references to the banking debate, tariff disputes, patents, nullification, President Jackson and other politicians, the song is, as Finson observes, partly a "political tract" touting Jacksonian politics (166). Importantly, while most politicians "tork sich nonsense," Jim Crow is straight-talking and deliberate, mocking and outwitting these members of the powerful governing class. When Dickinson names herself "Mrs. Jim Crow," the mask does not seem to offer the shield of "self-denigration," but rather it protects her with its weave of symbolic meaning. Dickinson casts herself in the role of political trickster, not pariah, and one, moreover, who always wins his (or her) point over other more impressive and powerful, politically minded men.

Dickinson's letter of early August 1860 to Samuel Bowles condenses a world of meaning in a few cultural references. The letter also thereby wraps together several of the concerns that are so pressing in Dickinson's verse: the possibilities for women in the public sphere, the benefits of the mask, and the problem of voice. In the letter, the mask of Jim Crow is joined by a second mask, that of the bobolink—or, rather, the Bob o'Lincoln—who sings heartily for one whose own public voice is controversial, to say the least. Dickinson's self-identification as Mrs. Jim Crow calls up a character but also a song (a tremendously popular song and one that has sparked its own controversies), another clue that Dickinson consciously or unconsciously desires a public voice as well as perhaps recognizes that a bold imagination is necessary for a woman to reveal that voice. Like the women she "reveres" and the ones at which she "smiles," Dickinson too is trying to forge a public presence, or to find a voice that can be heard. Whatever one accepts as its context and purpose, her letter to Bowles, with its culturally resonant references, places her within public political and cultural discourse.

The voices of minstrel entertainers were heard loudly in nineteenth-century America, and the experience of attending a performance was complicated by one's understanding of what exactly one was hearing and seeing. In Dickinson's poems too with their various singers, musicians, actors, and dancers, one contemplates the repertoire of voices and performers. What exactly do we hear and see when we notice her minstrels? In one poem, the minstrel hopes desperately that her furious playing will realize her most ardent desire; in another, the minstrel appears in a cataclysmic scene of violence and execution; in another, the musician calls neighbors to seasonal revelries; in another, a cunning speaker conjures herself as a minstrel-style dancer and sets the tropes of high art and those of popular entertainment spinning around each other. In these and other Dickinson poems, the most ordinary of speakers—a bystander, a beggar, a street musician, a child, a "tippler," a woman—has powers to enchant and persuade, to astonish, to rouse, to imagine the most mysterious and magical transformations. Present at scenes of mythic trial, of emotional furor, of gleeful fantasy, of revel and rowdiness, Dickinson's minstrels are figures of liminality standing at the precipice of great and fateful change or pressing for a moment of such consequence. Importantly, Dickinson frequently turns to music as her prompt or accompaniment, whether the transition commemorated in the poems be seasonal, mythic, imaginative, emotional, or political. Moreover, Dickinson identifies with her gallery of common but creative characters. It would seem that in the letter to Bowles, Dickinson's invocation of Mrs. Jim Crow marks her as bold, not small or shamed.

In general, the characteristic elements of the minstrel show—song, dance, masquerade, impersonation, riddles, satire—are repeatedly at play in many of Dickinson's poems. In "I cannot dance upon my toes" the speaker rehearses the role of dancer, burlesques it, denies

it, claims it, exults in it. In another poem of the same approximate
year (1862 or 1863), she presents a speaker who practices a role and
imagines a self-transformation similar to the ones conceived by speakers in other poems, that is, from a person of low status to a person of
exceptional accomplishment or high station. In "I'm saying every day,"
as in other poems, the private space of the home provides a kind of
theatrical space, in which the speaker practices a role, or a double role,
in her masquerade as beggar and her performance as Queen.

I'm saying every day
"If I should be a Queen, Tomorrow" —
I'd do this way —
And so I deck, a little,

If it be, I wake a Bourbon,
None on me — bend supercilious —
With "This was she —
Begged in the Market place — Yesterday."

Court is a stately place —
I've heard men say —
So I loop my apron — against the Majesty
With bright Pins of Buttercup —
That not too plain —
Rank — overtake me —

And perch my Tongue
On Twigs of singing — rather high —
But this, might be my brief Term
To qualify —

Put from my simple speech all plain word —
Take other accents, as such I heard
Though but for the Cricket — just,
And but for the Bee —

Not in all the Meadow —
One accost me —

Better to be ready —
Than did next Morn
Meet me in Arragon —
My old Gown — on —

And the surprised Air
Rustics — wear —
Summoned — unexpectedly —
To Exeter —

(F575)

The speaker practices her part as if she expects that the repetition of "saying every day" will trigger a magic spell. The anticipation that the commoner will awaken one morning as someone else, a member of the ruling class no less, carries the wonderment of the fairy tale and of narratives of newfound identity (and of an Emersonian belief in each person's unrealized glory). Because she seems to expect that she will one day "wake a Bourbon," she must rehearse her regal role. However, her decking and posing cannot help but seem a parody, her desired elegance undercut by buttercups and aprons, and her queenship mocked by her admission that she will try to mimic a more aristocratic way of talking: "Put from my simple speech all plain word — / Take other accents, as such I heard." Like the minstrel performer or carnival masquerader, this undistinguished persona—compared to a beggar in the marketplace—postures and impersonates, practicing a role reversal in which she assumes the bearing of royalty. Although located in her home and in the nearby meadow, this speaker is performing a kind of show, acting, imitating, affecting an accent, and singing. Halfway through the poem, the speaker identifies the singing voice as vital to her plan; with an image, both enchanting and troubling, she singles out her tongue for special lofty placement: "And perch my Tongue / On Twigs of singing." The image is surprisingly majestic, identifying the tongue, birdlike, as a metaphor for her high station, an instance of synecdoche that implies that her voice should be regarded as her most vital, natural self. However, the image of perching her "Tongue" high up in a tree is also odd and troubling, insinuating that the speaker and her tongue are now apparently separated, and, by implication, that her voice has become disembodied. Although she exudes confidence in her capacity to will her recognition as a monarch, this speaker, para-doxically, in casting her voice "rather high" finds that it alights among a chorus of other singers—the "Twigs" are alive with singing—and settles into a natural (not courtly) habitat. Sitting and singing "rather high" also carries the implication that, while she aspires to speak in august circles, she must be careful. The word "perch," with its con-notations of instability, presses the point. She may expect her voice to vivify this magisterial transformation, but her voice, however stirring, is placed most precariously.

Considering its likely date of composition (about 1862 or summer 1863), the poem seems weirdly detached from the realities of the country's experience. Entrenched in horrendous loss and devasta-tion, the nation experienced deep divisions and desperation in a war that seemed, as Lincoln continued to call up thousands of additional troops, endless. The proclamation for emancipation of the slaves that Lincoln presented in September 1862 was a source of jubilation by some and panic by others. Lincoln's attendant decisions to suspend the writ of habeas corpus and to authorize the arrests of anyone "disloyal" to the United States quelled protest as it increased the fear and anxiety that Lincoln was assuming dictatorial powers. In the early spring of 1863, Union forces were readying for a great offensive on several fronts against the Confederacy, but these battles were disasters for Union armies until July, when victories at Gettysburg and Vicksburg made, for a short while, an end to the war seem possible (Donald 354–447). Placed within this context of turmoil, the poem gathers an unexpected darkness that runs counter to the initial impression of its whimsy.

The poem's political references traject the speaker's vision into a set-ting far from 1860s America. This rustic dreamer imagines being trans-ported to another place and perhaps another time. Casting herself as "plain" and poor, the speaker conceives a fantasy of power and station as well as of something more: she awakens a queen, a sovereign leader, a ruler. The compulsive repetition of her fantasy—she muses on this metamorphosis "every day"—conveys an urgent desire to escape her present time and place. The reality of the nation's condition in 1862 and 1863 provides ample explanation as to why this speaker would want to experience different, more illustrious circumstances. Observing Dickinson's preference for a regal and aristocratic diction and her penchant for the narrative of "surprising elevation to noble rank," Jane Donahue Eberwein cites the legend of the Lord of Burleigh (*Strategies* 101). In the story (also noted by Patterson, as Eberwein indicates), a "humble village maiden" unknowingly marries into money and rank, becoming the Countess of Exeter (Eberwein, *Strategies* 101; Patterson, *Imagery* 87, 215n26).[30] However, a countess is not a queen, and being "Summoned" has connotations different from the pleasures of being drawn into an auspicious marriage. Moreover, in the chronicles of British history there is another Exeter, one associated with queens. This Exeter, Henry Courtenay, Marquess of Exeter, along with his wife, Gertrude, Marchioness of Exeter, was part of the high nobility in the court of Henry VIII. The Marquess of Exeter was Henry's first cousin, confidante, and member of the King's Council. As honorific head of the King's Privy Chamber, he had full access to all the plans, plots, suspicions, and machinations that characterized Henry's reign, and, thus, he was involved in the orchestration of some of Henry's marriages and divorces. To be summoned before this Exeter was likely to make one uneasy. The Aragon in this Exeter story is Catherine of Aragon, the daughter of two sovereigns—Queen Isabella of Castile and King Ferdinand of Aragon—and Henry's first wife.[31] Privy to the scheming that accompanied the annulment of this twenty-four-year marriage for Anne Boleyn to replace Catherine as Henry's wife, Exeter, later, was also fully aware of Henry's intentions to divorce Anne, an arrangement expedited by accusations of treason against her that were also used to engineer her trial and subsequent execution. The Marchioness of Exeter too had her hand in these events, apparently being among those who hated Anne Boleyn from the outset and was involved in designs to bring about her downfall. The Marquess and Marchioness both supported the marriage between Henry and Jane Seymour, hoping that this alliance would lead to the restoration of Princess Mary, Catherine's daughter, as heir to the throne. Unfortunately for them, they were caught in the tangle of accusations, arrests, and terror that sprung up and spread regarding these matters of power and succession. Exeter lost his privileged position with the King's Council and was ultimately executed in autumn 1538, accused of treason himself and suspected of plotting to kill the king (Starkey 297–98, 551, 587–88, 595–99, 708; Weir 380). The references in the poem to Exeter, Aragon, and Bourbon incant particular people and places and evoke a more generalized atmosphere of royal splendor and courtly convolutions far from Amherst. Juhasz concludes that the poem's references to Aragon, Exeter, and Bourbon signify a "state of mind" ("Big Tease" 33). Perhaps so, but one wonders what state of mind they signify. Invoking the kings and queens of British history summons tales of terror as well as of power. The mood of the poem oscillates wildly: on the one hand, the speaker's state of mind comes across as fancy-free and grandly optimistic; on the other hand, if one takes seriously the references, times, and context, the mood of the poem darkens and withers. Does the speaker frolic and pose for a crown of power and romance, or is her carnivalized promenading a sign of something more grim—the intimation of the everyday reality in early 1860s America of profound fear? It was a threat to be summoned before the Court of Henry VIII—it meant possible accusation, arrest, imprisonment, and death. These, in fact, were the very fears spreading across America in the early 1860s.

The poem "I'm saying every day" does not directly reference blackface performance, but the poem resonates with the conventions of the minstrel show. The speaker's bearing emphasizes costuming, acting, singing, and posing. The speaker practices other accents. She rehearses an identity that she clearly announces as a complete reversal of her perceived self. In minstrel shows, the performers parodied and satirized people and texts that enjoyed authority, fame, and public attention. Mock kings and queens have long been a mainstay of carnivals and community festivals; satires of the national aristocracy held a strong place on the minstrel stage. Similarly, embedded within the whimsy of the performance of the poem, there is a crosscurrent of political and social commentary: the speaker rehearses an upturning of social station, her language making clear her consciousness of class and rank, and her tropes convey a mindfulness of the perilous seas of power. Although beckoning coronations, the speaker's vision is imbued with shadows of threats and violence.

The blackface minstrel show exhibited this kind of incongruity, overlapping the jubilations of lively entertainment with questions that were serious and threatening. Observing this paradox, Lott proposes that the blackface minstrel figure derived from two key sources, the clown or harlequin and the slave trickster ("Blackface" 9–10). Blackface performance was seen everywhere in nineteenth-century America—on the serious theater stage as well as in circuses, traveling menageries, dime museums, and Ethiopian opera houses. Blackface performance was frequently part of Christmastime theatricals in the nineteenth century (Nissenbaum 125–26). Documenting the common and widespread presence of blackface performance on the legitimate American stage in the nineteenth century, Cockrell, in a list that he stresses is "incomplete," has counted over five thousand American stage productions involving blackface between 1751 and 1843, and estimates that about 25 percent of all American stage productions at this time involved blackface (*Demons of Disorder* 14–15). In one of those convergences of the highbrow and the popular, *Othello* rivaled "Jim Crow" as the most frequently performed blackface piece during that period (Cockrell, *Demons of Disorder* 27–28). These and other scholars argue for an expansive understanding of blackface performance. British scholar George Rehin, for example, views Jim Crow as an "archetypal clown," exhibiting characteristics of costume and physical feature typical of the type, and the minstrel show as an American example of European "popular theatre" ("Harlequin" 687–96). Articles, stories, and advertisements related to blackface minstrelsy appeared in the pages of newspapers and magazines such as the *Atlantic Monthly, Harper's Weekly,* and the *Boston Daily Atlas,* publications that came into the Dickinson household. The wide publication and distribution of sheet music also brought the minstrel performance right into the home. Although blackface troupes did perform in Amherst, as did minstrel troupes comprised of black performers, Dickinson would not have had to attend a minstrel performance to be informed of them.[32] In short, blackface minstrel shows were the most popular of entertainments during Emily Dickinson's lifetime. It would be astonishing if she were not well informed about them. As we have seen, she was informed, if verified only by the presence of several pieces of blackface minstrel music in her sheet music collection.

Dickinson's allusions to minstrelsy in her writing connect her to a wide and animated cultural conversation that addressed vital questions of personal and public identity and that debated the social struggles of her day. The minstrel show took on the contentious questions of identity, war, and nation in ways that were not straightforward; its mix of entertainment and social critique produced a language of crossings and costumings, riddles and ambiguity. Surprising as the unclarity may be to people of a later century, confusions regarding the race (and sometimes gender) of the blackface performers were sufficiently common that advertisements and sheet music covers frequently showed images of performers without their stage makeup—as white people— alongside images of how they appeared in blackface. Were the acts meant to be authentic depictions of black dance and song and legitimate recreations of black culture (as minstrel performers such as the Virginia Minstrels claimed), or were they intended as mocking caricatures? Just as important, what did audiences of the minstrel show think they were seeing and hearing? Historians disagree on this point. Some contend that audiences thought that blackface performers were actually black people (Lott, *Love and Theft* 20, 30, 39; Toll 38–40, 200). In his autobiographies, P. T. Barnum recounts an incident in which he felt compelled to appear on stage in blackface (when James Sandford [or Sanford], a "negro-singer" and main attraction, left the show) and was physically threatened by a man who was offended that a black man had spoken to him (*Life* 189–91; *Struggles and Triumphs* 89–90). Was minstrelsy obviously a "white man's charade" (Toll 40)? If so, what does it mean that by the 1860s, there were established minstrel troupes comprised of black musicians and black comedians, and some of these performers also used burnt cork make-up (Toll 195–269)? Whether the minstrel act connected or converged identities, whether it crossed identities out of hate, shame, guilt, curiosity, or other motivation, the blackface minstrel performer demonstrated the permeability of the borders of race, gender, and class.

The elaborate signification of minstrelsy complicates our perceptions of Dickinson and her verse. Her adaption of the minstrel trope, joined by a reader's recognition that Dickinson's penchants for impersonation, masks, riddles, and parody are mirrored in the minstrel show, propels Dickinson into a cultural space well beyond the ironic (and sometimes inflammatory) one cultivated by the Hutchinson Family with their mixing of music and politics and their conversions of minstrel melodies into anti-slavery songs. Dickinson's minstrels appear at crossroads, at sites crisscrossed with a rich array of cultural narratives. Her minstrels, with their mythic lineaments, appear at moments of vision or of violence. Witnesses to a world of conflict, her minstrels turn to misrule, trickery, a whirling of words, or a duel of wits to express the mash of uncertainty, chaos, threat, misery, glee, and hope that pervaded the nation. In hope that the entrancing airs of song and imagination will cast spells over difficult times and places and that words and wordplay will be the vehicles for propitious transformations, Dickinson and her minstrels specialize in the allure and variation of voice.

There is much singing in Dickinson's verse. A source of hope and strength in the poems, singing gives expression to an uplift of feeling. Her speakers sing for courage and for comfort, in glee and in steely defiance. In one poem of about 1862, she writes, "The first Day's Night had come — / And grateful that a thing / So terrible — had been endured — / I told my Soul to sing—" (F423). About three years later a speaker decrees, "Bind me — I still can sing — " (F1005). In a letter to her good friends the Hollands, Dickinson writes, "*My* business is to *sing*," ostensibly repeating the "sob" and words of a bird she saw "on a little bush at the foot of the garden" but also declaring for herself (Letter 269). Drawing again on bird imagery (as she does in scores of poems), Dickinson famously proposes that "'Hope' is the thing with feathers — " that "sings the tune without the words — / And never stops — at all — " (F314). Dickinson herself "perches" on "twigs of singing," aligning herself with singers and performers, musicians and dancers. For her, music is simply everywhere: "The Earth has many keys — / Where Melody is not / Is the Unknown Peninsula — " (F895). When she writes "Split the Lark — and you'll find the Music — " (F905), she professes the indispensable place of "Music": it is her trope for the quintessence of life, for the source and harmony of the self.

Dickinson's engagement with the most popular of musical entertainers and entertainments suggests that popular music served as an influence in her verse forms, but also that the racial, political, and class issues played out in popular music were relevant to Dickinson's writing. While her interest in the Hutchinson Family Singers, discussed in the previous chapter, discloses Dickinson's attention to the creative and musical expression of political views, acknowledgment of Dickinson's familiarity with minstrel music opens a new frame through which to peer at (and hear) some of her poems. Her minstrels are witnesses and commentators in both personal and public worlds of conflict; they appear at scenes of misrule or they beckon forces of misrule, resounding with the harmonies and dissonances of a culture's stories. Dickinson's minstrels exemplify the power of voice and convey her acute awareness of "singers." As if placing faith in her many birds who giggle and laugh, quibble and declaim, trill and quiver, witness, warn, strum, strike, dance, banter, and sing, Dickinson embraces her minstrel and welcomes the singer as another Orpheus who has the power to enchant and transform the world.

CHAPTER FOUR

CAPTIVITY AND LIBERTY

Haunted Tales of Emily Dickinson and Harriet Prescott Spofford

Nature is a Haunted House — but Art — a House that tries to be haunted.
🌸 Emily Dickinson in a letter to Thomas Wentworth Higginson, 1876

Bind me — I still can sing —
(F1005)

When Dickinson writes at the close of a poem composed around 1862 or 1863 that "Captivity is Consciousness — / So's Liberty — " (F649), she identifies the dichotomy that has marked the nation's history from its beginnings. Dickinson's aphoristic lines conjoin the experience of captivity—along with the threat of it so pervasive in the collective imagination—and the promise of liberty, a marriage of opposites that, by 1862, had tested the nation's moral elasticity, produced a troubled national story, and erupted into all-out civil war. The title "Emancipation" given by Higginson to the poem that includes these lines seemingly marks a direct connection to the fact of slavery and possibly to the historical moment that Lincoln created with his announcement, in September 1862, of the emancipation that would take effect on January 1, 1863. Recognizing in another poem of the same time the allure of difference—"'Tis Opposites — Entice" (F612)—Dickinson also warns of the dangers enlivened when opposites touch: "And Tinder — guessed — by power / Of Opposite" (F284).

So many forms of captivity persisted in nineteenth-century America that its forceful presence touched every community, household, and imagination. As an experience and a history, as a reality of law, as a system inventively justified and often ignored, captivity might be said to have haunted the nation. The fact and fantasy of captivity instigated many imaginative examinations of it: stories of abduction, enslavement, imprisonment, and servitude were commonplace on the stage, in song, and on the page. During the Civil War and afterward, newspapers and periodicals reported on the dreadful experiences of captured soldiers at Andersonville and other war prisons. The factory system that developed in nineteenth-century New England was commonly correlated with slavery in protest songs and reform writings. So many writers have described the domestic and familial "imprisonment" of women in the nineteenth century that Sandra Gilbert and Susan Gubar assert that "dramatizations of imprisonment and escape are so all-pervasive in nineteenth-century literature by women that we believe they represent a uniquely female tradition in this period" (85). The prominent place of captivity and confinement in the cultural discourse would certainly be evident in Dickinson's own reading of some of the popular authors of her time—writers such as Harriet Beecher Stowe, Rebecca Harding Davis, and Harriet Prescott Spofford—as well as of the now-revered British women writers—such as the Brontës, George Eliot, and Elizabeth Barrett Browning—on whom commentaries of Dickinson's reading preferences have frequently focused. Dickinson's own life, her interests and reading, her town and her family educated her about the permutations of captivity. Particularly worthy of close examination is Dickinson's encounter with Spofford's 1860 story "Circumstance," a tale that poses tangled visions of captivity and liberty, and one that apparently astonished Dickinson as well as frightened her. The story, and Dickinson's response to it, brings forth some of the specters and terrors of life in America as it materializes a great indeterminate, encroaching, clasping force that traps the woman in the story, agitates the reader (at least Dickinson-as-reader), and, arguably, haunts the nation. Dickinson's verse offers abundant evidence that she too was drawn into the effort to fathom something so menacing, so familiar, so confounding. Spofford's "Circumstance" conjures frightful figures and situations that Dickinson repeatedly—even compulsively—called forth: demons, fiends, confinements, and hauntings. That Spofford's short story garnered special attention from Dickinson suggests that "Circumstance" depicted something—a situation, a sensibility, a tactic—familiar to Dickinson. As the woman in Spofford's story tries to save herself, her voice is released and transformed, an all-too-real and fantastical experience rendered frequently in Dickinson's writing.

As the early days of the republic pushed into the nineteenth century, the experience of captivity was generally considered normal—as evidenced by the bastion of laws established to keep millions enslaved, to remove American Indians westward, and to stake claim on the lives of working people. The first census of the United States in 1790 recorded a slave population of 697,624 throughout the states and territories. By 1850 the number of slaves had increased to 3,204,313 men, women, and children, who were owned by 347,725 families (which is close to 10 percent of all families that were recognized in the census). By 1860, the slave population had increased by another 23.4 percent to a count of close to four million (*Century of Population Growth* 132, 135).[1] A focus of congressional legislation, so-called compromises, debates, conflicts, and protest since the origins of the United States, slavery certified its presence on the national stage through the first half of the nineteenth century as the nation expanded and demarcated its territory. By the 1850s, Congress and the judiciary had crafted key laws and heard cases related to the expansion of slavery into new territories as well as to matters of civil rights. While the outright abolition of slavery was generally a politically untenable position in 1860 and the presidential election campaign of 1860 exacerbated the ferociousness of the standoff between those who favored slavery's long reach and those who aimed to curtail it, in the summer of 1862 Lincoln shifted his advocacy of a more gradual emancipation to a call for quicker action, and the Emancipation Proclamation went into effect January 1, 1863.[2]

The enveloping forces of law, science, religious doctrine, custom, and language independently and collectively legitimized confinement and enslavement as a fact of life for vast numbers of people in the United States. One might think of the centuries-long history of trouble brought to Native American populations by Europeans and Americans that was justified by views of Indians as savages, killers, cannibals, and monsters.[3] One might think of the elaborate methods and efforts of natural historians such as Samuel George Morton and Josiah C. Nott to determine racial categories and human classifications, which were used in defining racial hierarchies and justifying slavery. The regulated experience of the girls and women who labored in factories and mills adds to the national story of de facto imprisonment. Characterizing factory work of the mid-nineteenth century as "wage-slavery," Catherine Clinton describes the unsafe and exploitive conditions in which women worked in textile mills in New England (21–39).[4]

The troubles and hazards of factory life were not unknown in Amherst during Dickinson's lifetime. In the nineteenth century, Amherst had many mills for the manufacture of paper, cotton, and wool. Fires plagued mills of all these types; one in 1857 at the Jones Factory was particularly terrible, forcing many of the workers—many of whom were women—to jump from second-story windows to save themselves (Carpenter 292). In his *History of the Town of Amherst,* E. W. Carpenter reports that fires ended the textile industry in the town: "The series of disastrous fires that destroyed so many mills proved a death-blow to the textile industry at North Amherst. After the year 1860, there is no further mention [in town records] of any attempt to manufacture either cottons or woolens in Amherst" (291).[5] Hatmaking, however, thrived in Amherst, and by 1872 the manufacture of palm leaf hats there had expanded so significantly that the town was considered "the hatmaking center of the nation" (Lombardo, *Tales* 52). Palm leaf hatmaking in Amherst began in the 1820s with Leonard Hills, who hired primarily girls and young women to braid and sew palm leaves into hats. The Hills Manufacturing Company became the leading employer in Amherst. However, serious health risks, especially to the lungs, were linked to hatmaking, so much so that by 1847 the braiding of palm leaf hats was cited as "*the* cause" of the high rate of premature deaths among young women in Amherst: the *Hampshire and Franklin Express* reported that "a few years of such labor and all that remains is a feeble youth, sickly womanhood, premature decline and early death" (quoted in Lombardo, *Tales* 53). An 1831 article in *the New-England Magazine* reported that girls as young as age four worked at making palm leaf hats ("Palm Leaf Hats" 177).[6]

Throughout the century, the riddling questions of human rights were reiterated in political and scientific debates. In his 1859 essay "Ought Women to Learn the Alphabet?," the ardent champion of human rights Thomas Wentworth Higginson reviews centuries of disparaging claims about women, noting the irrational reasoning that continued to deprive women of rights and opportunity: "We have, first, half educated women, and then, to restore the balance, only half paid them" (273–74). Also noting the illogic that served to demean women, Theodore Tilton, in his 1869 biographical essay on Elizabeth Cady Stanton, records that the Women's Rights Convention of July 1848 and "above all, its demand for woman's suffrage, excited the universal laughter of the nation." Noting that even Stanton's own father, Judge Cady, "fancied her crazy," Tilton reports that "wonder-stricken people asked each other the question, 'What sort of creatures could those women at Seneca Falls have been?'" (347). Similarly recognizing the ironic dynamic that would mock women for thinking themselves deserving of legal rights, Higginson further comments, "Man, placing his foot upon her shoulder, has taunted her with not rising" ("Ought Women to Learn" 276). Judgments, "proofs," and perceptions effectively maintained a system of restricted rights although the varied forms of disempowerment were often labeled opportunity, morality, knowledge, or freedom.

Perhaps not surprisingly, stories of captivity in its many forms—slavery, Indian captivity, high seas kidnapping, mill work, constrictions of women's lives—were widely narrated, and tropes of freedom and captivity were commonly imagined in productions of popular culture and mass entertainment. The contemporary prose fiction and verse narrative that comprised part of Dickinson's reading also reveal the prominent place of captivity and confinement in the national discourse, as narratives by the British and American authors that Dickinson read relate captivity, poverty, imprisonment, constricted means, and desperate lives.[7] We know, for example, that Dickinson likely read Rebecca Harding Davis's 1861 story of the wretchedly confined lives of iron mill and factory workers, for in a letter to her sister-in-law, Susan, of about April 1861, Emily asks Sue to lend her "Life in the Iron Mills," a story that had just been published anonymously in the *Atlantic Monthly* (Letter 231). Crammed with images of oppressive enclosed spaces such as a basement, prison cells, a smoky parlor, and a fiery hell-pit of a mill, the story portrays the mill workers, particularly the artistic Hugh Wolfe and Hugh's cousin Deborah, as, in effect, being buried alive. Rebecca Harding Davis depicts nineteenth-century industrialized America as a kind of underworld, a dreary borderland of the "free" and the enslaved, a place both suffocating and paralyzing. Eventually imprisoned for a petty theft that was committed almost accidentally (first through chance—in that Deborah takes the money and gives it to Hugh—and then out of a frantic desire for a different life), Hugh struggles to resurrect himself through his sculpting, such as the creation of a large korl woman, whose heavy, crouching, stretching form embodies the emotions that Hugh (and Deborah) cannot voice.[8] Placing Rebecca Harding Davis as well as Emily Dickinson within a nineteenth-century "rebellious American sisterhood," David Reynolds calls Dickinson the "highest product" of such literary "Amazons" as Fanny Fern (Sara Willis Parton), Lillie Devereux Blake, Elizabeth Drew Stoddard, Louisa May Alcott, Alice Cary, and Harriet Prescott Spofford (Reynolds, *Beneath* 397–433).

Dickinson's education of captivity and rebellion included her reading of Harriet Beecher Stowe's *Uncle Tom's Cabin,* the phenomenally successful and influential novel of which Dickinson's father seemed to disapprove.[9] Considering the extraordinary presence of *Uncle Tom's Cabin* in American culture, it is probably no surprise that there were numerous stage productions of the play throughout Massachusetts (in such towns and cities as Boston, Worcester, Lowell, Leominster, Milford, and Amherst) in the 1850s and later. While theatrical productions were generally disapproved of in Amherst until the 1870s, Rand reports that dramatizations of *Uncle Tom's Cabin* were a "perennial favorite" in Amherst (Rand 215).[10] Stowe herself was a presence in Amherst, having visited twice in the early 1850s (Pollak, *Dickinson* 195; Keller 104). Stowe's daughter Georgiana and son-in-law Henry Allen moved to Amherst in April of 1872, when he assumed the station of rector of the Grace Episcopal Church in town, and they lived there for the next five years (Lombardo, *Hedge* 18–19). Stowe spent the summer of 1872 in Amherst with her daughter and, in early October of the same

year, she returned to Amherst as part of a busy reading tour throughout New England (Lombardo, *Hedge* 18–19).[11] During the time that
Georgiana lived in Amherst, Susan Dickinson had opportunity to meet
Harriet Beecher Stowe and spend time with her. As described in her
"Annals of the Evergreens," Susan met Stowe at the home of Georgiana
Stowe Allen and apparently spent many fascinating and amusing hours
with her, remembering Stowe as a sociable and talkative guest, excited
by the "glory of the October morning."[12] Besides daughter Georgiana,
other members of Stowe's family had connections to Amherst and to
the Dickinsons. Stowe's husband, Calvin, preached in Amherst in the
early 1850s (Leyda 1: 205; Keller 104). Stowe's brother Henry Ward
Beecher had strong ties to Amherst through schooling—he attended
Amherst College from 1830 through 1834 (Applegate 77–81, 91–97,
102–3; Hedrick 92; Keller 104)—and through the Dickinson family—he
married Eunice Bullard, the sister of Asa Bullard, Edward Dickinson's
brother-in-law (Benfey, *Summer* 71–76; Leyda 1: xxxiii). Henry periodically delivered public lectures in Amherst (Leyda 1: 196, 209); in July
1862, he delivered the college commencement address, described by
J. G. Hall in the *Republican* as a great success: "Beecher was elo-
quent, earnest and right, and carried away the sympathies of the audience with him by storm" (Leyda 2: 62). Keller avers that Dickinson
heard the phrase "the Earthquake in the South" in Henry's address
and used it in her poem "At least to pray is left — is left" (F377; Keller
104). Stowe's literary depictions of desperate situations and of lives
constricted or overwhelmed by servitude and slavery infiltrated the
cultural consciousness of people throughout the country, and Emily
Dickinson, living in a town in which Stowe and Stowe's family had a
vital presence, is unlikely to have been exempt from that influence.

THE HAUNTED HOUSE OF NATURE

Dickinson's gravitation to the American poet and fiction writer
Harriet Prescott Spofford is also of interest here. A prolific writer,
Spofford was widely published in numerous popular magazines such

as the *Atlantic Monthly, Harper's Bazar, Harper's New Monthly Magazine, Scribner's Magazine, Lippincott's Magazine,* the *Galaxy, St. Nicholas,* and others. In an essay on Harriet Prescott's early writing that appeared in the *Springfield Republican* in 1903, Susan Dickinson addresses her own admiration for the author's writing and of her "distinct disappointment" if an issue of the *Atlantic Monthly* did not contain something by Prescott (or Spofford, as she was known after her marriage to Richard S. Spofford in December 1865). Describing "Circumstance" as "the most highly imaginative and thrilling tale I have ever read" ("Harriet" 19), Sue also records Emily's enthusiasm for the story. After reading "Circumstance," Emily immediately sent Sue the following note: "Dear S.: That is the only thing I ever saw in my life I did not think I could have written myself. You stand nearer the world than I do. Send me everything she writes" ("Harriet" 19).[13] Two years later Emily Dickinson wrote Thomas Wentworth Higginson that the story "Circumstance" was so haunting that she felt she must avoid Prescott's stories. In a letter of April 1862, she reports that "I read Miss Prescott's 'Circumstance,' but it followed me, in the Dark — so I avoided her — " (Letter 261). The discrepancy between the two accounts of Dickinson's response to "Circumstance" is curious. One account implies that Dickinson read many of Spofford's stories and the other states that Dickinson "avoided" them. What does the discrepancy suggest? Perhaps Dickinson underwent some change in the two years that shifted her reaction to the story from attraction to anxiety? One does wonder what it was about "Circumstance" that made the story so extraordinary to both Sue and Emily: "the most imaginative and thrilling tale I have ever read," Sue declared. What made it, by 1862, so frightening for Emily?

First published in the May 1860 issue of the *Atlantic Monthly* under the name Harriet Prescott (and republished three years later in *The Amber Gods and Other Stories*),[14] "Circumstance" tells a horrifying tale of abduction and captivity, of monsters and devils. Exploring the response to a terrifying situation, the story recounts a woman's confrontation with a shocking beast and her discovery of the astonishing power wielded by her voice. Set in the "eastern wilds of Maine," the story opens as a woman is starting home at twilight after visiting all day with a sick neighbor. With three miles to walk across copse, meadows, and woods, the woman proceeds, tired but steady and, with "her eyes wide-open," heads home to her baby and husband. Soon after she enters the woods, however, a "wild beast" swoops upon her and carries her high up onto the bough of a fir tree. As the animal claws at her clothing, the woman's screams assume a more musical sound, which calms the beast and eventually lulls him to sleep. Understanding that she must sing to survive, she does so continuously through the night. At dawn her husband (who has carried the baby along) discovers his wife trapped in the tree, still singing in what is described now as an "unearthly key"; with patience and some luck he manages to shoot the beast dead. On their return, the woman and her husband find that their home and those of their neighbors have been marauded in the night by Indians and burned to the ground.

Focusing on a dreadful predicament, the story replays a drama seen in myth, legend, and literature: the response of a person who, when confronted with danger, uses her voice to buy time or to defend herself. The woman in Spofford's "Circumstance" is a kind of Scheherazade, another woman with nerve and imagination, who postpones her death repeatedly by telling stories each night until (after a thousand and one) she has sufficiently charmed her husband the king so that he allows her to live.[15] The woman in "Circumstance" resembles the siren who can exploit her desirability and enchant men by her singing. She is the snake charmer whose melodies can mesmerize the serpent. She is the musical David whose harp soothes the troubled King Saul and who eventually slays the colossus Goliath (1 Samuel 16–17). She is the lucky Jack who, in *Jack and the Beanstalk,* escapes the giant who has been lulled to sleep with a magic harp. She is a female Orpheus, her music casting spells and helping her to navigate a treacherous otherworld. An unexpected cousin of Jane Eyre, who distracts and disarms the controlling Rochester with stories, songs, and other amusements (and thus also evokes Scheherazade, as Nancy Workman notes), the woman in the trap imagined by Spofford entertains her captor.

In Spofford's story, the woman finds herself in the landscape of nightmare. Alone, at night, in the woods, she is accosted by a wild creature with very sharp claws. The beast itself presents a quandary: What, pray tell, is it? An amalgamation of human, animal, and monster, the beast evokes the hybrid beings that P. T. Barnum would showcase in his American Museum. In Barnum's venue, the fantastical body was presented as a living puzzle, one that illustrated the mysteries and ambiguities of human identity. In Spofford's story the creature is described variously as "wild beast," "Indian Devil," "monster," and "swift shadow." On its first appearance, the narrator implies that this being is familiar to residents of the region: "It was that wild beast — the most savage and serpentine and subtle and fearless of our latitudes" (Spofford 85). Though ferocious and frightening, it is known. Some readers have referred to the creature as a panther (perhaps due to the reference to "panther tribes" in the first paragraph of the story) or a mountain lion (Fetterley 264; Gaul 35; Garbowsky 13; Wardrop, Gothic 84; St. Armand, "'I Must'" 101; David Cody 40).[16] The thought that the beast is a panther may also derive from a statement in Elizabeth Halbeisen's biography of Spofford that the story "Circumstance" was inspired by an experience of her great-grandmother, who "was said to have sung all night in the grasp of a panther" (12). Yet in Spofford's story, the beast's features and abilities suggest something far more fantastical. Said to resemble the "fabulous flying-dragon" (85), it comes equipped with lacerating claws, sharp "white tusks," and eyes that blaze like "balls of red fire" (86). Almost immediately, the trapped woman imagines the "fierce plunge of those weapons" (86) and soon she feels "the daggered tooth penetrating her flesh" (88). What is this being? Is it an actual terror of the wilderness? Is it a supernatural wonder? While seeming real enough, is it, nonetheless, an apparition? Described as a "shadow" on first appearance, the creature seems to have materialized out of an extraordinarily bad dream.

Moreover, this horror comes with startling erotic particulars: its hot breath washes over her face and body (86), long claws tangle in her clothing, and long lolling tongue "caresses" her (90). Often the narrator reports that the "long red tongue thrust forth again" (87). In case we doubt the erotic quality of this assailant's actions, we are told that

as he lay upon the woman and licks her face, "a half-whine of enjoyment escaped him" (90). He is physically upon her, embracing her,
holding her, lying on her, licking her. He stretches his paw "across her
with heavy satisfaction" (88), claiming her. The narrator's commentary
also connects the preying beast with a physical, sexualized self—it is
known by "our lower natures let loose." He is, the story reports, a "living lump of appetites," unleashed and demanding (89).

The woman and her captor are in a tight embrace for much of the
story. At one point, "both of her arms were pinioned in the giant's
vice" (90). That the beast has difficulty disentangling its claws from
the woman's clothing reinforces the image of them as entwined. In
her efforts to express the fear experienced by the woman, the narrator
muses that this kind of death, which seems unavoidable, would be
more horrible than death by fire, since fire is something "remote" and
"alien"—and therefore, in a sense, less personal; this monstrosity, the
narrator contends, is "half ourselves" (89). The apparent conflation of
captor and captive makes manifest one of the most pervasive concerns
for women in the wilderness: the possibility that a woman will turn
"uncivilized," her sexuality unloosed, her appetites untamed. In narratives in which white women come in contact with Indians, the pres-
ervation of a woman's chastity and her ladylike deportment are always
of concern.[17] While one might correlate the beast with male violence
(as Fetterley and Gaul do), the story intimates another possibility: the
fabulous flying creature is a reflection of the woman, the closeness
of their relationship most out in the open when most hidden. The
woman's response to her avatar can be read equivocally, her singing
as much a serenade as a frantic effort to ward off suffering. Recalling
Stuart Hall's observation regarding the fusion of self and Other (that
"the Other is not outside, but also inside the Self, the identity" [16]),
the close encounter of singing woman and flying creature manifests
the personal drama of perceiving oneself and knowing oneself through
whoever (or whatever) seems most different from oneself.

In Spofford's tale, the woman is sought after not only by her husband, but also apparently by the beast. For whatever purpose, the beast
has claimed her, a choosing that may be random or may be deliberate.

The creature is readily perceived as a horror by the woman and by the reader, but as has been discussed, it is as prismatic as a dream. It is truly a wonder of indeterminacy: monster, animal, devil, shadow. We do not really know that the creature intends to harm the woman. He has whisked her up a tree and she "instinctively" imagines a brutal mauling, but it is possible that the creature does not purposefully harm her. When his claws become caught in her clothing, the story reports, he tries to "disentangle" them. Understandably, the woman sees him as a "monster," but when she shrieks, he steps back. He actually seems comforted by her voice. When the creature folds itself around the woman's body, might this suggest something other than her victimization? Is it possible that this fantastical creature is not a threat? By detaining the woman, the creature consequently draws the husband and baby away from the peril of the night attack. Monster, shadow, redeemer? The woman's experience in the wilderness is fraught with conflicting images: the beast thwarts her return home, and the beast's actions also compel "home" to find her; her repertoire of songs mostly invokes adventure that is far from home in tales of war, of travel and seafaring adventure, of freedom and escape, although some songs recall her life to her—her child and husband, memories of her first communion, and her mother (Spofford 90–91).

In effect, the extraordinary creature appears out of the night air for the woman, a muse in a monster's mien. Despite the story of horror and assault, one might perceive that, in the shrewd way of doubles, the woman uncovers—at night, in the dark, alone, in the forest—a wild and shadowy part of herself. The situation recalls Gilbert and Gubar's theory of the "mad double" in women's writing; describing widespread images of confinement and submission in nineteenth-century literature written by women, they propose that the "female author enacts her own raging desire to escape from male houses and male texts" through the creation of doubles that embody violence, madness, and monstrosity, half-hidden presences that exhibit the anger and anxiety that a "normal" woman would feel required to repress (78–79, 85). In a similar vein, Jeffrey Weinstock professes that ghosts and other supernatural beings in American women's fiction of the nineteenth and early twentieth

centuries are "far less frequently sinister or horrific figures" than in stories written by men since they themselves are not threats but rather
often signal women's anxieties and common state of "disempowerment"
(19, 26). In a discussion of nineteenth-century women's gothic fiction
that includes Spofford's 1860 novel *Sir Rohan's Ghost,* Weinstock argues
that the "ghost in the parlor" (or any other gothic-inspired supernatural
creature) metaphorically dwells alongside or inside the woman: "The
ghost in the parlor, so to speak, functions in these works as a thinly
veiled metaphor for the living woman 'ghosted' by a culture that refuses
to recognize women as active agents in control of their own destinies
and which socially and legally sanctions misogyny" (27). While these
theorists and others, such as Kate Ellis, pay particular attention to the
Victorian home as a site of imprisonment for women, "home" might well
include the panoply of expectations and common experience that cir-
cumscribe and define many women's lives. For American women of the
nineteenth century, gothic mood or phenomena would appear to arise
from anxieties regarding the commonplace violence that encroaches on
women's bodies and minds, from the dispiriting recognition of being
treated as not wholly human, from the shock of dispossession, or, more
succinctly, from anxieties and troubles regarding their bodies, families,
children, and marriages. According to the reinforcing theories of Gilbert
and Gubar, Weinstock, and others, a gothic presence in women's writing
manifests women's doubled, divided, or splintered selves, whether or
not the accosting phantoms or goblins be menacing.[18] In her examination of the fantastic in literature (and the gothic as a form of the fantastic), Rosemary Jackson addresses the metamorphosing relationship
of self and threatening "other"—whether originating within the self or
outside the self—as well as the "strong desire" depicted in some gothic
tales (such as *Frankenstein*) to find union with one's "lost" or divided
selves (58–59, 100).

In "Circumstance," the coerced coming together of self and other—
whether as doubles, foes, confederates, or kin—conflates the realms
of the familiar and fantastical, the natural and supernatural. When
the woman finds herself singing lullabies to a monster, one implication is that the creature is her "baby," a being born from her and for

which she is responsible.[19] Through the story's confusion of imagery that entwines the maternal and the horrible, the woman retains what she is supposed to have (the legitimate domestic relationship) but also "escapes" the potentially imprisoning narrative of the demure silent woman: she releases something wild in herself—a peculiar other-worldly voice with which she saves her life.

Much of the critical commentary on "Circumstance" evaluates the woman's spiritual state, regarding the traumatic encounter in the woods as a test of the woman's faith in God and as a restoration of that faith (as has been asserted by Bendixen, David Cody, Dalke, Fetterley, Garbowsky, and Holly). Does it seem likely that Dickinson's response to the story (or Susan's for that matter) comes from such an orthodox view? As sensible as these readings that focus on the woman's relationship to a god are, the ordeal in the Maine woods suggests meanings other than the reaffirmation of religious faith. For example, the sudden appearance of the beast (devil, dragon, shadow) in Spofford's tale might mark the return of a demonized and ostracized Other, perhaps bent on retribution or on "testing" the woman's courage, resourcefulness, or stamina. From this viewpoint, the dreadful standoff high up in the tree summons the long history of captivities and insurrections in this nation, of innocents held prisoner, of power wielded ruthlessly, of graspings to survive. The story suggests that, unless rattled by deep personal trauma, we tend to live comfortably with these histories. Perhaps what is a memento of the ghostliness that has settled into the countryside—a "winding-sheet," so "cold, white, and ghastly" (85)—appears early in the story, although the woman is surprisingly undisturbed by a sight so spooky, as if she sees such things as floating corpses with regularity. Despite the sudden appearance of a "deathly blot," she is "happy in her situation" (85). Oddly, all of the strange sights and inscrutable creatures seem familiar to the woman, who, the story informs us, is not subject to "fancies" (85).

A careful attention to matters of dispossession, revenge, and ignored histories reinforces the link between Spofford's story and tales of Indian captivity and Indian lore. When Wardrop identifies the creature in "Circumstance" as a "half-human Indian beast" (*Gothic* 11),

123

she recalls the annals of Indian captivity, from Mary Rowlandson in 1676 onward, in which Indians are depicted as monsters and demons.[20] Spofford's story recalls "Panther Captivity," a surreal tale from the late eighteenth century in which a young "lady" is held captive by a "gigantic" man until, amazingly, she kills him in his sleep and decapitates and dismembers him. Curiously, in his account of captivity in the Maine woods in the 1690s, John Gyles writes that the Indians had many tales of the ghosts, devils, and fabulous creatures that inhabited their world. Gyles recounts one piece of lore that resonates with Spofford's story: the story of a gigantic bird that grabbed a boy and swept him up into its nest high up on a rock. The boy survived the threat of being clawed, bitten, and torn apart by the large bird and its babies (21–23, 30).[21] All of these narratives relate tales of ostensible assailants and specters that lurk in the natural world, ready to pounce on the child or woman who finds herself or himself in the midst of some known or unknown horror.

With monsters and ghosts potentially everywhere in "Circumstance," there is no secure place anywhere. In Spofford's narrative, a threatened home and an assaulted self must be reconceived. In the story, the family survives but must set out to build a new home; the woman herself has been changed ("She seems to herself like some one newly made" [96]) and, implicitly, the family must change as well. The threat to the woman in "Circumstance" instigates a stunning revelation: something wild in her is illuminated; something "unearthly" in her voice is released.[22] If one views the beast as the visible manifestation of the woman's unseen self, its death, by a panicked husband no less, would suggest that her voice and her "singing" need to be quieted, her desires and appetites suppressed.[23] And yet the story does not fully support these designs, since in "Circumstance," fantastic beings are not expunged; killing one actual or phantasmal monster does not eliminate apparitions or other forms of haunting. Specters persist in this world; possibly other "fabulous flying-dragons" survive, thus maintaining the possibility of recurring displays of women's unseen and unheard selves. The "singular foot-print in the snow" at the edge of the ruined settlement (96) marks another mysterious, uncanny presence.

In Spofford's story, the one "footprint" is not described in any way. Is the print barefoot or shod? Is it the impress of an adult or a child? It is not completely clear if the print is animal or human. Why is there only one? Are we to imagine an imprint of a phantom? The one footprint calls to mind another mythic narrative of a shipwrecked, stranded man: Robinson Crusoe. In a state of utter distress upon seeing the single footprint after fifteen years alone on his island, Crusoe worries and convinces himself that the footprint is, in turn, an apparition, a devil, a savage, or a cannibal, until one day he wonders if the print is his own, a contemplation that turns his most terror-inducing images of an alien other into himself. The invocation of the shipwrecked-man-who-survives holds meaning for Spofford's resilient woman. Not just far from home, but completely divested of a home and of everything connected to a "home," Crusoe constructs something new for himself out of the bits and pieces of the wreck of the ship and from the natural materials on the island. Spofford's answer to the crisis of the "imprisoning" home is, like Charlotte Brontë or, in a later day, Daphne du Maurier, to have the house burned down. Despite the woman's release from the beast's tearing claws, the family's home is still destroyed along with the rest of the settlement. This startling revelation in the story's final paragraph leaves us with a final image of the family alive but adrift. Perhaps the "monster," who has compelled the woman to sing, "has to" be killed so that the woman can be reunited with her husband and baby, but their home has been ruined nonetheless.

In a transmutation of faith into forms more mythic or magical than Christian, the woman in Spofford's "Circumstance" finds herself in a kind of otherworld: she is accosted in a forest wilderness and, placed dangerously high up in a tree, trapped in absolute darkness. Except for her abductor, she is alone. The smell given off by the creature's breath is described as a "hell-pit" (87). The beast tears at her clothing, injuring her, so that by the time her husband locates her she is "ghastly white" and "stained with blood" (94). The narrator of "Circumstance" implicitly refers to the Orpheus myth just as the woman begins to sing in an effort to save herself, or, perhaps more accurately, to delay what seems likely to be a painful and unavoidable death: "She had heard that music charmed wild beasts" (86). Spofford's story is filled with the language of spells and witchery (87, 93, 94, 95), and the beast is lulled temporarily into sleepiness by "the enchantment" (95). In addition to the charmed effect of her singing, the story also mentions specters, the wondrous image of the woman high in the tree, the fantastical creature itself. That the family has been saved from the nighttime Indian attack feels miraculous. The "unearthly key" in which the woman sings at the end of the story suggests that the woman's trial evokes something "otherworldly," her voice unnatural or supernatural.[24] These descriptions suggest that the events were partially hallucinatory, crossing boundaries of consciousness, dredging up repressed fears and desires, straddling worlds of recognition and delirium, implications made manifest when, as the woman wends her way home with husband and baby, we are told that "the night was a dream" (96). In addition to the underworld locales of Greek myth, Spofford's bewitched natural world aligns with the kind of dreamscapes displayed in the writings of such American authors as Cotton Mather, Washington Irving, Edgar Allan Poe, Nathaniel Hawthorne, E.D.E.N. Southworth, and Dickinson. In their invisible worlds, fanciful countrysides, toxic gardens, midnight forests, gothic plantations, and surreal spaces, nature is made very strange. In Spofford's story, nature *is* a haunted house, or, rather, it is "the" haunted house, a portal of mystery and dread, a parlor of enchantment.

When Dickinson or Dickinson's speaker announces "I see — New Englandly" in "The robin's my criterion for tune" (F256), she credits her immersion in a time and, especially, a place, with shaping her attitudes and judgments. Her viewpoint, she says, reflects her particular environment. While many scholars have understood Dickinson's claim to see "New Englandly" as her acknowledgement of the importance of the regional landscape or of a Puritan legacy, the same critics also note accompanying ironies. For example, Helen Vendler discerns humor in the speaker's recognition that all people have myopic perspective (or determined preferences): in the poem, the Queen of England is as "Provincially" posed as the speaker (86–87). Sewall perceives Dickinson's "New Englandly" characterization as out-and-out irony, asserting that there was "nothing provincial in her interests," as evidenced by Dickinson's wide circle of relationship and the depth of her observations and understanding of the world (1: 9). In discussing Dickinson's herbarium, Farr notes the irony of Dickinson's self-perception (or self-description): this woman who "liked to think that she saw 'New Englandly' was profoundly attracted to the foreign" (*Gardens* 99). In addition to these types of ironies (derived from Dickinson's suspect and dissonant self-description), seeing "New Englandly" might also invoke the macabre histories of the region, a climate of anxiety and accusation, or tales of sorcery. Dickinson writes in a short poem of about 1883,

> Witchcraft was hung, in History,
> But History and I
> Find all the Witchcraft that we need
> Around us, Every Day —
>
> (F1612)

Dickinson here announces her immersion in "Witchcraft," it being "Around us, Every Day." She summons a populace of mysterious beings and an invisible world of conjuration that lives alongside or within the boundaries of home and community. At the least, Dickinson's speaker seems unbothered by a world of apparitions and otherworldly forces and perhaps even takes pleasure in it. The poem's speaker sounds gratified that she has access to all the "Witchcraft" that she will "need," leaving open the question of what these needs might be. As in the poem "Sweet skepticism of the heart" (F1438), in which she writes of "the delicious throe / Of transport thrilled with Fear — " and of the pleasurable swing between comprehension and uncertainty, "Witchcraft was hung in history" testifies to a reality of shadow that slips in and out of view, and to a "New Englandly" perspective that recognizes, with both exhilaration and trepidation, a place inhabited by forces of the supernatural and vitalized by unaccountable occurrences.

The crisis so carefully detailed in "Circumstance" is one seen in many of Dickinson's poems: a speaker encounters a demon, a monster, a goblin, a ghost. As they do in Spofford's story, the ghastly and the familiar live side-by-side in Dickinson's poetic landscape. The streets where ladies stroll have become grotesquely blood-splattered, as "Scarlet Rain" falls and "sprinkles Bonnets — far below — " (F465). The neighborhood is not predictable or safe. A trip out to walk the dog becomes an occasion for navigating fantastical creatures: mermaids show themselves and stare; the sea, as charming as a stalker, chases the woman back home (F656). The domestic space preserves intimidating prospects: "I Years had been from Home / And now before the Door / I dared not enter, lest a Face / I never saw before // Stare stolid into mine" (F440). One's own mind bedevils one, hosting "a superior spectre," far more frightening than ghosts and murderers (F407). The most discreet life can be subject to desperate appetites, as described in the first two stanzas of this poem of about 1862:

> It would have starved a Gnat —
> To live so small as I —
> And yet, I was a living child —
> With Food's necessity
>
> Opon me — like a Claw —
> I could no more remove
> Than I could coax a Leech away —
> Or make a Dragon — move —
> (F444)

The meek speaker experiences an appetite as a gripping "Claw" that is as formidable as a "Dragon," images that invoke Spofford's tenacious beast in "Circumstance." Like the situation in Spofford's tale in which the beast compels the woman, intruders of various guises galvanize Dickinson's personae, inspiring them to sing, to speak, to see, to laugh, to remember. The presence of unwelcome or assailing forces stirs her speakers' courage, at least at times, and even those who seem the playthings of their tormentors can still express themselves, spinning fear into vigorous words and voice, such as the tortured speaker of "He fumbles at your soul" who can contemplate her condition while awaiting the final fatal "imperial — Thunderbolt" (F477). Others, like the speaker in "The first day's night had come," outlast the nightmare: "grateful that a thing / So terrible — had been endured — / I told my Soul to sing — " (F423). Like a magician's trick, Dickinson's speakers can, at times, extract power out of air, so that she or he can "easy as a Star / Look down opon Captivity — / And laugh" (F445). A speaker in another poem notes that "There's Ransom in a Voice" (F1300), the fact of speaking (or singing or laughing) making possible a deliverance from whatever entraps or terrifies. Not short of bravado, her assaulted speaker will sing: "Magnanimous as Bird / By Boy descried — / Singing unto the Stone / Of which it died — " (F1349). There are many possible responses to the experience of torment and captivity: endurance, acceptance, defiance, resistance, escape. In their varied experience of trespass, Dickinson's personae call upon courage or tenacity; some cope through luck; some rename the trial, converting it into something more congenial: "A Prison gets to be a friend — " (F456), one speaker blithely declares. Another advises "To learn the Transport by the Pain — " (F178) and another exalts in the paradox, "Joy to have perished every step — " (F739). In many poems, the speaker declares that she cannot be restrained: "No Prisoner be — / Where Liberty — / Himself — abide with Thee — " (F742); "No Rack can torture me — / My Soul — at Liberty — " (F649). One recalls the confident impounded bird-speaker mentioned above who simply decides to "Look down opon" (or "Abolish") imprisonment (F445).

Yet there is also the need for escape, upon which, the speaker muses—apparently repeatedly—in a poem of about 1875.

> Escape is such a thankful Word
> I often in the Night
> Consider it unto myself
> No spectacle in sight
>
> Escape — it is the Basket
> In which the Heart is caught

When down some awful Battlement
The rest of Life is dropt —

'Tis not to sight the savior —
It is to be the saved —
And that is why I lay my Head
Opon this trusty word —

(F1364)

This speaker "often" thinks about escape. She appears to lie awake at night, contemplating it, ever vigilant as if the need to run or hide could be upon her at any moment. Mindful of some threatening "spectacle" (or "Monster then in sight," Dickinson's alternative line 4), she is grateful for the idea of escape ("Escape is such a thankful Word") even if her vision of it offers limited relief: in the poem, something vital ("the Heart") is saved and something vital ("The rest of Life") is lost. Rescue and doom sit side by side. In this poem, unspecified but terrible dangers abound; battlements exist. There is the homey image of the "Basket," the woven or wood container that might hold flowers or breads, and which here catches "the Heart," yet the correlation in the poem—a "Heart" is saved as "the rest of Life" is lost—makes for the thinnest sort of hope. The reference to a "Battlement" (line 7) acknowledges the need for protection, although the battlement itself is "awful" and, in the situation envisioned by the speaker, is the site of devastating injury: "Life" has been or will be "dropt," deliberately or accidentally, from the tremendous height of the battlement. Such fortifications are worse than useless. Moreover, if one's life is "dropt" how is one's heart "saved"? The poem's formation of escape depends on or leads to a severe division of self—a split between mind and body or a psychic rift, part saved and part not. The speaker, sleepless, ponders such dramatic self-severance.

The speaker in Dickinson's poem "Bind me I still can sing" (F1005) also recognizes a divided sense of self. Similar to the woman in "Circumstance," Dickinson's speaker imagines herself as bound and killed, her singing a sign of resistance and, ironically, survival. A line from a

Covenant hymn that Spofford's trapped woman recalls ("Though He slay me, yet will I trust in him" [91]) also resonates with Dickinson's speaker's words in this poem: "Slay — and my Soul shall rise / Chanting to Paradise — " (lines 4–5). That their voices prevail and even honor the one who can "bind," "banish," and "slay" bespeaks a possible religious salvation, although so much in "Circumstance" sidesteps Christian allegory and so much of what we know about Dickinson would lead us in other directions. The vow of "trust" and the destination of "Paradise" may have spiritual import but spirit does not need a Christian provenance. The woman in "Circumstance" and the speaker in the poem have each endured torment, their singing voices extricating them from a nightmare and opening the way to a miraculous reclamation. Given the plentitude of constricting circumstances and blocked spaces in Dickinson's poems, the recurring mention of escape is not surprising, with a speaker's singing (or laughing or meditating or playing) as a source of defense.[25] In her discussion of closed doors, entrapping rooms, and hidden spaces in Dickinson's verse, Wardrop notes that Dickinson's speakers can appear enamored of confining sites or situations (as in "How soft this prison is" [F1352]), or at least comfortable (as in "The soul selects her own society" [F409]). For Dickinson, like Poe, a "Tomb" can resemble a "Home" (*Gothic* 28). Yet, one hears excitement in the contemplation of "escape": "I never hear the word 'Escape' / Without a quicker blood," (F144). Another of Dickinson's adventurers relishes "a Hairbreadth 'scape" (F1247). These mixed attitudes and the apparent necessity of a divided sensibility suggest that "escape," in the sense of flight or freedom, is extremely unlikely, if not impossible. "Escape" in these poems seems to require exceptional poise or an artful imagination that enables one to find comfort or delight in confinement. Moreover, what conditions or situations can one aspire to escape? How is one to even know? In discussing the "fictional shape Dickinson gave her life," Gilbert and Gubar describe a self-dramatization that is at times romantic and at times gothic: they posit that Dickinson depicts a woman's life as a "living burial," a view that is assembled out of the many images of graves, coffins, caverns, and chasms in the poems. For Dickinson, say Gilbert and Gubar, a woman's body was a place of entombment

(626–30). How can one hope or expect to "escape" one's own body? If, as Gilbert and Gubar assert, "psychic fragmentation" reflects "society's multiple (and conflicting) demands upon women" (622), the split or splintered self, depicted in so many Dickinson poems, may also provide a strategy for maneuvering within such disconcertingly contradictory roles: the "split" Dickinson persona may present herself as both restrained and rebellious, both "dropt" and saved, both compliant and bold. Despite her argument that Dickinson's speakers adjust to their entrapment, Wardrop also proposes that enclosed domestic spaces that constrain can also allow for "experimenting with new, raw, female power" (*Gothic* 30).

Other Dickinson poems depict scenarios as sensational as those in "Circumstance" and address comparable issues: survival, the comprehension of peril, and the tottering line between illusion and reality. In a poem of about 1862, Dickinson imagines an intrepid figure, someone willing to look directly at realities that remain unspecified but which are disturbing, disorienting, or worse.

When we stand on the tops of Things —
And like the Trees, look down,
The smoke all cleared away from it —
And mirrors on the scene —

Just laying light — no soul will wink
Except it have the flaw —
The Sound ones, like the Hills — shall stand —
No lightning, scares away —

The Perfect, nowhere be afraid —
They bear their dauntless Heads,
Where others, dare not go at noon,
Protected by their deeds —

The Stars dare shine occasionally
Opon a spotted World —

And Suns, go surer, for their Proof,
As if an axle, held —

(F343)

A meditation of particular urgency during wartime, the poem helps us to ponder the extent to which one can see the "reality" of a world that is damaged or diseased—"spotted." The poem depicts challenges of perception, of seeing through smoke and murk, of comprehending something that holds together only for the moment, or seems to hold, the "as if" in the last line emphasizing that cohesion may be an illusion. The confidence or certainty of "Suns" that "go surer" is likely misplaced, Dickinson's alternative word for "axle"—"muscle"—accentuating the tenuousness of the situation, since muscles tire and deteriorate. The speaker of the poem casts herself upward to an extreme height, overlooking "Things," the comparison in line two conjuring an image of one high up in a tree: "And like the Trees, look down." Although this vantage point must be remarkable—fresh, panoramic—to stand on "the tops of Things" must also be frightening, one's perch precarious and exposed, distant and likely far removed from one's familiar place. The position, however, apparently allows for keener vision. Noting that the "smoke" has "cleared," the narrator insinuates that ordinarily we mostly apprehend haze. Caught up in the usual fog, it is easy not to notice that we do not fully see the "spotted World"—or see it at all; high up, we have a prospect and perspective. The poem repeatedly refers to forms of illumination: "mirrors," "lightning," "noon," "Stars," and "Suns." Not that bright light ensures protection. The third stanza cautions that the full glare of sunshine would only make the hazards and pain more fully visible. Who, truthfully, could stand that? Perhaps the "Perfect" and fearless could, but the rest of us, the poem proposes, would not "dare" to venture into the light of "noon," a time that would potentially expose every risk. The poem imagines a "soul" courageous and clear-sighted, one willing to look honestly at the troubles and horrors of a darkened world. In Spofford's "Circumstance," too, the woman trapped in a tree demonstrates the need to confront the world directly, even if what one sees in that world is terrifying, even if what one sees are ghosts or demons, even if what one sees is not to be believed.

The unnerving poem "As the starved maelstrom laps the navies" itemizes a few of the ways that people ravage and are ravaged. Written about 1865, this poem describes a harrowing world occupied by predators:

> As the Starved Maelstrom laps the Navies
> As the Vulture teazed
> Forces the Broods in lonely Valleys
> As the Tiger eased
>
> By but a Crumb of Blood, fasts Scarlet
> Till he meet a Man
> Dainty adorned with Veins and Tissues
> And partakes — his Tongue
>
> Cooled by the Morsel for a moment
> Grows a fiercer thing
> Till he esteems his Dates and Cocoa
> A Nutrition mean
>
> I, of a finer Famine
> Deem my Supper dry
> For but a Berry of Domingo
> And a Torrid Eye —
>
> (F1064)

The poem depicts successive scenes of predation and destruction. The powerful and frenzied "Maelstrom" feeds itself on whole "Navies"; the "Vulture" preys on young birds; the "Tiger" has tasted blood but bides his time until he can feast on a human delicacy, the "Morsel" of a man. In the 1860s, the prevailing maelstrom was surely the Civil War; the images in the poem of killing and being killed, the repeated references to starvation and deprivation, the tumult all reinforce that context.

The opening line conjures the furor of battles between the Union navy and the Confederate navy, battles that spread along the Atlantic and Gulf coasts. In addition, in a wartime context, the reference to "Navies" evokes the Union naval blockades of Southern ports and of trade routes, especially from the Bahamas, Cuba, and Bermuda, which effectively disrupted trade and prevented the passage of all sorts of commodities, including arms and ammunition, clothing, household goods, medicines, cotton, tobacco, and food (Massey; Fowler). The "Dates and Cocoa" mentioned in line 11 more directly point to items of commerce, goods that must have seemed like luxuries during the war and were produced in the West Indies and other tropical locales or transported through those regions. Especially for the Southern soldiers and population, but also in the North, goods such as fruits and cocoa, coffee, tea, sugar, salt, vegetable seed, meat, butter, flour, and alcohol became increasingly scarce due to numerous factors including the naval blockades; the transport of these kinds of goods and other merchandise became the profitable, if dangerous, object of Confederate blockade runners.[26] In the poem, the terror of wartime is depicted as a rapacious vortex—the gigantic tongue-of-war scooping up ships and men, a tempest feeding on pitifully defenseless offerings.[27]

Though the animals and forces named in Dickinson's lines eat their prey, the predators themselves are described as hungry. The very "Maelstrom" itself is "Starved." A number of scholars have addressed the condition of deprivation frequently expressed in Dickinson's verse. Vivian Pollak, for example, argues that a Dickinson persona is often obsessed with food and drink and that "typically, her persona is starving, unaccountably and unjustly, in a world of plenty" ("Thirst" 74). Pollak very reasonably argues that this starvation reflects the cultural divestments of women and further posits that a woman's "shrinking vital needs" are a "defense against" the restrictions that women experienced in Victorian America (64).[28] However, in addition to the established cultural and legal constrictions of women's lives, the churning forces of war produced their own nightmares of scarcity. Starvation was a particular horror in war prisons during the Civil War. In newspapers such as *Harper's Weekly* in 1864 and 1865, numerous reports of the confederate military prison at Andersonville, Camp Sumter, describe wretched conditions, including the starvation of prisoners, that led to the deaths of thirteen thousand to fourteen thousand men there.[29] Throughout the duration of the war, newspapers were filled with reports, editorials, personal narratives, illustrations, and occasional poems about battles, prisons, and the terrible circumstances that soldiers and citizens endured.

While the speaker of Dickinson's poem distinguishes herself from the predacious beings she names, she too is famished. Hers is "a finer Famine," she says, proposing perhaps that her starvation incites less bloodshed and less brutality; her hunger is perhaps more spiritual or creative, as Weisbuch proposes, or more sexual, as both Vendler and Weisbuch suggest (Weisbuch, "Prisming" 201–2; Vendler 393). At the least, her self-description marks her hunger as different from that of the maelstrom, vulture, and tiger even if she places herself in their company. Both associating with and detaching herself from these cannibalistic animals and forces of the natural world, the speaker crafts a kaleidoscopic portrait of herself, a rotating image of "I" that obscures as much as it focuses.

When the speaker assesses her "Supper" as "dry," her seemingly straightforward statement quickly spins in different directions. Evidently renouncing water, whirlpools, and bloodshed, the speaker's acknowledgement of "dry" fare rebuts the outright deadly scenes set forth in the first three stanzas. And yet the image of a "dry" dinner quite plausibly intimates wartime and its consequent food shortages, the dryness of her meals implying that she does without butter and sweeteners, without wine or other alcoholic beverage. Perhaps the word "dry" does not describe the plainness of her food but rather characterizes the speaker's own attitude: she is dry-eyed, impassive, detached, or determined.

There is still a further twist to her supper that is "dry," except for "a Berry of Domingo / And a Torrid Eye — ." Here, again, the words "Domingo" and "Torrid" bring to mind the equatorial zone and the wartime strategies of trade blockades. For the speaker, moisture comes from a berry, its juice replacing blood. But what is "a Berry of Domingo"?

Ed Folsom and Kenneth Price propose that the "Berry of Domingo conjures up an image of blood and slave revolt." Wardrop, citing Folsom and Price, agrees that the word "domingo" in Dickinson's verse connotes slave insurrections or resistance and the market economy of slavery (Wardrop, "'Minute'" 73–77). Eliza Richards, also citing Folsom and Price, discerns in the poem a depiction of the "hunger" of slaves and their rage and desire for revenge through images that ultimately serve as tropes, Richards posits, for the speaker's own feelings ("'News'" 173–75). While Richards regards the speaker as solipsistic, "appropriating experience she cannot imagine for the sake of self-expression" (175), the speaker may be less crassly exploitative and more grappling in her efforts to understand her own constrained circumstances as well as the embattled state of the country. The speaker, presenting herself as small and unassuming (or as cunning and uncontainable), may be announcing her own incipient thoughts of revolution. Hers is a "Berry," a seed, a morsel of "Domingo," but Domingo—with its fullness of meaning—nonetheless. That her eyesight is "Torrid" suggests additionally that she sees things or reads about things that have been associated with the geographical Torrid Zone, that is, the locale of the West Indies and other tropical regions, or with other fiery locations, such as battlefields. The compressed phrase "Torrid Eye" might convey the speaker's effort to express something genuine about her relationship to such riving experiences as slavery or revolution: she may not have direct personal experience or the most brutalizing forms of experience, but she reads about such terrors and insurrections or she sees their consequences in her life.[30]

Both the hungry Maelstrom that "laps the Navies" and the Tiger who dines on "adorned" tidbits of a human being are variations of Spofford's clawed creature who haunts the Maine woods.[31] The poem's montage of sharp beaks and claws, teeth and wide-open mouths generally conjures the overall impression of predacious cats and birds, but also of something more undefinable—an ever-present, lurking, devastating power. For some readers, Dickinson's Tiger may summon William Blake's blazing Tyger, the "Tyger of Wrath," as discussed by Morton Paley, that embodies the apocalyptic visions of Old Testament prophets. Arguing that Dickinson associated an "aloof" and torment-ing god with a monstrous cat, St. Armand notes that such a correla-tion would be almost overwhelmingly terrible for "a poet who often thought of herself as a bird" or a mouse (*Emily Dickinson* 163–67). Vendler reads the image of the tiger in the poem as an expression of Dickinson's desires and, more specifically, Dickinson's desires for Susan Gilbert Dickinson: "Susan's tropic lips and torrid eyes—with the exoticism Dickinson attributes to Santo Domingo—have trans-formed Dickinson into a Tiger who, having tasted Blood, wants no more of the insipid Cocoa and Dates of the desert" (393). Setting aside the likelihood that cocoa and dates would not have been regarded as dull, especially during a war (and perhaps at any time), one can appreciate Vendler's perception of Dickinson "transformed" by pas-sions. While Vendler (like Weisbuch) focuses on Dickinson's personal feelings, she makes a more widely applicable and provocative point, that desires can be catalyzed by a combination of knowing and not knowing: the speaker (and Dickinson, apparently, too), like the tiger in the poem, "Grows a fiercer thing" on a "Crumb of Blood." While it is wholly understandable that a reader would try to identify the causes of the speaker's "famine" (as well as the causes of other hungers noted in the poem), a question that strikes closer to the roiling heart of the poem is something far more ambiguous and vexed: Is power (passion, fierceness, a maelstrom, a monster) vivified because it is starved or because it is fed? In addition, in this poem, Dickinson lines up the maelstrom, vulture, and tiger as equivalences for each other and for the speaker; the desolating beasts and energies stand as doubles for the woman or as segments of her divided self. There is something wild and ravenous in her that can be let loose, even if this power goes largely unrecognized or unacknowledged. All the more curious then that so many of the inhabitants of her poems are locked up, shut out, bandaged, shackled, stricken, and stalked. The women with glimmer-ing thoughts of "Domingo" evidently need to be deterred.

Dickinson's schooling in captivity and trauma came from many cor-ners and forces, including popular fiction and the kinds of stories she could (and did) read in the pages of the *Atlantic Monthly,* one of the many periodicals that came into the Dickinson home. David Reynolds suggests that the narratives of escape in Dickinson's poems display her intrigue with "sensational literature," her enthusiasm for it and familiarity evident in her imagery of violence, prisons, pirates, and alcohol ("Emily Dickinson" 175–78 and *Beneath* 428–35). Discussing the prominence of this motley genre—with its narratives of crime and criminals, court trials, tragedies, horrors, and perversities—in nineteenth-century American culture, Reynolds focuses on Dickinson's letters of the early 1850s to document her interest in such "lurid" stories as found in newspapers and in pamphlet literature (*Beneath* 429–32). The "sensation" vocabulary of "As the starved maelstrom laps the navies"—and which is evident in numerous other Dickinson poems—might well indicate a reading experience that, in addition to news accounts in newspapers and magazines, included the popular sensation fiction of the day, commonly published in these same newspapers and magazines.

The extreme violence of Spofford's story is matched by the extraordinary violence that marks many of Dickinson's poems. In so many Dickinson poems, a person confronts some form of a "ghastly Fright" or proclaims that, in this world, "Terror's free" and on "Gay, Ghastly, Holiday!" (F341). Critics have noted strong connections between Dickinson's "'Twas like a maelstrom with a notch" (F425) and Spofford's "Circumstance," citing, for instance, the shared vocabulary (such as the words "agony," "fiend," "creature," "stirred," "paws") (Garbowsky; Fetterley 264; David Cody 40–42). Garbowsky discusses their similar, "more than coincidental" depictions of a terrifying situation as well as of anguished helplessness.[32] In Dickinson's "He fumbles at your soul," the speaker again depicts pure terror, with God and nature twin tormentors who aim to "scalp" souls.

> He fumbles at your Soul
> As Players at the Keys
> Before they drop full Music on —
> He stuns you by degrees —
> Prepares your brittle nature
> For the Ethereal Blow

By fainter Hammers — further heard —
Then nearer — Then so slow
Your Breath has time to straighten —
Your Brain — to bubble Cool —
Deals — One — imperial — Thunderbolt —
That scalps your naked Soul —

When Winds take Forests in their Paws —
The Universe — is still —

(F477)

In "He fumbles at your soul," as in "As the starved maelstrom laps the navies," Dickinson envisions humans as alarmingly slight entities, helpless in the grip of a colossal merciless wild thing. Much in this poem is also reminiscent of Spofford's story "Circumstance." The speaker describes a slow process of torture in which a powerful and tenacious "He" first "fumbles at," then "stuns," and then "Hammers" away at "your Soul." Again, Dickinson conjures a powerful clawed beast, a big-pawed force of nature that is able to contain the Universe: "When Winds take Forests in their Paws — / The Universe — is still — ." Nothing resembles comfort in the poem, the Universe held "still," as if holding its breath, paralyzed with fear, held captive by "Winds"— great gusts of air, spectral-like and metaphorized (or manifest) as the biggest cat in the cosmos. The pummeling of the soul depicted in this poem culminates in a scalping, an evident allusion to marauding Indians that would seem to imagine the experience of profound soul- or self-revelation as something terrifying.[33] In the poem, such battering experience is also linked to music: the violating "He" is compared to a musician improvising or warming up on a keyboard, the musical instrument and music generally rendered as an instrument of personal torment.

In addition to related contemplations, Dickinson and Spofford have connection through the coincidence of people. Some of those in Dickinson's most intimate circle also admired Spofford's writing. Susan Dickinson herself spoke and wrote enthusiastically about Spofford as well as noted the admiration of others: "The late Mr. Bowles keenly felt her originality and power and frequently sent me brief extracts from her manuscripts given him by his friends in the editor's sanctum" ("Harriet" 19). Especially significant in Spofford's career was the "Preceptor" himself, Thomas Wentworth Higginson. As might be inferred from Spofford's numerous publications in the *Atlantic,* Higginson was a friend, teacher, mentor, and promoter of Spofford. Rodier recounts his caretaking of her writing career, not only through supporting publication but also through trying to negotiate with editor James T. Fields a higher payment per page for her in the *Atlantic* (55–57).[34] Higginson called Spofford "a wonderful genius" as well as "a demure little Yankee girl" and "the little authoress" (Higginson, *Letters and Journals* 103). If his descriptions of Spofford, while full of praise and support, still place her in the safe terrain of Victorian femininity, his descriptions of Dickinson often suggested that she existed in some realm of the bizarre: Dickinson is "much too enigmatical a being" to understand quickly or easily; she is "strange, solitary, morbidly sensitive" (Higginson, "Emily" 453; Higginson and Boynton 130). And yet these two women, the "demure," "humble," grateful one (Higginson, *Letters and Journals* 103–4) and the odd, "partially cracked" one (note to Letter 481), both placed trust in him. One might even credit Higginson with bringing the two women together, so to speak, through the pages of the *Atlantic Monthly.* Dickinson's disclosure about being "followed . . . in the Dark" by "Miss Prescott's" story appears to have come in response to a query from Higginson.

How is one to understand the allure and power of Spofford's haunting horror story for Dickinson? Both Spofford and Dickinson contend with elusive many-headed personal and cultural threats: their sensationalized depictions evince captivities and freedoms, insurrections and quiet rebellions, terrors and mysteries. Nature, nation, home, and body all house demons and ghosts.

One answer to the mystery of Dickinson's changing and disturbed response to Spofford's story is that "Circumstance" accrued a mythic status for Dickinson. Emanating Greek myths, folk tales, fairy tales, song, literary fictions, poems, histories, and captivity narratives,

Spofford's "Circumstance" itself is "haunted" by stories of captive or
constrained persons who manage (or at least imagine) their escape.
Spofford's narrative, refracted with social and cultural reference, itself acts as a ghost, persistently present, for Dickinson. The poet reveals that it stalks her, worries her, frightens her. It haunts her. In
so many of Dickinson's poems, one can sense the ghost of Spofford
and of other writers who ponder women's desperate efforts to live, the
ghostly half-hidden lives of women, the spectral presences that inhabit
families and homes, the ghosts of national history. With their share of
assailed, stranded, famished, and frightened individuals, the poems
also conceive an American woman's narrative that, as in Spofford's
tale, bespeaks both threat and allure. The Soul may be "Bandaged"
but it still gleefully "dances like a Bomb" (F360). One queenly speaker,
abandoned on an apparently sunless island, with "Oceans — and the
North" on "every side" (F596), recalls a blissful if short-lived marriage
to another Queen. "Most — I love the Cause that slew Me — " (F841)
attests another heroic (or mad) speaker. Dickinson, like Spofford,
brings together the horror tale, the gothic tale, and the domestic tale.
Alarm and delight resolutely reside together.

In addition, many Dickinson poems and the Spofford story present
similar disturbing conundrums: How is one to know with any confidence what is phantasmagoric and what is not? What is shadow and
what is light? What is escape and what is doom? What's a prison and
what's a friend? And, perversely, what is liberty and what captivity?
There are so many twists of meaning, so many ways that borders are
crisscrossed and smudged, that the ostensible stories told in these texts
are interlaced and refashioned by other stories. The seemingly endless
permutations of meaning keep one questioning what is "aberrant" and
what is "ordinary." In this chapter, I have noted a few in the long procession of thinkers who have examined the riddles and shadows of
American "freedom" and "captivity." Enigmatic and illusory, ubiquitous
and terror-ridden, these topics haunt American narrative and experience, the meaning of freedom and of captivity subject to constant individual and cultural interpretation and reinterpretation. In discussing
the "Africanist" presence in the American imagination, Toni Morrison

deftly describes the entwined existences of freedom and enslavement: "The concept of freedom did not emerge in a vacuum. Nothing highlighted freedom—if it did not in fact create it—like slavery" (38).[35] As Morrison deduces, the culture's expositions of freedom and captivity are determined by calculating rhetoric and political manipulation. How else to understand complacency over the shocking constraints on people's lives, or mockery of women's supposed frivolous demands, or contradictory judgments about the look and state of freedom. "Captivity is Consciousness — / So's Liberty — ." In numerous poems, Dickinson displayed this paradox, this muddle, this rift.

If a reader of Dickinson acknowledges that she lived in a time and a place, many of her poems will reverberate with the struggles of freedom and captivity so overwhelmingly present in the nineteenth century, both in the home and in the nation. Read within social and cultural contexts, so many of her words and references radiate the complexities of the times, sometimes quite unexpectedly. Many of the poems that I have discussed throughout this book reveal this effect. Another example is an 1873 poem that is typically understood as a laudation of the pleasures of reading. In the poem, Dickinson compares a book to a "Frigate," that is, to a warship. In "There is no frigate like a book" (F1286), the act of reading and, just as readily, the act of writing are transposed into dangerous and deadly arenas—battles, blockades, piracy. During the Civil War, steam frigates were the dominant type of warship, armed and maneuverable and eventually well-armored.[36] The initial decisions in the new American republic to rebuild a navy and construct frigates came in response to pirates of the Barbary States who, especially in the late eighteenth and early nineteenth centuries, repeatedly threatened American merchants and sailors with attack and abduction (Canney 2, 5). As reported in a December 1860 story in the *Atlantic Monthly,* "Moorish pirates" demanded "gifts" of jewels, money, guns, and frigates in exchange for the safe passage of American sailors ("The United States" 641–57). In the nineteenth century, waters were extremely dangerous territories. There is no frigate like a book? Oh dear. This is a vision of books that anticipates dangerous prospects for a reader and a writer. A writer or reader boarding the "frigate" must be prepared for confrontations with a ferocious world. In Dickinson's conception, a "book" can save and a "book" can destroy. A writer-reader will need to summon boldness and valor, patience, and courage.

Dickinson and her speakers confront the maelstrom, the tiger, the fiend, the dark, and they sing in response—to comfort, assert, and save themselves and others. Her speakers will "sing to use the Waiting" and sing "To Keep the Dark away" (F955). "Let Emily sing for you because she cannot pray," she writes her cousins Louise and Frances Norcross in January 1863 upon the death of their father, Dickinson's Uncle Loring (Letter 278). In this solemn and tender letter, Dickinson's admission that "she cannot pray" even as she ruminates on grief suggests a profound sense of abandonment or detachment; her offer to "sing" comes in the form of a poem that Dickinson includes in the letter. It begins, "It is not dying hurts us so, — / 'Tis living hurts us more;"—not exactly words of consolation, but compassionate words that acknowledge the pain experienced by "the birds that stay." In the April 1862 letter to Higginson in which Dickinson reveals that Spofford's "Circumstance" "followed" her "in the Dark," Dickinson describes herself as singing past the cemetery to quell the "terror" that she had kept private for several months: Dickinson informs Higginson, "I had a terror — since September — I could tell to none — and so I sing, as the Boy does by the Burying Ground — because I am afraid" (Letter 261). She sings because she cannot "tell," her voice both suppressed and released.

The challenges of speaking, praying, and telling pervade her verse and apparently some people perceived them in her behavior. Higginson may have heard a "soft frightened breathless childlike voice" on first meeting Dickinson at her home in August 1870 (Letter 342a), but this is the same person who likens "Melody" and "Witchcraft" in her inquiry to him of "how to grow" as a poet (Letter 261). In Gertrude Graves's reminiscences of her cousins the Dickinsons and of her father, John L. Graves, who would stay at the Dickinson home whenever Edward Dickinson was away, she records that her father was often awakened during the night by Emily's "heavenly music": "Emily would explain in the morning, 'I can improvise better at night'" (Graves 41).

Among the powers that Dickinson seemed to find "in the Dark" was a creative voice that could be harmonious and inspired as well as one that could be tortured. In the poem "One joy of so much anguish," the speaker wonders why the birdsong of summer feels like "Dirks of Melody" (F1450). In Dickinson's poem "The saddest noise, the sweetest noise," spring birds adopt the role of necromancers, their "siren throats" exhuming ghosts: "It makes us think of all the dead / That sauntered with us here, / By separation's sorcery / Made cruelly more dear" (F1789). Breaching a border between the living and the dead, the birds' early morning singing is extremely painful: "We almost wish those siren throats / Would go and sing no more." Yet the birds' singing bewitches "us," and the natural world opens a door into the spectral world, providing a portal into another reality, a space apparitional and mythic, the reference to sirens suggesting that this enchanted realm has been conjured by female voices.

In "Sang from the heart, sire" (F1083), a poem of 1864 or 1865, Dickinson's image of "telling" requires self-inflicted trauma: having "Dipped" her "Beak" into her heart, like a pen into an inkwell, the bird-speaker practices an "Awkward" and "faltering" tune. "Telling" is clumsy and bloody business. Through a mysterious musical alchemy, her speakers confront demons and fiends with songs of torment that are also songs of salvation. The woman in "Circumstance" also becomes a bird-siren, her singing incantatory. High in the tree, the wild creature grasps and claws the woman, but she holds him spellbound with her voice. Can a monster be a muse? What happens during the traumatic encounter in the Maine woods for Spofford's neighborly woman is recreated repeatedly in the spaces of Dickinson's poems. Her poems may house an unwieldy accumulation of peril, injury, and haunting, but, like a ghost rising, her voice beckons, an emissary into iridescent realms. A woman is restrained, but her voice can be heard.

THE EXHIBITION
OF EMILY DICKINSON

I must tell you about the *character* of Amherst.
🌼 Mabel Loomis Todd, in a letter to her parents in 1881

Photographs, which cannot themselves explain anything,
are inexhaustible invitations to deduction, speculation, and fantasy.
🌼 Susan Sontag, *On Photography*

A Charm invests a face / Imperfectly beheld —
(F430)

Nineteenth-century America blazed with entertainments that celebrated wonder-inspiring individuals, enigmatic creatures, technological phenomena, and other marvels of the times. Demonstrating their
wide appeal across class lines, the "democratic" entertainments of the
dime museum, the traveling circus, and the minstrel show seemed
to offer something for everyone and benefitted from their promotion
as educational. This was the age of Barnum and his seemingly endless "curiosities." This was the era of the minstrel show extravaganza,
which combined the pleasures of lively musical expression with satiric
and serious critiques of varied American experiences. It was an age of
exhibition, a distinctive time of so-called wholesome family entertainments that reveled in spectacle, certified the display of non-normative
bodies for public inspection, exulted in the magical and the mysterious, and dramatized a nation's anxieties. Successful popular entertainments of the nineteenth century inspired delight and wonder, their
easeful and enjoyable mingling of truths and fantasies capable of concocting narratives that could not only arouse astonishment but also

express genuine concerns regarding complex national and personal identities.

Emily Dickinson herself has long been presented as a spectacle, a person turned into a "curiosity," a mystery spurring creative public speculation. In the preface to the 1931 edition of *Letters of Emily Dickinson,* Mabel Loomis Todd writes of this disappearance and dramatization: "The Emily legend has assumed a shape unrecognizable to one who knew her. Her life is revamped to suit the taste of the times, and Emily herself has all but vanished in the process" (x). As many have noted, even before Dickinson's death, she was already being cast as a curiosity. In her well-known letter to her parents in 1881, Todd renders a description of Dickinson, "the *character* of Amherst," that makes her sound utterly strange and more than a bit phantasmic.[1] In her collection of unpublished letters and "reminiscences," Dickinson's niece recounts that "various fantastic tales were circulated about her" (Bianchi, *Face to Face* 37). Bianchi contributes to the image of Dickinson as a conjurer of magical spells: "In thinking back over the past now, nothing is more striking than the actual glamour Aunt Emily seems to have cast over us—all the way from childhood on" (*Face to Face* 43). In Bianchi's telling, Dickinson is an entrancing, spell-spinning figure, a "fable." She is an unexpected and strange story as much as a person: "It became something of a boast to have seen her" (*Face to Face* 36).

The "fantastic tales" of Emily Dickinson have also been promoted by special attention given to specific objects associated with her. Items such as daguerreotypes and other pictorial images, a white dress, fragments of envelopes on which Dickinson set down lines of verse, and flowers included with poems and letters sent to family members and friends have accrued status, each a shorthand for conveying Dickinson's distinctive imagination and each a putative key to the mysteries of Dickinson. As metonymic representations of her, these curiosities in Dickinson's cabinet have been treated with reverence, the objects observed and studied with the highest of expectations—the revelation of Dickinson to us. What precisely each object might disclose about Dickinson's writing and life has been a matter of ongoing interpretation, management, and marketing by her family, editors, biographers, and scholars since the 1890s. These objects and the stories of Dickinson that they carry or inspire—whether in biographical, scholarly, or literary forms—participate in the shaping of a persona, the alleged vanishing of Emily followed by her reappearance in any number of guises.[2] Through the intermingling of facts and fictions, of postulations and speculations, a person we call Emily Dickinson has been "called forth."[3] While many forms of popular entertainment of the nineteenth century entwined the pleasures of performance and of story with the serious business of social critique, the exhibition of Emily Dickinson herself has focused on perceptions of her and on the efforts to guide or manage those perceptions. The overall aim may be something understood as "revelation," although the ongoing exhibition of Emily Dickinson has largely enhanced her mystery and mystique.

MIRROR WITH A MEMORY

Visual depictions of Emily Dickinson have been invested with extraordinary meaning and emotion. The elaborate efforts exerted to control the pictorial representations of Emily Dickinson demonstrate this powerful investment of meaning, implicitly acknowledging the expectation that photographic images of Dickinson (as well as images of a woman or women who might or might not be Dickinson) will influence our understanding of her. The vital questions of how we *see* Dickinson and how we compose her are literalized in the icon of the daguerreotype.

Among nineteenth-century innovations in technology, the development of the daguerreotype and the photograph in mid-century created dramatic new possibilities for visual culture. According to historians of early photography, the first daguerreotypes, first seen in the United States in 1839, were regarded with utter "awe" (Trachtenberg, "Mirror" 60). In essays published in the *Atlantic,* Oliver Wendell Holmes calls the daguerreotype "an inconceivable wonder" ("Stereoscope" 127). As conveyed by Holmes and others, the advent of photography felt miraculous, the impression of images on a metal plate seeming to happen magically, springing out of thin air. Or they were attributed to the mysterious workings of nature, the evidence of "nature's painting" or "sun-painting" (as the images were sometimes called), which made them no less "audacious," "improbable," and "incredible" (Holmes, "Stereoscope" 126; Holmes, "Sun-Painting"; Marien 1–4). The daguerreotype, Holmes wrote, "has fixed the most fleeting of our illusions" ("Stereoscope" 126), seemingly able to capture what we barely see or even think. Holmes further attributes to early photography the "divine gift" of immortality: "shadows last" as "their originals fade away" ("Sun-Painting" 170, 178). While Holmes's account of this creative wonder suggests that looking at a photographic portrait is, in effect, comparable to looking at the actual living person,[4] his description of the daguerreotype as *the mirror with a memory* suggests that the pictorial image is a living thing, an entity with consciousness, not only holding a moment in time but remembering a moment over time ("Stereoscope" 129). The "memory" of the photographic image is better than any person's actual memory, being more nuanced and longer lasting. Some early commentators also credited the photographic image with delivering perhaps unexpected revelations of people we thought we knew: "Each new picture gives us a new aspect of our friend; we find he had not one face, but many" (Holmes, "Sun-Painting" 170).

In the 1850s, technological developments made possible multiple inexpensive paper prints of a photograph; by the early 1860s, cartes de visite, 4 x 2½-inch mounted photographs, were easily produced and extremely popular, bought as postcards and souvenirs. Many people collected cartes de visite and preserved them in personal photo albums. Inexpensive, easily attainable, and pervasive, the carte photograph extended the reach and value of the photograph: According to Marien, "the carte photograph increased the fetishistic qualities of the photograph," its easy availability expanded the possibilities of whom or what one could know and, in a sense, possess (81). Calling the daguerreotype one of the "two most miraculous discoveries of the age" (the other being "magnetic telegraphic communication"), Barnum housed a photography studio for visitors among the marvels in his American Museum (quoted in Kunhardt 267). Barnum also made a practice of sending his performers across the street to the studio of

Mathew Brady to sit for daguerreotypic and photographic portraits, a practice that generated a pictorial history of his "living curiosities" as well as provided sought-after images for the lucrative cartes de visite business (Kunhardt vii, 196; Bogdan 11–12; Dennett 77–78). The daguerreotype could be unexpectedly beautifying, but the technology could also be frustratingly non-cooperative and produce disappointing results, a sitter's facial expression, for example, unattractively frozen or morphed into a skeletal lifelessness. Ralph Waldo Emerson was apparently perennially displeased by daguerrean portraits of himself, he and his family agreeing that they made Emerson look "supremely ridiculous" (Pfister 142). Still, the new pictorial technology proved irresistible and prosperous. In his *The Daguerreotype in America,* Beaumont Newhall reports that by 1860 virtually every city and town had at least one photography studio and "itinerant daguerreotypists traveled to remote backwoods and frontier areas" (34).

We have one authenticated photographic image of Emily Dickinson, the daguerreotype taken in the mid-1840s. Measuring 2¾ x 3¼ inches (a sixth plate), the daguerreotype has been an object of critical attention since the first editions of Dickinson's poems and letters were being prepared for publication. The identity of the photographer of this portrait remains in contention, some scholars leaning towards Otis H. Cooley, others pointing to William C. North, others uncertain.[5] If one accepts the dating of Mary Elizabeth Kromer Bernhard, who identifies North as the photographer, Emily Dickinson was sixteen years old when her image was chemically fixed on a silvered copper metal plate. She is a teenager, a schoolgirl in her last year at Amherst Academy, anticipating beginning her studies at Mount Holyoke Female Seminary in a few months. It is an Emily Dickinson who has recently experienced a severe bout of influenza. This Emily has written her friend Abiah Root about her current courses at Amherst Academy ("am studying Algebra, Euclid, [Ecclesiastical] History & reviewing Arithmetic again" [Letter 15]), and presses her to visit soon. It is an Emily who, in describing a new teacher at the academy, Miss Woodbridge, writes Abiah that "I am always in love with my teachers." The face we recognize as Emily Dickinson is the face of the sixteen-year-old girl. As we read and wonder over poems she composed as a young woman or a middle-aged woman, it is the face of the teenager that we have in mind as Emily Dickinson. The story of this photographic image offers mystery and surprise. It is a story constructed on the decisions of family members and friends, decisions meant to be protective or manipulative or aesthetic. After Dickinson's death, the 1846/1847 daguerreotype had its share of alterations, intended apparently to create an image of Dickinson that looked more like her.

In addition, over the past 120 years, photographic images of Dickinson have been gradually accumulating, introduced (and sometimes published) as depictions of her, the people who present them seemingly certain that the images are authentic. However, with the exception of the 1846/1847 daguerreotype, all of these photographic renderings remain questionable. These images include the photographic portrait of a woman identified as "Emily Dickenson 1860" used as a frontispiece in volume two of Richard Sewall's *The Life of Emily Dickinson;* the photograph that scholar Philip Gura purchased on eBay in 2000; and the daguerreotype of two women, found in a junk shop in western Massachusetts in 1995, dated 1859 and speculated to be Emily Dickinson and her friend Kate Scott Turner Anthon. Dickinson's response to Higginson in July 1862 that she had "no portrait, now" has seemed reserved or coy or, at least, not quite truthful. If any of these found photographs are of Dickinson, her demurral to Higginson is even more quizzical. The claims that any (or all) of these additional photographs are Dickinson carry the implication that by 1862 she sat for daguerreotypes or photographs possibly four times. A fifth time is posited by John Felix (who identifies Cooley as the daguerreotypist of the 1840s image): Felix reports that teacher Susan L. Tolman's journal entry for January 1, 1848, refers to the "excitement" caused by an "itinerant photographer" who had set up a temporary studio outside the grounds of Mount Holyoke Female Seminary. Felix states that Emily Dickinson "has been widely assumed" to be among the students who sat for this unidentified photographer (10).

Each serendipitous find of a previously unknown photographic image of a woman who might be Emily Dickinson has generated a flurry of excitement and attention, both among scholars and in the media. The public announcement of the 1859 photograph in August 2012 by Martha Nell Smith at an academic conference propelled a whirlwind of news stories in September 2012. On the *CBS Evening News,* anchor Scott Pelley reported that "researchers at Amherst College believe" that they have identified Emily Dickinson in the photograph ("Researchers": September 6, 2012). The *New York Times* ran a story entitled "Still No New Pynchon Photo, but Here's Emily Dickinson" (Itzkoff: September 5, 2012). An article in the *Guardian* announced that "Emily Dickinson gets a new look in recovered photograph" (Flood: September 5, 2012). While a number of headlines pose questions, such as the headline for the story in *Ms. Magazine*—"Is This a Photo of Emily Dickinson? And Will It Tell Us Who She Loved?" (Enszer: September 11, 2012)—the stories accompanying these querying headlines also tend to answer the question affirmatively by referring, for example, to the "new photograph of Emily Dickinson" (Enszer) or noting that examiners of the image are convinced of Dickinson's identity.[6] Stories about this suddenly discovered Dickinson photograph ran in newspapers and on media sites across the country and around the world.[7] The news of the Gura photograph—purchased by the Dickinson scholar on eBay for $481—was greeted with much fanfare as well as caution, the astonishing circumstances of its appearance making for a story that seems nearly miraculous (Gleason; Habegger 634–37; Marta L. Werner 485–86). The Gura photograph has been published in biographical studies of Dickinson with little (or no) indication that the identification of the woman in the photograph has not been settled: Wineapple presents the Gura image as Emily Dickinson in her *White Heat* (261); and Habegger adds a caption testifying to his and Gura's belief that the image does "represent Dickinson" (Habegger, portraits following 366). The acceptance of the much-contested Gura photograph by some biographers and scholars is in itself a curious development. Is this acceptance an act of faith, a sign of hope, an embrace of the mystery that marks so much of Dickinson's life and writing? For others, the relatively easy acceptance of the Gura photograph has been a cause of concern and an impetus for greater scrutiny. Authorized by the Emily

Figure 7. Daguerreotype, dated 1859, found in a junk shop in Massachusetts in 1995 by a private collector. The two women are speculated to be Emily Dickinson (*left*) and her friend Kate Anthon. Published with permission of the private collector. Courtesy of Amherst College Archives and Special Collections.

Figure 8. Albumen photograph of a woman speculated to be Emily Dickinson, found by Philip Gura in 2000. Courtesy of Philip F. Gura.

Dickinson International Society to investigate the photograph's authenticity, attorney George Gleason puts forward his findings and conclusion that the image purchased by Gura is "not of Emily Dickinson": he points to suspicious details of the sale, a gap in provenance of about a century, mysterious features of the photograph (such as the missing cardboard backing), and inconsistencies of facial features when compared to the 1846/1847 daguerreotype. The Sewall frontispiece photograph (for volume 2) identified as Dickinson (or "Dickenson") has also been questioned. In his investigation of this photograph, Joe Nickell has determined that there is no evidence to identify the woman in the portrait as Emily Dickinson.[8]

Each appearance of a new Dickinson photographic image generates wonderment and speculation, testaments of belief as well as of disbelief, and evidence of the desire for more ways to *see* Dickinson. Each find is sensational, both improbable and believable, tapping into our restrained expectations that there must be more photographic images of her out there somewhere. However, rather than being clarifying, each found photograph multiplies the mysteries around Dickinson. Each new "Dickinson" photograph enhances her mystique.

The expectation that a found photograph that may or may not be Dickinson could reveal anything about her taps into assumptions and attitudes about the powers of photography. Susan Sontag suggests that this particular kind of visual display offers opportunities to speculate and fantasize on a life: "Photographs, which cannot themselves explain anything, are inexhaustible invitations to deduction, speculation, and fantasy" (*On Photography* 23). The daguerreotypic and photographic images that we have of Dickinson or that purport to be Dickinson illustrate this allurement. Putting aside the mystery of why no family member seems to know anything about any daguerreotype or photograph of Emily other than the daguerreotype of 1846/1847, any new image that might possibly be of her, and even images that have been assessed (by some) as fake, affects how we perceive Dickinson and how we think about her. The willingness to believe that any of the unauthenticated portraits are of Dickinson supports Sontag's claim regarding the wooing effects of photographs. Similarly, the alterations of the 1846/1847 daguerreotype illustrate the intention to set "deduction, speculation, and fantasy" in particular directions.

The efforts to find portraits of Dickinson that could be included in early editions of poems and letters spun around the same vexing question and standard voiced by Lavinia: Does the picture represent Dickinson "truthfully"? The orchestration of Emily's public image by her brother and sister contributed to the shaping of a persona. What images of Dickinson would Austin and Lavinia permit people outside their immediate circle to see? What images would editors and biographers promote? According to Bingham, Lavinia and Austin strenuously opposed the public use of the 1846/1847 photographic image of their sister. Described by Bingham as "the only picture taken from life" of Emily Dickinson (*Ancestors'* 268), the 1846/1847 daguerreotype was judged by them as "unsatisfactory" and "too solemn," with "none of the play of light and shade in Emily's face" (*Ancestors'* 224–25, 294). They objected to it because it was "not like her," wrote Mabel Loomis Todd to publisher Thomas Niles (*Ancestors'* 227). Because of the siblings' dissatisfaction with the 1846/1847 daguerreotype, when Niles pressed for a picture of Dickinson to be used as a frontis-piece to the 1894 *Letters of Emily Dickinson,* to be printed eight years after her death in 1886, the decision was made to use the head of Emily as a child from the 1840 oil painting of the three Dickinson siblings by O. A. Bullard. Dickinson is no more than ten years old in this painting and may be as young as seven or eight, as Todd indicates in a letter to Niles in September 1893 (Bingham, *Ancestors'* 239). Ironically, Bingham also records that both Austin and Lavinia thought that the child in the Bullard painting "did not resemble" Emily either (*Ancestors'* 273).[9] Appar-ently in agreement, Bingham describes the painting of the children as "generic," that is, "more the artist's idea of what children should look like" than recognizable renderings of the three Dickinsons (*Ancestors'* 224). On April 3, 1893, Lavinia wrote to Mr. Niles that both options—the photo-graph of the daguerreotype and the oil painting—were inadequate: "Em-ily had a most interesting & startling face but neither of these pictures represent her truthfully" (Bingham, *Ancestors'* 225). According to Bianchi, Lavinia later regretted the use of the Bullard painting for the frontispiece: "she felt the child face insufficiently indicates the later Emily Dickinson of the *Poems*" (Bianchi, *Face to Face* 17–18n). Even so, Bianchi used the Bullard painting of Austin, Emily, and Lavinia as the frontispiece to her *Emily Dickinson Face to Face*.

Before the final decision to use the head of the child Emily from Bullard's painting as a frontispiece, Lavinia and Thomas Niles tried to produce other options. In the April 3, 1893, letter to Niles, Lavinia expresses her hope that "a likeness may be secured by the suggestion of a child portrait & the picture at sixteen." In addition to the collection of letters, Niles was arranging to publish a combined volume of the first and second series of Dickinson's poems, and Lavinia wanted to know, "How early would the likeness be required for the double volume?" In the letter, Lavinia seems to propose finding an artist who could render a "likeness" of Dickinson by working with the Bullard painting and the 1840s daguerreotype.[10] Her plan is more clearly stated in a letter to Niles the following month: "It is possible a genious [sic] with crayon might create a likeness, with the help of this early picture [the daguerreotype] & family suggestions—can *you* mention a skillful artist?" (Bingham, *Ancestors'* 226). The plan to create a more "truthful" portrait of Dickinson involved culling from a selection of sources: the 1840 Bullard painting (for a better "expression"), the disliked 1840s daguerreotype, a daguerreotype of a cousin whose hair was arranged in a way that Lavinia and Austin liked, and "family suggestions" (Bingham, *Ancestors'* 225–27, 273; Longsworth, "'Whose'" 37). Niles did enlist an artist who produced a preliminary sketch ("to shew the proposed arrangement of the hair") and wrote to Mabel Loomis Todd for permission "to work on the likeness" (Bingham, *Ancestors'* 226). The "artist's composite sketch" of Dickinson "did not please" Austin and Lavinia "because it did not look like her at all" (Bingham, *Ancestors'* 269). The disagreements regarding a portrait of Dickinson continued:

> Lavinia favored the sketch in preference to the raw daguerreotype, but Austin would not allow a manifestly doctored picture to go into the book. And the child portrait, though both considered it more "good looking" than the other two, had as my mother [Mabel Loomis Todd] said, "nothing to do with Emily's real appearance." (Bingham, *Ancestors'* 269)

156

As has been described in a number of places (and with some discrepancies), two or three years after the efforts involving Niles and an artist, Lavinia was still anxious for a likeness of Emily. Bianchi recounts a story told to her by Gertrude Graves in 1931 regarding this purpose: During a visit to the Graves's home in autumn 1896, Lavinia expressed a wish for a portrait of Emily and enlisted the help of her cousin Gertrude, who arranged for Laura Hills to make a miniature portrait of Emily with "Aunt Lavinia's directions." Lavinia, apparently delighted with the portrait, wrote to Gertrude, "Emily has come back to me!" Bianchi reports that Lavinia "always" repeated those words whenever she showed the painted miniature to friends (*Face to Face* 17–18n). However, Bingham attests that Laura Hills told her that she did not paint a miniature and only "retouched the photograph": "She softened the appearance of the hair and 'rearranged the neckline of the dress.'" Further, Bingham reports that in a letter of May 11, 1897, to Gertrude Graves, Lavinia wrote in regard to Hills's picture, which is not a painted miniature, "It really seems as if Emily was here" (*Ancestors'* 270).[11]

A mystery persists about the source of an extensively modified portrait of Dickinson that has been published. For the frontispiece to Bianchi's 1924 edition of *The Life and Letters of Emily Dickinson,* a bust portrait of a curly-haired Dickinson clothed in a white dress with a large showy ruffled collar was used. Although the image in this edition appears to be credited to Hills ("From a photograph retouched by Laura Coombs Hills") and Bianchi implies in her collection of unpublished letters and reminiscences that this is the portrait made by Laura Hills (*Face to Face* 18), Bingham maintains that this version of the Dickinson portrait is not the one "retouched by Miss Hills," but was made after Lavinia's death in 1899. Citing an article written by Louise Graves and published in the *Harvard Library Bulletin* in 1947, Bingham explains that someone reworked the Hills version of the "retouched" photograph:

Louise Graves is of the opinion that that "miniature" was made after Lavinia's death, not before, and was painted by someone

Figure 9. Modified portrait of Emily Dickinson, used as frontispiece to Bianchi's 1924 editions of *The Complete Poems of Emily Dickinson* and *The Life and Letters of Emily Dickinson*. From the Louise B. Graves collection of reproductions of the Emily Dickinson daguerreotype, MS Am 1118.15, (5), Houghton Library, Harvard University.

not known to her or to Miss Hills, *upon* a photographic enlargement of the little print sent by her sister [Gertrude Graves] to their Cousin Lavinia, and which the latter acclaimed with the words, "Emily has come back to me!" (Bingham, *Home* 519–20n)

Bingham also reports that Laura Hills told her she did not paint the much-modified portrait of Emily that has appeared in print (as the frontispiece in two books edited by Bianchi and published in 1924—*The Complete Poems of Emily Dickinson* and *Life and Letters of Emily Dickinson*): "The grotesque picture used as Emily's likeness in the current edition of her collected poems was not the work of Laura Hills, on her own authority" (*Ancestors'* 271).[12]

The many altered pictures of Dickinson, accompanied by the uncertain accounts of their origins, all seem to have been developed out of a desire for a portrait of Dickinson that her family thought was more recognizably her. In the correspondence regarding the composite portrait, the purported aim of creating a "likeness" of Dickinson—and the repetition of the word "likeness"—perhaps offer a clue as to this curious situation. Austin and Lavinia did not consider the actual photograph of Dickinson a good enough likeness, whereas an artist's rendering, created from different images of Emily (and of a cousin) and from the family's "suggestions" was intended to produce a portrait that would be more like her. What is connoted by the word "likeness"? In her cultural history of nineteenth-century photography, Mary Warner Marien discusses the significance of "likeness" in the early decades of photography: "The concept of likeness was widespread in photographic portraiture. It referred not only to physical resemblance but also to the idea that the photograph and the person pictured shared personal qualities" (75–76). In her discussion of European portrait photography of the mid-nineteenth century, Elizabeth Anne McCauley also addresses the concept of "likeness" and the debates concerning what a portrait was supposed to convey: exact physical resemblance or "interior" qualities. McCauley explains that mid-nineteenth-century portrait photographers who viewed themselves more as artists than technicians tended to understand "likeness" as a "portrayal of moral character" or as the revelation of the mind of the sitter (2–3, 12).[13] The strong objections of Lavinia and Austin to the daguerreotype of sixteen-year-old Emily implies that, for them, the image was a deception: according to them, it did not look like her, or, perhaps, it was not her, in that it did not convey qualities that were vital to their sense of her, especially perhaps to their sense of the woman who wrote the poems. It was not a good "likeness." If the belief was that the photographic image and the actual person "shared personal qualities," the apparent expectation was that traits perceived in the person—"moral character" or personality or the cast of a mind—ought to be strikingly evident in the photograph. A belief in the concept of likeness could help explain the persistent dissatisfaction with the 1846/1847 daguerreotype. The plan to concoct a composite portrait would perhaps not seem so ludicrous if the hope or expectation was that something vital to Emily's mind and character would be revealed through the combination of features.

Alan Trachtenberg has posited that, in the world of early photography, the concept of "likeness" connoted something akin to "identity": a daguerrean image seemed close to a mirrored reflection of the sitter. The image could feel like a "living presence" ("Likeness" 175). Focusing on "the trope of the living portrait," Trachtenberg discusses how changing light and shifting viewing angles affect the appearance of the daguerrean image: the image will fade away and reappear, this "flickering" creating a sense of movement, and thus, of life. Trachtenberg proposes that the daguerreotype "behaves like a ghost," fluctuating between absence and presence, seeming to be "dead and alive at once" ("Likeness" 173, 176). The perception that the daguerreotype was "alive" formed one of the main discourses of this new visual form. The conception and language of the "living portrait" also tied the daguerreotype to realms of magic. Referring to the "eerie presence" of the "absent subject," Marien stresses the association of early photography with illusion, the double, the uncanny, and the occult (8–9, 12–15, 176n32). She notes that nineteenth-century literary texts "often alluded to the connection between photography and magic," an idea explored in detail by Susan S. Williams.[14] Perceived by some to be a kind of magic mirror or magic memory in that it functioned as a better, more complete memory, the daguerreotype was thought, wondrously, to reveal the inner truths of the sitter. Referencing the essays by Oliver Wendell Holmes that were published in the *Atlantic,* Marien explains that in the nineteenth century, daguerreotypes and photographic images were regarded as enhancements of memory, allowing one both to "remember" the past in exceptional detail and to witness the present moment with preternatural vision: "The photographic externalization of memory promised to reveal moments of time and aspects of appearance undiscerned by normal human perception and attention" (77). With portrait photography, Marien posits, "the sitter's presence seemed to be almost palpable to the viewer" (76), the photographic image wondrously animating the sitter and evoking something more— a revelation of things "undiscerned by normal human perception and attention." One can hear associations with the magical in statements like Marien's, that is, the inexplicable expectation that things could be revealed in the daguerrean portrait that were not easily viewed, that something beyond physical appearance would be illumined in a "likeness," something unseen, such as character or moral sensibility.

Trachtenberg further posits that nineteenth-century perceptions of the daguerrean image as a magic mirror or as an enchanted "living presence" of an absent person drew ties to the realms of shadows and apparitions. Trachtenberg observes that the "popular slogan of daguerreotypists"—"Take the shadow ere the substance fade"—directly suggests that the daguerreotypist aimed to capture some "immortal part of self" in the image, or at least they often presented themselves as being able to do so ("Mirror" 68). In her essay on "Dickinson's Unknown Daguerreotypist," in which she quotes from William North's advertisement that appeared in the *Hampshire and Franklin Express* in December 1846, Bernhard notes that this was North's approach. In his newspaper advertisement, North uses nearly the exact words of the slogan that Trachtenberg points out: "Secure the Shadow ere the substance fades" (Bernhard 595). The daguerreotype was promoted as a vehicle or as a miracle whereby something invisible—a soul, a spirit, a mind—would be made visible. The daguerreotype is a rich cultural artifact and a fitting trope for the complexity of efforts to see Dickinson clearly and fully, the dynamic of revelation, disappearance, and creation long at work in encounters with Dickinson and her writing.

The publication of the 1931 *Letters of Emily Dickinson* marks an important moment in the history of Dickinson iconography: for the first time, the 1846/1847 daguerreotypic image was used in its original form, without redrawn face, hair, or clothing. Bingham describes the decision that led to the first publication of the undoctored portrait as the frontispiece to the 1931 *Letters,* edited by her mother, Mabel Loomis Todd:

As a frontispiece she reluctantly decided to reproduce the 1890 photograph of the daguerreotype. Even if not a flattering likeness it was at least authentic. Poor as it was, it would be preferable to the doctored "miniature," with curled hair and fancy ruff, which had been published in 1924 by Emily's niece and used thereafter as the frontispiece of the collected poems. For that doctored picture not only misrepresents Emily's appearance, it belies her character. Furbelows and Victorian ornateness were not a part of her nature; she would not have worn such a ruff. (Bingham, *Home* 520)

By 1931, the original daguerreotype was judged a more truthful depiction of Dickinson, at least more true to her "nature" and "character" than the fussily modified versions of the portrait. Todd's attitude (as expressed by her daughter) very much reflects a belief in photography's revelatory and uncanny capabilities: that a daguerreotypic or photographic portrait can reveal a sitter's inner self (a mind, a character, a nature) and hold it through time.

The 1846/1847 photographic image published in the 1931 *Letters* is quite faded, so much so that the table, chair, book, flowers, and fingers of Dickinson's left hand are effectively "cropped" out of the picture. Details of the dress are not easily seen, nearly flattened into a solid darkness, especially across the bodice. A clearer photograph of the daguerreotype surfaced unexpectedly in May 1932 through Austin Baxter Keep, a cousin of the Dickinsons. He wrote to Mabel Loomis Todd and sent along two prints made from his photograph of the daguerreotype of Emily. In the third printing of the *Letters,* the Austin Keep photograph replaced the previous one for the frontispiece, and it became the "standard likeness" of Dickinson for a number of years (Bingham, *Home* 520–21).

Another mysterious chapter in the story of the original 1846/1847 daguerreotype involves its disappearance, likely sometime in the 1890s.[15] Bingham reports that any thoughts of finding the original daguerreotype had "long since been given up" when a letter arrived from Saginaw, Michigan, in June 1945. Wallace Keep, Austin's brother, wrote to Millicent Bingham that he had the original daguerreotype, and that he had had it since June 1892, when, he explains, Lavinia had given it to him as a gift. "I am turning it over to your care," Wallace Keep wrote to Bingham, which he did, and the 1846/1847 daguerreotype was "soon" in Bingham's possession (Bingham, *Home* 521–22).[16] While the daguerreotype was returned through Wallace Keep, a conflicting story regarding the possession of the daguerreotype persists—that the original daguerreotype had been given to Maggie Maher, a longtime family domestic maid. The daguerreotype is referred to as "Maggie's daguerreotype" in Lavinia's diary entry for April 2, 1893, and, according to Bingham, Lavinia told Mabel Loomis Todd (Bingham's mother) that the daguerreotype had been given to Maggie Maher (Bingham, *Home* 519). Longsworth proffers a sequence of events in which the daguerreotype, "long assumed lost," was discovered when Maggie Maher "brought forth" the daguerreotype in the early 1890s, and speculates that Lavinia gave it to Wallace Keep in June 1893, a year later than he claims (Longsworth, "'Whose'" 37, 38).[17] In addition to the questions arising from the conflicting stories, one wonders why Lavinia would have given away the daguerreotype of Emily, whether to the devoted Maggie or to the twenty-two-year-old cousin Wallace or to anyone else for that matter. How extremely surprising that Lavinia would part with the only known daguerrean portrait of Emily in 1892 or 1893, especially as Dickinson's poems and letters were then being published and prepared for publication.[18] The convolutions of the story of the portrait, its many alterations, and its disappearance and reappearance enhance the portrait's mystique. It is a phantasmagoric thing, changed and changing, fading in and out of sight, replicating and literalizing the phenomenon of seeing and not seeing Emily Dickinson.

Staring at the portrait of the poet as a teenager, one can easily feel a mix of awe and mystery. Here she is, the young person who, in a few years, will begin to write verses and who, in about thirteen years, will become prolific at it. In this face we see the future poet, the person who over the next several decades will write hundreds of poems and who, in another hundred years or so, will have become established as an icon of American poetry. Here she is before the fact, a portrait of the poet as a girl. Since the 1846/1847 daguerreotype is the only certified photograph that we have of Dickinson, it seems evident that this is now how most people visualize her and have visualized her, although the person pictured is not precisely the person who wrote the poems. The person pictured has not written any poems, as far as we know. In line with Wardrop's proposition that a reader "superimposes" Dickinson's famous white dress onto the body in the 1846/1847 photographic image (*Labor* 10, 28), we can contemplate what else we impose onto the photograph. At the least, we conflate the image of the teenager with the woman who wrote the hundreds of poems. We invest the photographic image with our knowledge of who this teenager would become. Amending what T. S. Eliot said about the past and the present in "Tradition and the Individual Talent," we have a knowledge and an "awareness" about Dickinson "in a way and to an extent" that she could not have had about herself.

How does any particular image of Emily Dickinson affect our awareness of her? All of the investigations, speculations, judgments, and alterations contribute to a set of questions regarding perceptions of Dickinson. Does the image match the person one expects to see? How do authenticated images of Dickinson, possible images of her, and images that are assessed to be fake affect how we perceive her and think about her? If the image depicts a child, one described as a "generic" child, what does that contribute to one's views of Dickinson? If people who knew Dickinson tell us that these images do not look like the Emily they knew, what does that perspective and information do to our understanding?

That we want and even need portraits of Emily Dickinson speaks directly to photography's powers of enchantment. The singularity of the authenticated image of Emily Dickinson surely enhances its preciousness, even if it appears that to Lavinia and Austin the daguerreotype was not a precious possession. For others outside her immediate family and removed by time and space, this one authenticated portrait of Dickinson might fulfill any number of expectations or represent a variety of experiences: it is a factual record of an actual person; it invites meditation on creative brilliance; it functions as a talisman; and it serves as a devotional icon. Sontag contends that "all photographs are *memento mori*" (15), although the photograph of Dickinson is not only that or even mainly that. On the contrary, the photographic image imbues life. Lavinia is said to have exclaimed, "Emily has come back to me!" upon seeing a modified miniature portrait, and she wrote in a letter to Gertrude Graves, "It really seems as if Emily was here." Lavinia's words suggest that Emily has been found or resurrected. Emily has returned home. Through the portrait, Emily is alive and perpetually young.

Whether a daguerreotype or photograph serves as memorial, remem-

brance, talisman, or imprint of immortal "shadows," does it matter that Dickinson appears to be posed and surrounded by studio
props? That she *is* posed becomes evident when the portrait of Emily
Dickinson is placed next to other daguerrean portraits of seated women.[19]
As one example, the separate daguerreotypes of Emily Dickinson and
her mother appear to be a matched set. Venturing that the portraits of
mother and daughter were taken at the same time, both Longsworth
and Bernhard note that a table, a chair, and a book are set in the same
position in both portraits. In addition, they appear to be the same table,
chair, and book. Marta Werner asserts that these items "belong to a cultural field of objects instantly familiar to the genteel Victorian viewer"
(477). The patch of tablecloth visible in both portraits also appears to
be the same (Longsworth, *World* 40–41; Bernhard 596).[20] The similar
posture of each woman—sitting, face forward, looking straight ahead,
appearing to make eye contact with the viewer, right arm propped on
a table (and next to a closed book)—and the similarity of camera angle
reinforce the sense that the two Dickinson women have been placed
in this pose. How does posing complicate what one perceives in the
photographic portraits? One might think that Emily's straight-ahead
stare reveals an attitude or offers a glimpse into the "mighty Freight" of
that mind (F1187). It might be tempting to assume that the presence of
a book or the small bouquet in Emily's left hand illumines something
about Dickinson's interests or temperament, but these items are common studio furnishings—generic props. While the objects in the portrait
may encourage one to make assumptions about Emily, one is less likely
to extend the same assumptions to Emily Norcross Dickinson, although
the same objects appear in the portrait of her.

Even if "conventionally coded," as Werner states, the photographic
image still invites speculative contemplation. Further, modifications of
a portrait through cropping raise more complicating issues. If one accepts a daguerrean or photographic portrait as a reflection of a person or,
moreso, as a revelation of a person (as the concept of "likeness" posits),
alterations through cropping would potentially alter reflection and revelation. Along with affecting tone, cropping can revise the "story" signified in a portrait. A viewer's perception of Dickinson potentially shifts

as the portrait presentation changes, if the portrait includes her body or does not include her body, if her hands are visible or not visible. In her meditation on Dickinson's "motionless hands" in the daguerreotype, Marta L. Werner reads them symbolically, as signs of "the powerful cultural system of fixations and inhibitions confronting the female subject, and especially the female writer, in the mid-nineteenth century" (479). In addition to reading Dickinson's hands as social signs, Werner projects the future onto the image of Dickinson, adding to it our knowledge of the work done by these hands that are here "in repose" (479). In Werner's reading, Dickinson's hands figure the tension between an oppressive "cultural system" and a woman who challenged such constraints "all of her life *through* writing" (479). If Dickinson's hands are erased or faded out of the photographic portrait (as they have been in some variants), Werner's narrative loses its animating focus. Similarly, the ethos conveyed in the portrait changes with the presence or absence of the table and other objects. Interestingly, in the portrait of a glamorized Dickinson, the hair and clothing—all curls and frills and overweening whiteness—along with the erasure of everything except her head and bust, draw attention away from the actual person. This version of the portrait seems largely a study in feminized excess, the ruff of the large stand-up collar mirrored in the curls of hair. Despite their common origin in the 1846/1847 daguerreotype, all of the versions are, in a sense, portraits of different Emily Dickinsons.

Since the 1890s, these adjustments of fact and fiction have been creating someone we identify as Emily Dickinson. The daguerreotype—with its many modifications and mysteries—well illustrates this dynamic. Austin and Lavinia aimed to create an image of their sister that they regarded as more "truthful" by literally combining fact and fiction. Ironically, fact and fiction become so entwined (or so elusive) that which is which changes depending on one's perspective. What was it that Austin and Lavinia thought would make Emily look more like herself? Were "softened" features and ruffled collars intended to make Dickinson seem more beautiful or elegant, fashionable or feminine? In the original daguerreotype, Dickinson does look feminine. It is the ultra-feminine versions that surprise and perhaps disconcert, partly because the fussed-over, frilly Dickinson does not easily match the un-frilly personae of her poems. No one who knew her ever described Dickinson as being this girlish. In memoirs and biographical studies, family members and friends have at times remarked that Dickinson's drollery or mischievous self was sometimes not recognized by people or readers who did not know her.[21] It is possible that these are some of the qualities that Austin and Lavinia thought were absent from the 1846/1847 daguerreotype. And yet, the modifications to the daguerrean portrait, even ones that prompted Lavinia apparently to feel Emily's presence, do not obviously depict her as a mischief-maker or a droll wit. Even if artists were engaged to change the portrait because the original daguerreotype was such an inadequate representation—apparently so much so that Lavinia gave it away and Austin would "not hear of that portrait of Emily being used anywhere . . . on any account" (Bingham, *Ancestors'* 294)—it is likely that to our eyes, all of the efforts to modify the portrait make Dickinson look less like herself. The problem of "likeness" has continued to linger, and perhaps become only more complicated.

These ever-expanding observations and questions in regard to the Dickinson daguerreotype—and its many variants—underscore the elusive and illusory dynamic of both comprehending Dickinson and creating someone we identify as Dickinson. These entanglements of fact and fiction, of whole and part, of authentic image and altered image mirror the experience of viewing a daguerreotype, the picture sliding in and out of sight, angles and light creating shadows or clarity as well as ensuring that the viewer's own face will also be reflected back.

Beyond her well-known claim to Higginson in July 1862 that there existed "no portrait, now" of her (although her father "has Molds of all the rest") (Letter 268), is there any sign in Dickinson's poems or letters of her recognition of dageurreotypy or photography? Scholar Daneen Wardrop discerns a reference to daguerreotypy in two poems—Dickinson's 1862 "The outer from the inner" (F450) and the 1860 "Portraits are to daily faces" (F174). Asserting that Dickinson "worked hard to manipulate perceptions about her appearance," and so preferred "a verbal portrait" to photographic ones, Wardrop states that "The outer from the inner" reflects Dickinson's "concern with the daguerreotype" (Wardrop,

Labor 22, 209n18). Proposing that Dickinson was well "aware" of the "new technologies" of the daguerreotype and the stereograph, Melanie Hubbard identifies references to this new media of the nineteenth century in several poems, such as "It dont sound so terrible quite as it did" (F384) and "Before I got my eye put out" (F336).[22] Hubbard posits not only that Dickinson referenced these forms in poems but also that her writing practice of retaining variants for words or phrases replicates the "logic" and mechanism of the stereograph, whereby an enhanced picture is created with "side-by-side images" of a scene; Hubbard also correlates the "unstable medium" of the daguerreotype with the elusiveness of Dickinson's poems (Hubbard 115–16, 120–21, 131).[23]

While not directly or necessarily invoking portrait photography, words that are easily associated with portraits occur frequently in Dickinson's poems, words such as "eyes," "mouth," "lips," "brow," "cheeks," and "hair." The words "face" or "faces" appear in over 150 poems. In various poems, faces are described as "dim," "vague," "veiled," and "Imperfectly beheld." Dickinson denotes a face as "Image" or as "Evidence." She refers to "translated faces," a "transfigured" face, an "italic Face." One speaker refers to "The face I carry with me."[24] None of these words or phrases specifies the production of photographic images, but they do express a sense of the mystery and malleability of a person's most identifying feature—the face. In Dickinson's poems, faces are seen but often not clearly. Faces change; faces offer clues. The curious word "italic" (F1071) associates the face with language, or, more specifically, with writing, suggesting that a face inscribes or transcribes the self. A speaker suggests that her face is detachable and portable, something she can "carry," as if her face can be packed up or worn like an item of clothing. The third stanza of the 1860 poem "I have never seen 'volcanoes'" refers to "the stillness" of a "human face":

> If the stillness is Volcanic
> In the human face
> When opon a pain Titanic
> Features keep their place —
>
> (F165)

While the stanza most overtly addresses the anguish hidden behind the "stillness" of a face, the image of "stillness" could bring to mind a daguerrean portrait, the taking of which typically required the complete stillness of the sitter and the maintenance of a composed countenance for at least a few seconds and up to several minutes. In her study of early photographic portraiture, McCauley discusses the propriety of maintaining "the most fixed and calm facial expressions" and the impropriety of "laughter" or expressions of "despair" (5–6).

Whether or not the poem "The outer from the inner" references a daguerreotype or photograph, it presents images and analogies that depict the relationship between internal states and external manifestations.

> The Outer — from the Inner
> Derives it's magnitude —
> 'Tis Duke, or Dwarf, according
> As is the central mood —
>
> The fine — unvarying Axis
> That regulates the Wheel —
> Though Spokes — spin — more conspicuous
> And fling a dust — the while.
>
> The Inner — paints the Outer —
> The Brush without the Hand —
> It's Picture publishes — precise —
> As is the inner Brand —
>
> On fine — Arterial Canvas
> A Cheek — perchance a Brow —
> The Star's whole secret — in the Lake —
> Eyes were not meant to know.
> (F450)

The poem's imagery aligns with some nineteenth-century theories regarding the phenomenon of early photography, specifically those theories that attribute the source of the daguerrean image to spirit, mechanics, art, or nature. In the poem, the word "Outer" correlates with a body or a face and, by extension, a portrait. The opening lines assert that the compulsive force of the "Inner" determines the "magnitude" of the "Outer": "'Tis Duke, or Dwarf, according / As is the central mood — ." This "mood" shares the contours of its own size and importance, controlling its expression in visible form. In stanza three we learn that "The Inner — paints the Outer — ," an even more overt attribution of agency to whatever interior qualities are connoted by the word "Inner": "mood," mind, character, soul. The image of the "Arterial Canvas"—on which the "Inner" first "paints" and then "publishes"— merges the blood, heart, and skin of a human body with the materials used by an artist, specifically the cloth on which a painter creates a picture. While the words "paint" and "Canvas" invoke the medium of painting, the idea of a person being brought to life in artwork recalls also the nineteenth-century sensibility regarding the "living presence" of the daguerrean portrait. The mention of specific facial features ("A Cheek — perchance a Brow — ") reinforces the "coming to life" of a person on a "Canvas." The first fourteen lines present a direct relationship between "Inner" and "Outer": one's inner self controls its own "precise" reflection on the human "Canvas." In the last two lines of the poem, the relationship between Inner and Outer becomes more tangled, producing a Dickinsonian riddle difficult to unravel: "The Star's whole secret — in the Lake — / Eyes were not meant to know." Is the "secret" visible, reflected on the mirror-surface of the water? Or, conversely, is the secret submerged "in the Lake"? The semantic sleight-of-hand manipulates a concurrent appearance and disappearance, the "whole secret" both perceivable and unseen. The final line adds to the puzzle: "Eyes were not meant to know." Again, the ambiguity of the phrasing melds opposing ideas, leaving open the question if can one detect the "secret" or not.

Perplexities of seeing and not seeing, and of knowing and not knowing arise in so many Dickinson poems, this condition of uncertainty—in which a "secret" or face or one's own sense of self bobs in and out of view—persists as one of Dickinson's quintessential experiences. In the internal and external worlds that Dickinson endeavors to fathom, clear truths and shadows entwine. Her advice, in a well-known poem, to "Tell all the truth" obliquely, that is "slant," proclaims the necessity to shade "truth": the "Truth's superb surprise" is "Too bright for our infirm Delight" (F1263). Efforts to know and to tell benefit from obscuring angles. In this epistemological frame, in which we are not only unable to apprehend whole realities but also "not meant" to grasp them, Dickinson undermines the validity of empirical evidence. In poem after poem, because we cannot trust what we see, Dickinson calls for a different kind of vision, one that credits angles and indirection, parts rather than wholes. Dickinson's plane of truth honors uncertainty, mystery, obscurity: "I know the Whole — obscures the Part — " (F751); "That knows — and does not know — " (F1438); "Not seeing, still we know" (F1566); "Knows how to forget!" (F391); "Safer not to know — " (F1334); "We never know we go when we are going" (F1546); "We do not know the time we lose" (F1139); "That those who know her, know her less / The nearer her they get" (F1433); and "But we, who know, / Stop hoping, now" (F341). In scores of poems, Dickinson meditates the uneasy alliances between knowing and not knowing.

In the poem "The outer from the inner," the mystery of the "whole secret" is linked to the light of a distant celestial body, a "Star." In the discourse of cosmology, the concept of magnitude alludes to brightness and to a system of ranking determined by the intensity of light, so that the mention of "magnitude" in the opening lines conceivably references a level of illumination: how brightly does the "Inner" light up the "Outer"? As in the poem "Tell all the truth but tell it slant," brightness may be stunning, but stunning brightness compels deflection—or submergence "in the Lake." The image of the "whole secret — in the Lake" conjoins surface and depth—another version of Outer and Inner—as well as beckons the effects of water on perception: distortion and obfuscation. The final line ("Eyes were not meant to know") can be read as a head-shaking reprimand for the overly curious or as a tantalizing overture to witness something "not meant" to be seen; either way, temptation is tempered by the cold watery reality of "the Lake," which engulfs, half-hides, and changes whatever it contains. The ostensible revelation of secrets and of self, proposed in the poem, takes on illicit tones and the ghostly shapes of things prohibited and of things only partially seen. Yet, the transposition in the poem of face to Star, with its allusions to galactic mysteries, recalls the nineteenth-century view of daguerrean portraiture as a miracle of nature—"sun-painting," as Oliver Wendell Holmes declared—and a cause of astonishment. With the daguerreotype, the "Outer" reflection of the "Inner" was thought to have transcendent origins.

Dickinson's epistemological teetering between the empirical and the mystical, as seen in "The outer from the inner," offers a surprising demonstration of the mystique generated by the phenomenon of the daguerreotype. Emblemizing the tension in Dickinson's poem, the indisputably empirical daguerreotype (a physical object that can be held, seen, and examined) generated explanations that surpassed or challenged the empirical. What a viewer would see in a daguerrean portrait is precisely what nineteenth-century commentators debated: Does a viewer witness a miracle of nature, experience an illusion, gain access to the realms of "shadow," behold a sitter's moral character? In the physical object, one ostensibly sees something that transcends the object; thus, the form was perceived as magical or mystical. We too keep faith in the enchantments of photographic images, for example, in our expectation that they allow us to hold more closely the person (or place or experience) pictured. Susan Sontag succinctly links action and effect: "To photograph is to appropriate the thing photographed" (4). As did many amazed viewers in the nineteenth century, we accept the photographic image as a magic mirror or magic memory, the act of photography producing a lasting replica of a person (or place or experience) that seems real and revelatory. Sontag refers to "talismanic uses" of photographs, that is, the trust that photographs can (ritualistically and magically) help us "to contact or lay claim to another reality" (16). Lavinia and Austin may have disliked the daguerreotype of Emily and have thought that the image did not truthfully represent her, but for many others, there is something talismanic about the portrait of Emily Dickinson. Through the portrait we do imagine "another reality." We presume to know something about Dickinson from this image;

we think it helps us to relate more authentically or more deeply to her poems; we treat it as a looking-glass for an Emily in her twenties, thirties, forties, and fifties. The daguerreotype of Dickinson enhances the sense that one knows her—or can know her. The portrait brings Dickinson closer to us. We look at her and she looks at us.

Conundrums of self and identity infuse much of Dickinson's writing. In addition, pictorial images of Emily Dickinson—whether the 1846/1847 daguerreotype, its many variants, or other portraits that are proposed to be her—also set spinning questions of self and identity. In the 1862 letter to Higginson in which she disavowed the existence of any portrait of herself "now," Dickinson, now so famously, referred to the "I" of the poems as a "supposed person" (Letter 268). The history of Dickinson scholarship, biographical study, and sleuthing leads to the revelation that for us too, she is a supposed person. We have made her such, through our amalgamation of facts and theories, postulations and speculations. The history of Dickinson studies has been a narrative of efforts to peer into the many mysteries that characterize her words and life and to materialize the person and poet we call Emily Dickinson.

THE ENIGMA IN WHITE

The conjuring of Emily Dickinson and the exhibition of the person perceived have been promoted through the great regard granted to objects associated with her and through the many stories that portray her as mysterious, ethereal, or at least highly unusual. The cabinet of Dickinsonia houses a number of puzzle pieces—the daguerreotype, the dress, the house, the items included in some letters (a cricket, an autumn leaf, a crocus, and others), the poems themselves and the fragments of poems—pieces that are as mesmerizing as runes. Assigned divinatory powers, these items seem to promise special entry to Dickinson's world and into her mind. In addition, these iconic images contribute to the management and marketing of Dickinson as a curiosity on public exhibition. The objects carry stories, and the stories

CHAPTER FIVE

supply pieces of the constructed legend of her life and to the portrayal of Dickinson herself as "the Myth."

The singularity of the white dress, paralleling the singularity of the authenticated daguerreotype, ensures its treasured status in the Dickinson cabinet. Numerous scholars have ruminated on the signifying radiance of the white dress. Some chroniclers and scholars have read the whiteness of Dickinson's dress as a marker of mourning or yearning or renunciation. Dickinson's niece Bianchi explains that "the family" perceived Dickinson's "habitual wearing of white," as "a sort of memorial to the man she loved, and whom she renounced" (*Face to Face* 52n). Walsh directly refers to the dress as a "bridal gown" that signaled Dickinson's "spiritual" marriage to Otis Lord (82, 93). Speculating that the three letters Dickinson addressed to an unknown "Master," now collectively known as the Master letters, during 1858 and 1861 (as dated by Franklin) were written to the newspaper editor and Dickinson's dear friend Samuel Bowles, Sewall muses that an image of Dickinson wearing white that occurs in one of the Master letters "may be a trope for her longed-for rank as a published poet" (*Life* 2: 524). Arguing that the color white is "the color of renunciation" in Dickinson's poetry, Wolff proposes that Dickinson's white dresses "became a visible sign of perpetual mourning" (409, 507). Patterson calls it a "shroud" (*Riddle* 233). Connecting Dickinson's white dress to a spectrum of Victorian iconography, Gilbert and Gubar testify that Dickinson gives her life a "fictional" and emblematic shape: "By defiantly gathering all the implications of Victorian whiteness into a single shape of white around her own body Dickinson announces that she herself incarnates the paradox of the Victorian woman poet— the Self disguised as the Other, the creative subject impersonating the fictionalized object—and as such she herself enacts the enigma that she perceives at the heart of her culture" (621). Farr posits that Dickinson divulges her spiritual affinities through her white clothing and in her "women-in-white poems," noting that nuns frequently wore white in the nineteenth century and that "brides did not customarily wear white in the United States until the late 1870s" (*Passion* 33). Proposing a more secular observation, Pascoe suggests an association

174

between Dickinson and the celebrated singer Jenny Lind, who wore white when performing. A neighbor of the Dickinsons, Eugene Field, reportedly points to Dickinson's wearing of white as "one of her peculiarities" (Leyda 2: 114). Bianchi writes that her "first definite memory of my Aunt Emily is of her coming to the door to meet me in her white dress—looking to me just like another little girl" (*Face to Face* 3).

Wardrop argues that the critical and cultural allure of the "fabled white dress" has nearly hidden a "stylish" Emily Dickinson who wore clothing of many colors and was "vitally concerned with how she dressed" (*Labor* 6, 15, 34). Describing the young woman wearing the dark dress in the 1846/1847 daguerreotype as "fashionable," Wardrop observes as well that many a reader "superimposes" a white dress onto the picture of the sixteen-year-old (*Labor* 10, 13, 28). In the version of the Dickinson portrait that was heavily modified by a person not definitively identified, Dickinson's dark dress is literally painted over and replaced with a white dress. The persona of the Enigma in White—the figure of mourning or ghostliness or reclusiveness—superseded the "fashionably engaged" woman who was attentive to her self-presentation. Keenly aware of the nearly forgotten reality that Dickinson wore clothing and dresses in a number of colors, especially brown, blue, red, paisley, and calico, Wardrop sums up the mythologizing effect of the white dress: "The white dress has for decades coded Dickinson's mystique for us, signifying the seeming nature of the recluse" (*Labor* 34). What does it mean that the white dress assumed such grand metonymic power? The charismatic energy of the white dress has galvanized particular views of Dickinson so successfully that every quality that has been associated with the white dress has been associated with Dickinson herself. The presumption that interpretive readings of the dress reflect back on the woman who wore the dress flirts perhaps with animism, the sensation that Dickinson's spirit inhabits her dress.

Stepping onto the second floor at the Homestead Museum and approaching the white dress on the seamstress block recreates as closely as possible the experience of encountering Emily Dickinson herself in her home. The phantom Emily, standing outside her bedroom at the Homestead, is conjured by the dress and by the mind-trick in which a believer might envision the dress as embodied rather than disembodied. That the dress one encounters is not the original one, but an exact copy (with a second copy at the Amherst Historical Museum),[25] does not seem to hinder the visioning, but rather further attests to the alchemical properties of the dress, the object casting a spell and calling forth Dickinson's presence. Imbued with Dickinson's spirit and laden with signifying bounty, the white dress not only plays a role in shaping our comprehension of Dickinson but also sparks her apparition.

Despite the summoning effects of the white dress, the varied interpretive readings of it—cited as evidence of apparent idiosyncrasy, reclusiveness, "perpetual mourning," depth of sacrifice, fanatical passions, and more—magnify the mystery of Dickinson. As with the 1846/1847 daguerreotype (and its many modified forms) and other pictorial images considered as possible depictions of Dickinson, the dress and its signifying aura generate crisscrossing views, both enlightening and befuddling our understanding. That the color of the honored dress is replicated by the "dainty white casket" in which Dickinson was buried pushes one toward at least mulling over the ironic convergence by which the white dress and white casket seem to mirror each other, each a trope for the other, both functioning as dual markers of death and life.[26] Dickinson certainly conflates a woman's life and a woman's burial in a number of poems, including "Title divine is mine!" (F194), "Because I could not stop for death" (F479), "I felt my life with both my hands" (F357), and "A solemn thing it was I said" (F307). Women, it seems, according to Dickinson, are spectral in life and spectral in death.

Citing Habegger, Wardrop notes that the extant white dress has been dated sometime between 1878 and 1882 (*Labor* 29), when Dickinson was around fifty years old, a detail that renews the matter of perception: Whom does one envision wearing the dress—a fifty-year-old Dickinson or the sixteen-year-old, or someone who floats in between these ages? The dress has been irresistibly attractive to inquisitors of many sorts, who ponder it from different angles and use it to delineate one persona or another as Emily Dickinson, much as with the daguerreotype. It is perhaps this kind of unfixed view, or the wonderment prompted by absence or the changeableness of the objects themselves, that allows for such malleable perceptions and varied understanding. In her poems, faces that are "vague," "Veil[ed]" and "Imperfectly beheld" are spellbinding: "A Charm invests a face / Imperfectly beheld — " (F430). The focus is on the face, but also on the person gazing upon it. It is the perceiver's view, however partial or "imperfect," that adorns the "face" with "Charm." Whether this "Charm" connotes fantasy, desire, or some other form of entrancement, the ability to bestow a face with any of these dimensions also suggests extreme adaptability, as the "face" can conceivably reveal almost anyone. Similarly, the dress vivifies Dickinson's presence, and it even more blatantly presents an Emily more "Imperfectly beheld"—an Emily more phantom than person.

An abundance of dramatizing stories further reinforces images of Dickinson as a ghost or spirit, a figure extraordinary but not wholly human, a curiosity, a character of lore. In a letter to Lavinia in 1892, Bishop F. D. Huntington recalls Emily in otherworldly terms: "The image that comes before me when I think of her is hardly more terrestrial than celestial,—a Spirit with only as much of the mortal investiture as served to maintain her relations with this present world" (Leyda 2: 479). In his *The Village of Amherst,* Frank Prentice Rand suggests that Dickinson was incomprehensible to her "neighbors," perceived by them as a bizarre recluse in their midst (230). Higginson's description of Emily as "too enigmatical" hints that she was a puzzle that could not, perhaps, be solved at all, even if Higginson records only that a one-hour visit was not sufficient time to understand her: "I could only sit and watch, as one does in the woods" ("Emily Dickinson's Letters" 453). Among her reminiscences, Bianchi includes Cornelia Mather Kellogg's childhood memory of vigilantly keeping an eye on Emily's window from across the street: "She used to watch for a light behind 'Miss Emily's' window-shade at night and tell herself, with a shiver of excitement, 'I have seen Miss Emily's shadow!'" (*Face to Face* 38). It seems that Dickinson was frequently viewed or remembered as a distinctively unusual person, someone to be watched for, and if sighted, studied from a distance. Neighbor Clara Bellinger Green has written that meeting the "mythical" Emily "had the element of unreality."

Green recalls being "in a flutter of anticipation" at the prospect of meeting Emily when Clara and her sister and brother were invited to the Dickinson house to sing and play the piano on a "warm June evening." Although Emily and Lavinia listened to the performance from upstairs, afterward "a tiny figure in white darted to greet us" in the "dimly lighted" library (291). The "unreality" that Green associates with the occasion may derive in part from the hoped-for but unexpected meeting with this reclusive town celebrity but also from the ghostly aspects of the moment—Dickinson speaking with a "breathless voice" and seen in a dim light (and almost not seen at all). All of these recollections contribute to an image of Dickinson as a fantastical figure, alluring in her elusiveness.

In her introductory commentary to the 1924 *The Life and Letters of Emily Dickinson,* Bianchi mentions the exaggerations and "lurid misinformation" about Dickinson that have shaped her into something mysterious, peculiar, or fantastical. As her life has been "revamped" (as Todd claimed) by scholars, biographers, and readers, and "Emily herself as all but vanished," we have construed someone we identify as Dickinson, a shimmering figure, elusive and uncontained. In reading the multiplicity of biographies and scholarly studies, in examining the increasingly varied presentation of the poems, in recognizing scholars' scrutiny of Dickinson's process of composing, in noticing the attention turned toward her alternative words and lines and toward the actual pieces of paper (whether stationary, envelopes, or scraps) on which Dickinson wrote, one discerns the continuing and elaborate efforts to gather the innumerable parts of a puzzle and to determine possible arrangements. What can one glean from these mosaics of fact and fiction, theory and speculation, angle and shadow?

The 1846/1847 daguerreotype, the primary object with which I began, is a fitting trope for the varied accounts of Emily Dickinson, the story of this image illustrating the dynamics of seeing and seeing anew, of creating and re-making. Every single image of "Dickinson"— whether found, false, retouched, or authenticated—holds elements of mystery and fascination. The many evaluations of the portraits recall responses to some of the star attractions of P. T. Barnum's museum and circus, exhibitions that invited patrons to look, scrutinize, and judge. Similarly, the various images claimed or speculated to be Dickinson share features with some of the attractions that P. T. Barnum showcased, such as Joice Heth or "What Is It?" or others of his "nondescripts," all of which advertised the ambiguous identity of the presented marvel and which became hugely popular due to the intrigue of the conundrum. His human riddles provoked wonder and fascination. As discussed in chapter one, people returned repeatedly to Barnum's exhibition spaces to see Joice Heth, the proclaimed 161-year-old nursemaid to the infant George Washington and, eventually, the curiosity who was announced, as a promotional tactic, to be an automaton. One of Barnum's most popular attractions—"What Is It?"—was another version of the same kind of puzzle. Of the photographic images posited to represent Dickinson, we can and do ask the same questions: literally, "Who is it?" and, in a sense, "What is it?" in that we are forced to consider how the image has been conceived. We study the clothing, the hair, the face, the eyes, the chin, the hands, the lace, the ribbon necklace, the book, the flowers, the shadows, the light, and the pose in an effort to glean something about Dickinson. As with Barnum's museum attractions, repeated viewings and consequent assessments assist in enhancing the mystery and the mystique.

The white dress, too, demonstrates the overwhelming talismanic power of an object attached to Dickinson, achieving the very effect that was credited to the daguerreotype and other forms of early photography—that the absent person becomes uncannily present. The evocative effect that Marien claims for the early portrait photograph—that the person in the photograph "seemed to be almost palpable to the viewer" (12, 76)—is surely experienced by at least some of the visitors who stand before Dickinson's white dress. As reported in the arts section of the *New York Times* on May 22, 2014, restoration work on Dickinson's bedroom uncovered "floorboard ghosts," evidence of patterns of walking on the flooring underneath the twentieth-century floorboards (Kahn: May 22, 2014). In holding its own "memory," the bedroom flooring that makes visible Dickinson's pattern of movement contributes to the palpability of Dickinson's presence.

One can appreciate the irony that Dickinson's association with domestic space has contributed to the creation of Dickinson as a public spectacle. Positioned in the home, her bedroom, the kitchen, the conservatory, and the garden, Dickinson has often been perceived as excessively tied to domestic spaces. Perpetuated by stories and by analyses that place her forever in the house, her home has been regarded by some as a two-story brick emblem of Dickinson's personal oddness, illness, or inscrutability. However, for Dickinson, domestic realms are sites of stories and visions, passions and ghosts. For Dickinson, the domestic space is where the ordinary, the marvelous, and the aberrant encounter each other. Notwithstanding Victorian ideals of a domestic sphere of comfort, love, and piety, American literary narratives have also chronicled a long history of the domestic space as the location of all manner of diabolical, surreptitious, and unholy doings. In works ranging from captivity narratives to family melodramas, home is depicted as a bastion of violence and conflict, corrupting secrets and illicit acts, nightmares, deception, and demons. The domestic spaces that Dickinson portrays in her writing are frequently such places. A speaker of one poem, returning home after a long absence, is paralyzed by fear before "the Awful Door" and flees "gasping — from the House" (F440). Little girls are locked in closets: "They shut me up in Prose — / As when a little Girl / They put me in a Closet — / Because they liked me 'still'" (F445). Familiar spaces are haunted, occupied by hidden assassins, goblins, ghouls, and other terrors. The "Old Home" mentioned in the last line of "I felt my life with both my hands" materializes as the residence of anxious feeling. Looked to as a place of past comfort, however dubious and short-lived, "Home" cannot protect the speaker from the worry that she is disappearing.

> I felt my life with both my hands
> To see if it was there —
> I held my spirit to the Glass,
> To prove it possibler —

I turned my Being round and round
And paused at every pound
To ask the Owner's name —
For doubt, that I should know the sound —

I judged my features — jarred my hair —
I pushed my dimples by, and waited —
If they — twinkled back —
Conviction might, of me —

I told myself, "Take Courage, Friend —
That — was a former time —
But we might learn to like the Heaven,
As well as our Old Home"!

(F357)

As if the speaker and her "life" were fading in and out of view, the speaker attempts to ascertain if she exists: "I felt my life with both my hands / To see if it was there — ." Is she "there"? Is she real? Is she visible? Apparently seeking evidence that she is not a phantasm, the speaker turns to a "Glass"—either a mirror or a photographic image—in order "To prove it possibler" that she is "there." The reassurance the speaker hopes to find in the reflected image of herself recalls the powers of animation attributed to early portrait photography—that the daguerrean or photographic image was a "living presence" or a magic mirror capable of surpassing ordinary human powers of observation.

The statement in stanza two that "I turned my Being round and round" plausibly portrays the speaker insistently inspecting an object that depicts herself, a photograph perhaps, turning it and studying it from different angles. The activity of studying a photographic image merges with a metaphoric image of walking, moving in this direction and that direction ("round and round"), possibly walking in circles. This roving, self-examining speaker reports that she "paused at every pound," an acknowledgement, it would appear, that she inhabits the "pound" (pen, prison) as well as approaches it. She both experiences many confinements and, with detachment, observes them. By the end of the poem, we understand that "Old Home" has been replaced by a new home (wryly called "Heaven"), a place where she will need "Courage." She "might learn to like" this new home or she might not. Home can be a very inhospitable place, and yet Dickinson's speaker, in this poem as well as in others, has resources, including powerful objects, to assist her in her struggle to be more visible and to be more fully herself.

The exhibition of Emily Dickinson is promoted by talismanic and entrancing objects and places, large and small, by which we attempt to see Dickinson and to see her anew as well as more completely. While she is integrally attached to a daguerreotype measuring 2¾ x 3¼ inches, to a particular white dress, to poems and letters and home-made fascicles, to a house and a room, these tangible entities do not contain or fix or explain her. While these physical items and specific spaces have invited meticulous study, the consequence has been ever-shifting visions of a person (or riddle) we call Dickinson. In the poem "I dwell in possibility" (F466), Dickinson's House of "Possibility" is imagined as a structure with "numerous" windows and doors, a place rich in portals and thresholds. This house is excessively open, its roof comprised of "Gables of the Sky." With the barest of enclosure, this house is as much outside as inside. The openness of the dwelling and its abundance of views resonate with the ever-unfolding panorama of lights and shadows, the panoply of meanings that we discern in Dickinson's life and writing. Emily Dickinson has provided seemingly "inexhaustible invitations to deduction, speculation, and fantasy," as Susan Sontag claims for the photograph. While Dickinson's directive to Higginson in that letter of July 1862 (Letter 268) stresses that the "I" speaking in the poems "does not mean — me," we readers presume that so much does "mean" Dickinson: the poems, the objects of Dickinsonia, the strange and curious stories. It all conjures Emily Dickinson, or someone we think of as Emily Dickinson, this "character of Amherst" who is most surely "Imperfectly beheld."

EPILOGUE

The Show is not the Show
But they that go —
(F1270)

"The Show"—a shorthand reference in Dickinson's poem likely for the traveling circus and, by extension, for the many forms of popular entertainment in the nineteenth century—provided arenas for the exhibition of the vast variety of human experience, from the delightful to the terrible, from the inspirational to the bewildering. The beckoning stages of popular entertainment widely displayed the social, political, and legal quandaries that enmeshed the nation in the nineteenth century—questions of personal and national identity, contests of human rights and law, definitions of normality and aberration. The preeminent nineteenth-century showman P. T. Barnum and the sensational attractions he presented at his American Museum and, later, in his traveling circuses exploited the nation's fascination with and fears regarding race and dramatized the ostensible puzzle of human identity. Circus sideshows showcased "living curiosities" and so-called freaks. Some of the century's most popular singers, such as the Hutchinson Family Singers, performed in the cause of social reform, such as for abolition and for women's rights. Blackface minstrel acts, in the spirit of either burlesque, racist vitriol, or earnest appreciation, created songs, sketches, and plays based on the presumed experience of black people in the United States. These "educative" entertainment opportunities became widely available, potentially viewed or heard by individuals or audiences whatever their age, race, class, or gender. As sheet music found its way into the parlors of the middle class, as circuses traveled the countryside, as dime museums were promoted as educational and

183

wholesome family entertainment, as minstrel acts evolved and black-face performance continued as part of standard holiday entertainment, every member of the family had venues in which to apprehend the vexed questions of rights and identity that were preoccupying the nation. All of these forms of entertainment demonstrated that the dual realities of captivity and freedom were widely observed in nineteenth-century America and that distinctions between these two seemingly opposite states were both maintained and completely smeared.

As I have tried to demonstrate in these chapters, noticing Emily Dickinson's active interest in the popular entertainments of her day makes available a more world-bound Dickinson. Sometimes viewed as reclusive or disengaged from the world, in reality Dickinson enjoyed circuses, knew popular songs, including the music and musicians of reform movements and of the minstrel stage, and read popular writers of the day. The assessment that Dickinson was unheedful of anything beyond the borders of her house (and the house next door) has been shifting in recent decades. Shira Wolosky's 1984 pioneering study that boldly proposed that Dickinson wrote about the Civil War initiated the serious possibility of perceiving Dickinson as a witness of and a commentator on the great struggles of her times. Acknowledging Dickinson's participation in the wide-reaching, often rambunctious, world of popular amusement not only reveals one possible access to conversations that agitated the nation but also makes more visible her social and political consciousness.

Dickinson lived in a turbulent time and place. One might expect her to be attentive to vital matters of her time: the roiling debates over rights, liberty, human identity, gender, and race that did not produce clear direction, but rather exacerbated the splintering of the nation since the terms and boundaries of any of these matters were not stable and settled. The challenge, as expressed so frequently in her poems, involves navigating, or even imagining, one's presence in the world, especially if the time and place are inhospitable, confounding, perilous, or if one becomes stranded or frightened. If one feels surrounded by "Oceans" (F596) or assailed by demons ("She feels some ghastly Fright come up" [F360]), entering public space makes demands on

one's capacity for courage or defiance or vision. As one of her audacious speakers declares, "I took my Power in my Hand — / And went
against the World" (F660). This speaker's encounter with "the World"
does not go well ("Myself / Was all the one that fell — "), and while
we do not know whether what she "holds" in her hand is a weapon or
a writing implement or an idea, "Power" assumes many shapes and
purposes. There is also power in a voice, a conviction (or possibility) that Dickinson repeatedly deliberates, imagining voices that she
(or her speakers) might wield, even if people prefer her confined and
"'still'" (F445). The realms of popular entertainment invite entrance to
this troubled and perplexing world, comingling the prosaic with the
marvelous, and endlessly examining—in song, theatre, literary fiction,
and exhibitions—what is real and what illusion, what is dangerous and
what harmless, and any number of other matters that one might think
easy to distinguish, but that are unexpectedly enigmatic. That Dickinson's verse contains many allusions to circuses and menageries, song
and dance, masquerade, theatre, riddles, wild animals, and ghosts suggests not just that Dickinson was well aware of the types and tropes of
popular culture but also that they assisted her in her own imaginative
explorations of a bewildering, sometimes ferocious, sometimes fantastical world, and in her efforts to give voice to her experience.

In my examination of Dickinson and her engagement with the
popular culture of her time, I have been surprised by the confluence
between the puzzles and problems exhibited so effectively by the attractions of popular entertainment and those addressed by Dickinson
in her writing. Both display a compulsive attention to matters related
to the fierce debates in the country: the struggles between suppres-
sion of voices and free expression, the seeming mysteries of a person's
identity, and the uncertainties of sensory perception. These three issues emerge as motifs in this study, every new direction returning one
to the same conundrums of vision and understanding.

An illustrative case is Dickinson's evident familiarity with the music, performers, and images of blackface minstrelsy, and her many allusions to these in her poems and letters. If twenty-first-century readers
experience difficulty comprehending the significance of blackface

performance to nineteenth-century audiences, it is perhaps in part because minstrel music and performance likely held different meanings for different spectators in the nineteenth century. Historians, musicologists, and scholars have posited widely varied views of the minstrel figure of the nineteenth century: as racist caricature, as trickster, as theatrical performer, as social satirist. Dickinson's "minstrel" figures are ordinary people with tremendous power to speak, to imagine, to disrupt, and to transform. They are bystanders or beggars as well as mischief-makers, rebels, drunken revelers, and fanciful dancers. In poems such as "It makes no difference abroad," "I cannot dance opon my toes," "If I could bribe them by a rose," and "The jay his castanet has struck," Dickinson's incorporation of the figures and tropes of the minstrel show can seem surreal or parodic, although her minstrels can wear larger-than-life lineaments, being figures that evoke folkloric tales or myths. As in "It makes no difference abroad," her banjo-playing minstrel opens portals into apocalyptic scenes, apparently a witness to a crucifixion in 1863 America.

The vexed issues of perception and identity are also evident with the astonishing new technology, at mid-century, of the daguerreotype, a phenomenon that, in its productions and in the theories that proffered explanations for it, directly addressed the marvels, as well as the instabilities, of perception. Visual depictions of Dickinson have been invested with extraordinary meaning, the 1846/1847 daguerreotype (as well as images of a woman or women who might be Emily Dickinson) sustaining intense ongoing critical examination, endless fascination, and much speculation. What does one see and not see in a daguerrean portrait? This is the question that commentators on "the mirror with a memory" have deliberated. With visual images of Dickinson—whether the authenticated daguerreotype or other discovered photographic images—we might feel enlightened, as though we have greater access to that imagination or that person and her poems, or just as readily feel something else less certain. With visual depictions of Dickinson (or those who *might* be Dickinson), facts and fictions encircle each other, demonstrating the difficulties of seeing and knowing with certainty. One may desire to see Dickinson more fully and more clearly, but she swings in and out of view, much like the daguerrean image that changes with shifting angles and light.

Paying attention to the ways that Dickinson participated in varied types of popular culture shifts the angles on our perceptions of her and of her writing; thus what slides into view is a Dickinson who engages a web of social and political forces and grapples with the array of anxieties, uncertainties, and traumas that people in America experienced during the nineteenth century. As in any of the lively popular entertainments of her time, in Dickinson's poetic theatricals—occupied by singers and dancers, animals and shape-shifters, impersonators and actors—earthly realities can converge with the wondrous and the wondrous can assist in the apprehension of an earthly time and place.

Notes

INTRODUCTION

1 The collection of materials—including manuscripts, portraits, photographs and paintings, newspaper pages from the 1860s, and personal objects—displayed at the Morgan are presented in *The Networked Recluse* (Kelly, et al.), a book published in 2017 as a companion to the exhibit.

2 *A Quiet Passion,* written and directed by Terence Davies, with Cynthia Nixon portraying the poet as an adult, was released in 2016.

3 Rand also notes that Martha Graham "paid tribute" to Dickinson in an "interpretive dance" (229). Rand is referring to the ballet that Graham choreographed based on the life of Emily Dickinson, *Letter to the World*. Performed by Graham and Merce Cunningham (and others), the ballet premiered on August 11, 1940, at Bennington College Theatre in Bennington, Vermont (Library of Congress catalog, www.loc.gov/item/ihas.200182830). As discussed by Joan Acocella in "An Unforgettable Photo of Martha Graham," perhaps the most famous photographic image of Martha Graham is the one taken by Barbara Morgan in 1940 of Graham performing in *Letter to the World* (*Smithsonian Magazine*, June 2011, https://www.smithsonianmag.com/arts-culture/an-unforgettable-photo-of-martha-graham-159709338/).

4 Other plays about Emily Dickinson are Ethelyn Friend's 2012 one-woman play *More Than Daisy Dares* and Emma Ayres and Brianna Sloane's 2014 *The Emily Dickinson Project*.

CHAPTER ONE: EMILY DICKINSON'S AMERICAN MUSEUM

1 The Feejee Mermaid and Wooly Horse were two of Barnum's most famous animal attractions. Barnum's preserved "veritable mermaid," which was said to have been found among the Fiji Islands, was created by artfully joining a monkey and a fish (Barnum, *Life* 232–35). Also see Kunhardt et al. 40–43; and Saxon, *Barnum* 119–23. Using the temporary disappearance of Colonel John Frémont, the American explorer, to his advantage, Barnum arranged an exhibit of what he called "Col. Fremont's Nondescript or Wooly Horse," which he claimed Frémont had discovered in California: a composite creature "made up of the Elephant, Deer, Horse, Buffalo, Camel, and Sheep" (Barnum, *Life* 350). Barnum also exhibited many acts billed as human-animal crosses: Leopard Girl, Dog-Faced Boy, and Frog Man (see Bogdan 98–100; Kunhardt et al. 188).

2 The "What Is It?" quotation in the epigraph comes from Saxon, *Barnum* 98.

3 Commentators disagree as to what Barnum purchased: Joice Heth herself or the right to exhibit her. For accounts of this transaction as well as of Heth's time with Barnum, see Barnum, *Life* 148–59; Kunhardt et al. 20–23; Harris 20–23, 25–26; M. R. Werner 28–35; Saxon, *Barnum* 20–21; and especially Reiss's excellent study of Heth's role in American cultural history.

4 In his 1855 autobiography, Barnum describes Joice Heth: "She was apparently in good health and spirits, but former disease or old age, or perhaps both combined, had rendered her unable to change her position; in fact, although she could move one of her arms at will, her lower limbs were fixed in their position, and could not be straightened. She was totally blind, and her eyes were so deeply sunken in their sockets that the eyeballs seemed to have disappeared altogether. She had no teeth, but possessed a head of thick bushy gray hair. Her left arm lay across her breast, and she had no power to remove it. The fingers of her left hand were drawn down so as nearly to close it, and remained fixed and immovable" (148–49).

5 The letter is reputed to have been written by Barnum himself (Harris 23; Kunhardt et al. 20, 22). Reiss asserts that the automaton controversy arose in New Haven, not Boston (116). Following her death in 1836, an autopsy placed the age of the woman called Joice Heth at around eighty. Afterward, she continued to be the object of hoaxes and jokes, false histories, rumors about her identity, and claims that she was still alive (see Barnum, *Life* 171–76; Saxon, *Barnum* 71–73; Kunhardt et al. 22–23; Werner 33–34).

6 The original "What Is It?" was apparently played by Hervio Nano, the stage persona of Hervey Leach. In his 1855 autobiography, Barnum reports that two unnamed American managers "stained his face and hands, and covered him with a dress made of hair, and resembling the skin of an animal. They then advertised him as a curious 'nondescript,' called 'WHAT IS IT?' and claimed that 'the strange animal' was captured in the mountains of Mexico" (346). In the autobiography, Barnum disassociates himself from Hervio Nano; Saxon, however, points to a letter of August 18, 1846, in which Barnum acknowledges his participation (Saxon, *Barnum* 360n28). Also see Saxon, *Letters* 35–37.

7 Lindfors cites 1859 ("Barnum" 20).

8 The caption from the Currier and Ives lithograph is quoted in Lindfors, "Barnum" 20.

9 Lindfors states that Johnson was "discovered" in Bridgeport, Connecticut, and was not mentally impaired, but rather remarkably gifted as an actor ("Barnum"). Saxon cites an interview with Johnson's sister, who

says that he was born in 1857 (Saxon, *Barnum* 98). Also see Dennett
30–31; Bogdan 134–42; Kunhardt et al. 149; and Cook. The variance
of detail would seem to support Cook's claim that we know "a manufactured image—a *character* called 'What is It?' rather than the actual
human beings who embodied these fictions" (140).

10 Barnum exhibited several "missing link" acts, such as Hoomio and Iola,
"Wild Australian Children" advertised as native to "a distinct race hitherto unknown to civilization" (Kunhardt et al. 209). Kunhardt et al. reports that the Wild Australian Children were siblings with microcephaly
from Circleville, Ohio (209). The first "missing link" or "man-monkey"
presented by Barnum in the 1840s was "Mlle. Fanny," an orangutan
(Saxon, *Barnum* 98; Dennett 30).

11 Barnum exhibited many so-called giants, most of whom were identified
by ethnicity, for instance, Colonel Routh Goshen, the Arabian Giant,
and Hugh Murphy, the Irish Giant (see Kunhardt et al. 162–75, 258–59).
Barnum felt compelled to invent backgrounds for many of his performers. General Tom Thumb, for example, was actually Charles Stratton
of Connecticut. Although Stratton was four years old when he went
to work for Barnum in 1842, Barnum attributed a greater age to him,
identified him as British, and bestowed on him a military title. In addition to Barnum's extensive accounts of Tom Thumb's career in *Life* and
Struggles and Triumphs, see Saxon, *Barnum* 123–34, 140–45; Harris 43,
48–52, 93–102; Kunhardt et al. 48–57.

12 The quotations are from a letter dated August 9, 1882, that Barnum sent
to numerous "officials" (Saxon, *Letters* 226–27). Adams argues that the
1884 Ethnological Congress of Nations was built on "multiple, contradictory interpretations of race" (182), with all manner of cultural and
physical difference signifying "race" (175–85). Also see Kunhardt et al.
296.

13 For example, Elizabeth Phillips perceives many poems as dramatic
monologues reflecting the lives of Dickinson's friends, literary characters, and historical personages; Joanne Dobson examines voices of
"reticence" and "insignificance," especially the little girl and the wife
(*Strategies*); Paula Bennett attends particularly to the child and bride
personae (*My Life*); John Emerson Todd catalogs Dickinson's poems by
four types of personae: "little girl," "lover-wife-queen," those experienc-
ing "death and eternity," and "the divided personality." Also see Pollak,
Anxiety; Wolff; Homans; Mossberg; Gilbert and Gubar; Weisbuch,
Poetry; Runzo; and Patterson, *Imagery* and "'Double' Tim."

14 Rebecca Patterson argues that before 1862 the male identifications in
the poems are implicit, but that Dickinson clearly adopts male personae
in specific poems beginning in 1862 ("'Double' Tim" 170). Also see
Patterson's *Imagery*, especially the first chapter, "The Boy Emily." As ex-

amples of poems with a male persona, see F225, F284, F451, F547, F597, F734, F856, F937, F1096, F1271, F1472, and F1538.

15 As other examples, see F283, F550, and F670.

16 The words "bird" and "birds" appear 161 times in the poems, not including numerous references to individual species—sparrows, robins, orioles, larks, wrens, bobolinks. See *Concordance*.

17 Unless otherwise indicated, all letters will be cited from the three-volume *The Letters of Emily Dickinson*, edited by Thomas H. Johnson and Theodora Ward.

18 Also in note to Letter 405.

19 As example, see poems F288, F336, F340, F341, F407, F423, F484, F841, F867, F1088, and F1310.

20 For discussion of the types of entertainment available at the American Museum, see, in addition to Barnum's autobiographies, McNamara, "Congress of Wonders"; Kunhardt et al.; and Saxon, *Barnum*. Dennett discusses a more general array of the entertainments found in dime museums of the late eighteenth century into the twentieth century.

21 Letters 318, 372, 390, 412, 506; Leyda 2: 11, 113, 200, 274; Bingham 122; Carpenter, 455; Lombardo, *Hedge Away* 171–72.

22 Quotations taken from broadsides for George Bailey & Co. and for Van Amburgh (American Antiquarian Society and Readex Digital Collections).

23 Broadsides for the North American Circus included accounts of the Apollonicon that had been published in the public press. One press report described the instrument in some detail: "The exterior of the Apollonicon presents something of the appearance of a two story house, and is decorated with elaborate oriental designs upon Berlin wire (by Messrs Lee & Co.) which protects the musical directors within from the public gaze, and imparts to it the air of an automaton. The arrangement of a forest of musical pipes, varying in size from the diameter of a man's body to that of a slender pipestem, so as to be adapted to a colossal chariot, built for its reception by Mr. John Stephenson of this city, is one novel feature" of the instrument ("North American Circus" broadside). Proving far too cumbersome to continue being conveyed from town to town, the Apollonicon was eventually placed on a riverboat on the Mississippi, creating, in effect, the showboat (Marian Murray 166–68).

24 On sideshow entertainments, also see Thomas Frost 248–51; and McNamara, *Step Right Up* 40.

25 Renowned for his remarkable skill as a trainer of lions and other wild animals, Isaac Van Amburgh became one of the world's most celebrated animal trainers and menagerie operators. Van Amburgh would, for example, put a lion, leopard, and panther together in a cage and proceed to "play" with each. Thought to have magical powers or at least

an extraordinary rapport with the animals, Van Amburgh is "generally credited with the distinction of having been the first lion-tamer of modern times" (Thomas Frost 89) and the "most famous trainer in circus history" (Speaight 126). Hyatt Frost joined Van Amburgh's business in 1846, and after Van Amburgh's death in 1865, he managed the business under Van Amburgh's name for over twenty years. Van Amburgh and Co.'s Menagerie and P. T. Barnum joined their operations by 1866. See Speaight 126–27; Kunhardt et al. 196–97; Marian Murray 136; Adams 78; M. R. Werner 300–01, 303, 306.

26 *The Boston Daily Atlas* reported that a horse in a hurdle race "fell and broke his neck, and killed his rider, a female, almost instantaneously" ([Sarah Sands; Plymouth] June 14, 1853). *The Barre Patriot* (Barre, Massachusetts) reported on "several most unfortunate accidents" at the New York Hippodrome: "They occur to the females who ride the chariot and horse races. In one case more than a week ago, a chariot wheel came off, and the female driver was thrown, and so badly injured that she has since died" ([New York Hippodrome] June 3, 1853).

27 As other examples of poems that draw on circus or museum show imagery and reference see F257, F305, F319, F321, F507, F696, F1102, F1678. In addition, the many references to tents throughout the poems suggest overlapping images of theatrical shows, revival meetings, and military camps.

28 Julien-Joseph Virey, for instance, proposed that in a system of two human species, one white and one black, Africans, Indians, and Asians all comprise one species (Sollors 62).

29 Wardrop further observes that in the poem Dickinson acknowledges the value civilization attaches to a particular "gold standard" and more generally that, in this and other poems, Dickinson is "concerned with portraying a Midas-like nineteenth-century economy in which greed could turn a person into a 'thing'" ("'That Minute Domingo'" 82–83).

30 In his meticulous classifications, Morton places the Circassians within the Caucasian branch of the Caucasian family of the Caucasian race. In *Crania Americana* he extols the Circassian people: "The *Circassians* have long been celebrated for superior personal endowments. . . . The women have attracted the attention and commanded the admiration of all travellers; nor can there be a question that in exquisite beauty of form and gracefulness of manner, they surpass all other people. They are distinguished by a fair skin, arched and narrow eyebrows, very long eyelashes, and black eyes and hair. Their profile approaches nearest the Grecian model, and falls little short of the beau-ideal of classic sculpture" (8). Although Morton concludes that people he categorizes as Caucasian display all variety of skin color (from white to black), he describes the Circassians as the fairest in color (7–37).

31 In a letter of May 14, 1864, Barnum instructs Greenwood on how much to pay for one or two Circassian women. Although Greenwood apparently returned to New York without such a woman, Barnum soon thereafter exhibited his first Circassian Beauty. In a footnote to the published letter, editor Saxon states that Greenwood "presumably . . . obtained the beautiful slave girl Zalumma Agra" in the slave market (Saxon, *Letters* 125–28).

32 On the Circassian Beauties, see Linda Frost, *Never One Nation* 62–85, and "Circassian Beauty." Some scholars assert that the Circassian Beauties were another of Barnum's hoaxes; that is, the Beauties were local women whose hair and skin color were made to match a prototype (see Bogdan 238; Kunhardt et al. 181).

33 The skin of the Leopard Girl was mottled due to a skin pigmentation disorder (Kunhardt et al. 188).

34 See poems F121, F248, F418.

35 Pearls are commonly thought of as white, but come in many colors (beige, golden, yellow, pink), usually in pale shades. One theory holds that white pearls are formed in deep waters (Landman et al. 35, 52, 54).

36 Some pearl poems do have a direct link to Susan Dickinson: a version of "The feet of people walking home" (F16), headed "Darling," was sent to Sue in 1859; the earliest copy of "Your riches taught me poverty" (F418) was sent in letter form to Sue about 1862.

CHAPTER TWO: DICKINSON, POPULAR MUSIC, AND THE HUTCHINSON FAMILY SINGERS

1 As described in Dickinson Family Artifacts (the guide to that collection in the Houghton Library) Dickinson's piano was a "Renaissance revival square piano" made of Brazilian rosewood, with "floral and scroll carved legs and apron." Bianchi describes the piano as "an old-fashioned square in an elaborately carved mahogany case" (*Face to Face* 34). Made by the Boston piano manufacturer Hallet, Davis and Co. circa 1845, the piano is now located in the Dickinson Room of the Houghton Library at Harvard University. Clara Newman Turner, a Dickinson cousin who lived at the Evergreens between 1858 and 1868, refers to the "modern 'Chickering'" in the parlor at the Homestead: "When I knew her, her Repertoire was quite limited—consisting of but three tunes. One of these she called 'The Devil,' and it was weird and quaint enough to warrant the title. She had learned it on an old-fashioned piano, two octaves shorter than the modern 'Chickering' which then stood in her home parlor, and always before seating herself to play, she covered these superfluous octaves, that the keyboard might accord with her education" (Sewall *Life* 1: 272). The whereabouts of the Chickering piano are unknown.

2 Ann Elizabeth Vaill Selby was the niece of Sarah Vail Norcross, grandfather Joel Norcross's second wife.

3 Dickinson refers to playing the piano in letters throughout the 1850s. In
a letter of December 15, 1851, Dickinson writes to her brother, Austin:
"Thank you for the music, Austin. . . . I shall learn my part of the Duett,
and try to have Vinnie her's" (Letter 65). The next month, Dickinson
asks her brother to exchange the sheet music for another arrangement:
"You sent us the *Duett,* Austin. Vinnie cannot learn it, and I see from
the outside page, that there is a piece for *two* hands" (Letter 71). In
April 1856, Dickinson writes to her cousin John Graves, "I play the old,
odd tunes yet, which used to flit about your head after honest hours
— and wake dear Sue, and madden me, with their grief and fun . . ."
(Letter 184). In the April 25, 1862, letter to Higginson, Dickinson writes,
"The noise in the Pool, at Noon — excels my Piano" (Letter 261).

4 In the preface to *The Single Hound,* Bianchi recalls, "In these earlier
days Aunt Emily often came over, most frequently in the evening,
and always when Mr. Bowles, Mrs. Anthon of London, or some such
cherished guest, was here. She played brilliantly upon the piano, and
travestied the descriptive pieces popular at that period with as much
skill as wit. One improvisation which she called *the Devil* was, by tradition, unparalleled. She had no idea of the passing of time when at the
height of these frolics and not until my revered Grandfather appeared
with his lantern, would the revel break off" (xi). Carolyn Lindley Cooley
proposes that Dickinson was a "highly accomplished pianist," which
she judges from the level of difficulty of Dickinson's collection of sheet
music (13–14). Millicent Todd Bingham is more reserved in her assessment of Dickinson's skill: "Whether or not Emily Dickinson was
really musical is hard to say" (*Home* 153). Kate Anthon Scott Turner had
extended visits to the Evergreens in early 1859, October 1861, and January 1863 (Johnson, *Letters* 933; Sewall, *Life* 2: 442, 467; Habegger 373).
The birthdates of MacGregor Jenkins (April 1869), Martha (November
1866), and Ned (June 1861), all of whom recalled hearing Dickinson play
the piano, would imply that she was still playing possibly into the 1870s.
MacGregor Jenkins was the son of Sarah Jenkins and the Reverend
Jonathan Jenkins, who preached at the First Church of Amherst beginning December 1866 and was pastor there from 1867 to 1877.

5 Also see letters 7, 8, 9, 12, 14, 20, and 23.

6 In a letter to Frances Norcross in May 1873, Dickinson refers to the
Boston concert and describes the experience of hearing Anton Rubinstein perform: "Glad you heard Rubinstein. Grieved Loo could not hear
him. He makes me think of polar nights Captain Hall could tell! Going
from ice to ice! What an exchange of awe!" (Letter 390). Clara Bellinger
Green recounted a visit to the Dickinson home in 1877 at the request
of Emily at which Clara, her sister, Nora, and brother, Nelson, performed a song for Emily and Lavinia, who both listened from upstairs.

Afterward, Emily met with them and expressed her "pleasure" at their singing. Green reported that Dickinson "told us of her early love for the piano and confided that, after hearing Rubinstein [?]—I believe it was Rubinstein—play in Boston, she had become convinced that she could not master the art and had forthwith abandoned it once and for all, giving herself up then wholly to literature" (Leyda 2: 273). Green described the visit with the "mythical" Dickinson in "The Sketch Book: A Reminiscence of Emily Dickinson." Scholar Judy Small doubts that Dickinson heard Rubinstein perform, and speculates it was another pianist (228n20). In 1872 and 1873 Rubinstein, conductor of the Russian Imperial Court Orchestra and renowned pianist, toured the United States as a promotion for Steinway pianos (Sanjek 369; Loesser 515–16). Johnson records that he performed in Boston in 1873 (note to Letter 390). Rubinstein also performed five concerts in Boston in October 1872 (Sablosky, *What They Heard* 86–92). Loesser describes Rubinstein as "the most fiery, most fabulous, and most hypnotic of living pianists, the true inheritor of Liszt's crown" (515).

7 Barnum arranged for Jenny Lind to perform one hundred concerts for one thousand dollars a concert. On June 9, 1851, Lind broke her contract with Barnum after ninety-three concerts, but performed forty other concerts without Barnum's sponsorship. See Ware and Lockard; Kunhardt et al. 88–102; Barnum, *Life* chapter 11. Charles Hamm identifies Jenny Lind as "the most popular singer of the entire nineteenth century" (*Yesterdays* 76).

8 The concert was held at the First Congregational Church of Northampton (Longsworth, *World* 46).

9 Bingham recounts, mostly through Dickinson's letters, the Dickinsons' responses to Jenny Lind in her *Emily Dickinson's Home* (143–44, 149–53). Also see Letter 44.

10 England and Sparrow state that "the formal influence in all her poetry is the hymn" (119). Porter confidently asserts "that Isaac Watts was the principal transmitter of the verse forms which Emily Dickinson uses seems indisputable" (58), although he also proposes that she "manipulated with wit and ironic effect the tonal connotations of the hymn" (57). As Cooley observes, "That the hymn is the basic influence in both the meter and the message of Dickinson's poetry is generally accepted by Dickinson scholars" (22–23). Throughout her *Emily Dickinson: Daughter of Prophecy*, Doriani argues that Dickinson models the majority of her poems on the structure and style of the sermon or on such literary forms of the scriptural prophets as the psalm, the hymn, the prayer, as well as on the meters of Isaac Watts's hymns. While Thomas Johnson identifies a variety of meters that Dickinson used in her poems, stating that they all "derived from English hymnology," he notes, too,

Dickinson's innovations and her significant divergences from these metrical patterns: "Her great contribution to English prosody was that she perceived how to gain new effects by exploring the possibilities within traditional metric patterns. She then took the final step toward that flexibility within patterns which she sought. She began merging in one poem the various meters themselves so that the forms, which intrinsically carry their own retardment or acceleration, could be made to supply the continuum for the mood and ideas of the language" (*Emily Dickinson* 84, 86). Similarly acknowledging the general agreement among scholars that the hymn forms "provided a frame of associations within which to work," Domhnall Mitchell, like Johnson, notes the diversity of hymn meters and the possibilities for combining them (224, 226). Mitchell observes that "traditional hymnology might have provided Dickinson with a greater mixture of rhythmical and stanzaic forms and combinations than is always acknowledged" (227). In challenging the well-established claim that Dickinson's stanzaic forms were shaped by Watts, Judy Jo Small argues that hymn meters are found throughout English poetry and "have always been the mainstay of popular poetic forms including songs and hymns" (44). Small associates Dickinson's verse forms with the ballad, also noting resonances of the nursery rhyme in some of her verse (45–46). While Charles Anderson cites the Protestant hymn meter as Dickinson's basic formal structure, he also relates her stanza form to the popular ballad of England and Scotland as well as to Mother Goose rhymes (24–25). Wolff, too, briefly notes that the "rhythmic configuration of hymns" is easily seen in nursery rhymes (186). See also Miller, *Poet's Grammar* 141–43; and Porter 55–74.

11 Common meter refers to a four-line stanza in iambic tetrameter or mixed iambic tetrameter and trimeter, rhyming either abcb or abba. Although the common meter may be most typical, the eighteenth- and nineteenth-century hymn displays a variety of meter: for example, the long hymn measure contains four accents in each line (4-4-4-4); the short meter follows a 3-3-4-3 accent pattern; the half meter has a 3-3-3-3 pattern. In addition, the variety of hymn meters includes the six-line particular meter (4-4-4-4-4-4), the common particular meter (4-4-3-4-4-3), and the short particular meter (3-3-4-3-3-4). For a fuller definition, including variant forms of the common meter, see the *New Princeton Encyclopedia of Poetry and Poetics* and Lewis Turco's *The New Book of Forms*.

12 Turco posits that the rhyme scheme of long measure (abcb) differs slightly from the rhyme scheme of the long hymnal stanza (abab) (120). In *The New Princeton Encyclopedia,* both rhymes are identified as typical of ballad meter (119). The entry also explains the relationship between the hymn and the ballad: "In the 15th and 16th cs., when ver-

nacular hymn-writers such as Sternhold and Hopkins in England sought to appeal to the hearts and minds of the religious laity by setting the Psalms to music, they did so by the natural expedient of casting their new hymns into the meters, and sometimes the melodies as well, of those songs the laity knew best—the ballads" (*New Princeton Encyclopedia* 119).

13 Dickinson's personal album of sheet music is housed at the Houghton Library, Harvard University. Carlton Lowenberg identifies the contents of this album in appendix one of his *Musicians Wrestle Everywhere* (119–24). Boziwick identifies the titles of a few songs that either Emily Dickinson or Lavinia Dickinson references in letters but which are not included in Emily's personal sheet music collection, such as, "Long, Long Ago," "Oh the Merry Days When We Were Young," and "Are We Almost There?" (133n12, 141).

14 The family library also included Lowell Mason's *The Boston Handel and Haydn Society Collection of Music,* Mason and David Greene's *Church Psalmody: Psalms and Hymns, Adapted to Public Worship*, Asahel Nettleton's *Village Hymns for Social Worship*, Charles Seymour Robinson's *A Selection of Spiritual Songs*, and Isaac Watts's *Christian Psalmody in Four Parts*. See Lowenberg's Appendix Two: Music and Books on Music in the Dickinson library (125–128).

15 Dickinson's personal album of sheet music contains two copies of "Believe Me, If All Those Endearing Young Charms," one of these with "variations for the piano-forte" arranged by Thomas Valentine. The family collection also contains a third separate copy.

16 "The Old Arm Chair, A Ballad" (music by Henry Russell and words by Eliza Cook [Geo. P. Reed, 1840]) and "Our Native Song" (music and words by Henry Russell [Firth Hall & Pond, 1841]).

17 Hamm states that *The Bohemian Girl* "was unquestionably the most successful and enduring musical stage work in English of the entire nineteenth century, before Gilbert and Sullivan" (*Yesterdays* 84).

18 In a jovial letter of January 1850, in which Dickinson declares that "Amherst is alive with fun this winter," she tells her Uncle Joel Norcross that, because he enjoys singing, she will try to learn two new piano pieces "by close, and assiduous practise." One of these new songs appears to be Stephen Collins Foster's "Oh! Susanna!," a popular minstrel number, connected particularly to the Christy Minstrels (Richard Jackson 152; Finson 182). Dickinson asks Uncle Norcross, "Have you found *Susannah* yet?" (Letter 29).

19 In 1843, Marshall S. Pike, L. V. H. Crosby, and brothers James and John Powers initially formed the Albino Family, appearing in whiteface and "flaxen wigs." When they became a blackface singing group, they became known first as the Harmoneon Family and then as the Harmo-

neons or the Boston Harmoneons. The Harmoneons sang for President
Polk in the White House in 1847 (Rice cites both 1846 and 1847). Pike,
who wrote over one hundred songs, was also one of the first blackface
female impersonators (Rice 28, 50, 51; Finson 185).

20 The *Tribune* carried an announcement of a Hutchinson Family Thanksgiving concert in Amherst (the date November 22, 1848 [or possibly
1847], is handwritten at the bottom of the clipping): "The Hutchinsons
are to give a Concert at Amherst, Mass. on Thanksgiving Evening, as
the first of a Fall campaign in which they are about to embark. It is
rumored that they intend to spend the most of the coming Winter in
Ohio and the West. We wish well to the 'Tribe of Jesse'" (Hutchinson
Family Scrapbook 8). John Hutchinson states that the Hutchinsons performed at Amherst College (I: 230; Brink 60). On November 30, 1859,
John's splinter group of the Hutchinsons—comprised of John, wife
Fanny, and children Henry and Viola—performed at the Baptist Church
in Amherst, Massachusetts. An article in the *Hampshire and Franklin
Express* implies that there had been other Hutchinson Family concerts
in or around Amherst: "We believe these singers have always been well
received by our citizens, and we hope that now they will receive a hearty
welcome. Their style of music, and the list of songs from which they
make their selections never becomes wearisome. They are pure and
simple and touch the heart more than the most scientific music of Ital-
ian masters. Their music is emphatically home music, and while it can
be appreciated by children, it is equally acceptable to older persons. We
hope and expect that they will have a full house" ("The Hutchinsons").
My thanks to Tevis Kimball, Curator of Special Collections at the Jones
Library, for locating this article.

21 One might consider an earlier concert as the first public concert of
the Hutchinsons. John Hutchinson records that all thirteen children
performed at the Baptist Meeting House in Milford, New Hampshire,
on Thanksgiving evening 1839 (Hutchinson, *Story* 1: 35); whereas the
first concert (of the thirteen children) listed in *Excelsior,* edited by Dale
Cockrell, was on November 6, 1840. Cockrell's extensive compilation
of posters, programs, and newspaper reviews would make his dating
seem reliable. However, John Hutchinson places the first concert on a
Thanksgiving Day, a day that one would think him unlikely to mistake.
Scott Gac follows the dates in *Excelsior*; Jordan and Roberts follow the
dates in John Hutchinson's family history. John, Judson, and Asa traveled throughout New England performing as a trio until eleven-year-old
Abby joined the group in 1841. (Gac reports that Abby joined the group
in January 1842, following the Cockrell chronology in *Excelsior* [19–20].)
For a detailed account of the lives and careers of the Hutchinson Family, see especially John Wallace Hutchinson's two-volume *The Story of*

the Hutchinsons (Tribe of Jesse). Also see Gac, Jordan's *Singin' Yankees*, Roberts, Brink, and chapter seven in Hamm's *Yesterdays.*

22 John Hutchinson reprints Nathaniel Rogers's description of the scene and the performance of "The Old Granite State" from the *Herald of Freedom*: "Phillips closed his speech at the highest pitch of his fine genius, and retired from the platform, when the four brothers rushed to his place, and took up the argument where he had left it, on the very heights of poetic declamation, and carried it off heavenwards on one of their boldest flights. Jesse had framed a series of stanzas on the spot, while Phillips was speaking, embodying the leading arguments, and enforcing them, as mere oratory cannot, as music and poetry only can, and they poured them forth with amazing spirit, in one of the maddening Second Advent Tunes. The vast multitude sprang to their feet, as one man, and at the close of the first strain, gave vent to their enthusiasm in a thunder of unrestrained cheering. Three cheers, and three times three, and ever so many more—for they could not count—they sent out, full-hearted and full-toned, till the old roof rang again. And throughout the whole succeeding strains they repeated it, not allowing the singers to complete half the stanza before breaking out upon them in uncontrollable emotion. Oh, it was glorious!" (1: 77). For a detailed account of this appearance, including newspaper accounts from the *Liberator* and the *Herald of Freedom*, see Hutchinson, *Story* 1: 73–78. Also see Gac 60–62; Jordan 53; Hamm, *Yesterdays* 149.

23 In his introduction to the 1896 *The Story of the Hutchinsons,* Douglass recounts the mesmerizing effect of the Hutchinsons' singing: "There was something almost miraculous in the singing of these three brothers and one sister. I have heard them, in a time of great excitement on the slavery question, calm to silence and order a turbulent and determined mob when it was in full blast and fiercely bent upon breaking up an anti-slavery meeting. We had, in the old Tabernacle in Broadway, New York, an instance of this power. One of the most furious mobs that I ever saw, confronted the American Anti-Slavery Society and determined that its speakers should not be heard. It stamped, shouted, whistled, howled, hooted and pushed and swayed the multitude to and fro in confusion and dismay. It silenced the platform and threatened the speakers with violence; and when neither the prophet-like solemnity of Garrison nor the sublime eloquence of Phillips could silence that tempest of rowdyism and wrath, the voices of this family came down from the gallery of the old Tabernacle, like a message from the sky, and in an instant all was hushed and silent. Every eye was raised and every ear attent" (xvi–xvii). In her profile of Abby Hutchinson in *Eminent Women of the Age*, Elizabeth Cady Stanton commends the Hutchinson Family Singers as effective voices in the cause of abolition: "Early in the anti-slavery

cause, [Abby] with four brothers, began to sing in the conventions. In all those stormy days of mob violence the Hutchinson family was the one harmonizing element. Like oil on the troubled waters, their sweet songs would soothe to silence those savages whom neither appeal nor defiance could awe" (Stanton 387).

24 See Hutchinson, Story 1: 105, 378–98; Jordan 89–90, 230–36; Brink 133, 206–10; McMurtry 5, 8–13.

25 At the urging of Lucy Stone, in 1867 John Hutchinson agreed to go on a campaign for universal suffrage in Kansas with Susan B. Anthony, Elizabeth Cady Stanton, and others. John, son Henry, and daughter Viola traveled and sang for suffrage for ten weeks beginning September 2. In preparation for the campaign, John apparently tried to enlist "a large number of our American song-writers" to compose suffrage songs, but with few responses, John wrote some songs himself, including "Vote It Right Along" (Hutchinson, Story 1: 436–55). In May 1868, John, Henry, and Abby performed at the second anniversary of the Equal Suffrage Society in Cooper Institute, New York, sharing the occasion with Stanton, Anthony, Frederick Douglass, Lucy Stone, Henry Blackwell, and others (Hutchinson, Story 1: 460–61). In 1874 John's family group performed at the National Convention of the Woman Suffrage Association in New York (Hutchinson, Story 2: 33; Jordan 265); in March 1888, John attended the fortieth anniversary of the Seneca Falls Women's Rights meeting, held in Washington, D.C., again in company with the pioneers and luminaries of the movement: Anthony, Stanton, Stone, Blackwell, Julia Ward Howe, Frances Willard, Clara Barton (Hutchinson, Story 2: 146–48; Jordan 265, 280; Hamm, Yesterdays 153–54; Gac 45–46).

26 In a review of a June 2, 1843, concert in Boston printed the following day in the Boston Daily Evening Transcript, the reviewer proposes adding a verse to "The Old Granite State" with the lines "We support Emancipation / But like not Amalgamation" ([Old Granite State.] June 3, 1843, 2). In 1859 members of the Hutchinson Family and the Luca Family, a black family of singers, performed together throughout Ohio. While the singers received mostly favorable notices, some reviewers expressed discomfort or shock at the performance. A news story out of Fremont, Ohio, for example, states that the "abolition proclivities" of the Hutchinson Family Singers are too "startling" as well as comments that "respectable white persons (we presume they are such) travelling hand in hand with a party of negroes, and eating at the same table with them, is rather too strong a pill to be gulped down by a democratic community" (quoted in Southern, The Music 107). Southern also suggests that the Luca Family as a performing group was modeled on the Hutchinson Family Singers (The Music 106).

27 For example, the Congo Melodists (also known as the Buckley Family

and later as Buckley's Minstrels) were said to sing in the "style of the Hutchinsons": this phrase was printed on their publicity handbills in 1844 (Cockrell, *Excelsior* 297). Nathan claims that a group assembled by Dan Emmett in 1845—the Operatic Brothers and Sisters—evoked the Hutchinson Family Singers (216). Noting the Hutchinsons' use of "humor" and "rhythm," Meer refers to their "musical proximity to minstrelsy" (25). Also see Winans 146, 161; Jordan 166; Brink; Moseley 716, 718; and Mahar 20, 22, 218.

28 Some reviews declared that the Hutchinson Family's political songs were not suitable for respectable audiences. For example, in early March 1852, handbills were posted around the city of Baltimore and at Carroll Hall, where the Hutchinsons were scheduled to perform on March 8. Addressed "To The Citizens of Baltimore," the handbill asks, "Are you willing to be insulted by a band of abolitionists, singing strains of fanaticism?" (reported in *the Liberator* March 26, 1852). The same *Daily Atlas* news story that rebukes the singers for "foisting their Abolition songs" on others, continues the reprimand: "The Hutchinsons have more music than manners. They ought to be taught better than to nauseate the greater portion of those who patronize them with the songs with which, at Liberty Party Conventions, they helped on the election of Polk and the Annexation of Texas" (reprinted from the *Utica Gazette*) ([Hutchinsons] March 27, 1845). Also see Douglass's review "The Hutchinson Family"; reviews quoted in *Excelsior* (Cockrell 258–59, 308–309); and reviews quoted in Roberts 357–58, 367–68.

29 Dickinson also owned the sheet music to several songs that were performed by the Hutchinson Family, although these songs are not as strongly attached to the group. For example, the Hutchinson Family performed "Irish Emigrant's Lament" frequently in concerts over the years. Their repertory also included Edward L. White's "The Home That I Love," Thomas Moore's "The Last Rose of Summer," and "Home, Sweet Home."

30 Hamm notes that after 1843, "The Old Granite State" was "a standard and even necessary part of the program" (Liner notes 4). Also see Hutchinson, *Story* 2: 298; Jordan 72, 125,161; Hamm, *Yesterdays* 146.

31 The sheet music cover for "The Grave of Bonaparte" (published by Oliver Ditson in 1843) identifies the song "as performed at the Principal Concerts of the Hutchinson Family." S. Foster Damon includes "The Grave of Bonaparte" in *Series of Old American Songs* (no. 35).

32 Isochronism "refers to the rhythmic organization of speech into equal intervals of time" (*New Princeton Encyclopedia* 635).

33 The metrical association of popular ballads and hymns stretches back to the fifteenth and sixteenth centuries: "In the 15th and 16th cs., when vernacular hymn-writers such as Sternhold and Hopkins in England

sought to appeal to the hearts and minds of the religious laity by setting the Psalms to music, they did so by the natural expedient of casting their new hymns into the meters, and sometimes the melodies as well, of those songs the laity knew best—the ballads. Hence the meters of the popular ballads passed into Protestant hymnals, where they influenced centuries of not only hymn singing but also the writing of literary poetry" (*New Princeton Encyclopedia* 119).

34 The Dickinson family library also had Webb and Mason's *The Odeon* and their *The Vocalist*, two singing books of secular music. *The Vocalist* contains "Maiden, Weep No More," another song that Dickinson specifically identifies as one that she played on the piano (Letter 7).

35 Similarly, Dickinson, at the age of thirty-one, described herself in a letter to Higginson as "small, like the Wren" (Letter 268).

36 William Miller, a farmer and preacher from Vermont, prophesized that Christ was scheduled to return in 1843 or 1844 (Holifield 301).

37 Verse seven of Dickinson's copy of "The Old Granite State" is as follows:

> Liberty is our motto
>
> Liberty is our motto
>
> Equal liberty is our motto
>
> In the "Old Granite State"
>
> We despise oppression
>
> We despise oppression
>
> We despise oppression
>
> And we cannot be enslaved.

38 These four songs in Clarke's *The Harp of Freedom* are "The Free State Debate," "The Free Soil Voter's Song," "Raise a Shout for Liberty," and "We've Had a Cordial Greeting" (285, 288, 304, 305). *The Liberty Minstrel* includes another variation: "We're for Freedom Though [*sic*] the Land" (173–76). In regard to Lincoln's campaign songs, see John Wallace Hutchinson's *Hutchinson's Republican Songster, for the Campaign of 1860* which includes "For Freedom and Reform" and "Have You Heard the Loud Alarm?," both sung to the tune of "The Old Granite State." The chorus of "For Freedom and Reform" mimics the Hutchinsons' original song: "We're a band of freemen, / We're a band of freemen, / We're a band of freemen, / We're for Freedom and Reform" (24). The lyrics of "Have You Heard the Loud Alarm" are particularly vivid, such as in verse two:

> Steeped in infamous corruption,
>
> Sold to sugar-cane and cotton,
>
> Lo! A nation's heart is rotten,

And the vampires suck her blood;

O'er our broad and *free* dominions

Rules the Cotton king whose minions

Clip our fearless eagle's pinions

And invite Oppression's reign.

(54)

39 I thank musicologist Anna Nekola for sharing her knowledge of nineteenth-century hymn music and popular music.

40 Some scholars have argued that Dickinson was shaped and driven by a strict sense of social class boundaries that led her to withdraw from the social and political trials of her time. Seeming to fault Dickinson for not being more politically active and publicly visible, Erkkila argues that Dickinson's elitist class consciousness spurred her resistance to social and political change and her retreat into ever-narrower spaces (161). Also see Morse and Aífe Murray.

41 The Hutchinsons also rewrote Dan Emmett's "Jordan Is a Hard Road to Travel" (1852–53) into another of their emancipation songs, "Slavery Is a Hard Foe to Battle" (Nathan 223). In addition to "Get off the Track," *The Harp of Freedom* includes two other versions of "Old Dan Tucker" rewritten as anti-slavery songs: "Down with Slavery's Minions" (Clark 316) and "Strike for Freedom and for Right" (Clark 312).

42 In his editorial "'Abolition' Extremism Denounced" Whitman wrote, "'Liberty, a nation's glory!' sang the Hutchinsons at their concert last evening, (4th)—whereupon certain zealous persons felt themselves called upon to *hiss*. Is not 'liberty a nation's glory?' Even more—is not slavery in this Republic an evil which the good and farsighted men not only in the North, but in the South—in Virginia, in Tennessee, and in North Carolina, where 'emancipation' has many plump, bold advocates—consider to *be* an evil, and one demanding the anxious consideration of every American Democrat—every American politician?" (1: 191–92).

43 On March 19, 1845, a reviewer for the New York *Evening Express* wrote that the Hutchinsons' songs "must be highly offensive to a New York audience": "We have long known that the male part of this family were Locofoco Abolitionists, but we had always supposed they had shrewdness enough not to embody so gross an expression of their sentiments in music, intended to be sung in public. If they persist in rousing the prejudices of the people by these appeals, they had better return to New Hampshire" (quoted in Cockrell, *Excelsior* 308–09). Also protesting the Hutchinsons' abolition songs, the *Mississippi Free Trader and Natchez Gazette* reports that "These infamous panders [*sic*] to abolitionism, who 'face the music' at every abolition convention [in] the North,

have had the unblushing effrontery to appear in St. Louis and advertise concerts. They have been warned away from that city" (June 18, 1851). Also see Cockrell, *Excelsior* 258–59, Roberts 305–06, Jordan 107–08, 143.

44 John Hutchinson describes the "uproar" provoked by the group's performance of "Get off the Track" at Niblo's Gardens and at Palmer's Opera House in New York City in March 1845 (1: 138). Brian Roberts also addresses the worry of mob violence over the performance of "Get off the Track" at these same concerts (305–07, 352–53).

45 Richard Jackson includes this exact version of "Old Dan Tucker" in his *Popular Songs of Nineteenth-Century America.* Jackson identifies this 1843 Charles Keith version of "Old Dan Tucker" as the first edition of the piece (278). Mahar records eight 1843 publications of "Old Dan Tucker," although he quotes from the Keith version (Mahar 229 and 397n40). The members of the original Virginia Minstrels were Dan Emmett, William Whitlock, Frank Brower, and Richard Pelham.

46 In his "Early Minstrel Show Music, 1843–1852," Robert Winans identifies the songs most frequently performed on the minstrel stage. He calculates that between 1843 and 1847, "Old Dan Tucker" was performed in 49 percent of all minstrel shows (148).

47 The 1844 Turner and Fisher songbook, *Dandy Jim and Dan Tucker's Jawbone,* contains five versions of "Old Dan Tucker": "De Bran New Old Dan Tucker," "The Newest of All the New Verses of Old Dan Tucker," "Old Dan Tucker," "De New Ole Dan Tucker," and "The Latest Version of Old Dan Tucker."

48 The 1856 Clarke anthology *The Harp of Freedom* includes two rewritings of "Old Dan Tucker" that turned the minstrel melody into anti-slavery songs: "Down with Slavery's Minions" and "Strike for Freedom and for Right" (312, 316). Dennison discusses the relationship between blackface minstrelsy and anti-slavery songs in chapter four of his *Scandalize My Name* (157–86).

49 Dickinson signed her last known letter to Bowles "Your 'Rascal'" (Letter 515). She adds the postscript "I washed the Adjective." Johnson's note to this letter cites "A Cousin's Memories of Emily Dickinson" in which Gertrude M. Graves recounts the occasion on which Bowles apparently upbraided Dickinson for initially staying upstairs when he had come to visit. Johnson interprets Dickinson's final line to mean that "Bowles had said 'You damned rascal.'" Louise Graves relays Lavinia's account in which Bowles "went to the foot of the stairs and called in a loud and insistent tone, 'Emily, you wretch! No more of this nonsense! I've traveled all the way from Springfield to see you. Come down at once'" (41). In her version of the incident, Bianchi reports that Bowles called "you rascal!": "Aunt Lavinia said that once, when [Bowles] had driven from Springfield to see her, she refused to come down from some whim, and

he ran part-way up the stairs calling, 'Emily, Emily, you rascal!–come down here!'" (*Face to Face* 62).

50 See Brown's *The Anti-Slavery Harp; and Clark's The Harp of Freedom* and *The Liberty Minstrel*.

51 Dickinson's collection includes "Gems from *The Bohemian Girl*." The song "I Dreamt I Dwelt in Marble Halls" (which Dickinson owned) inspired a number of parodies: "I Dreamt I Dwelt in Kitchen Halls," I Dreamt I Dwelt in Hotel Halls," and "I Dreamt I Had Money to Buy a Shawl." Several different blackface groups—including Buckley's Serenaders, Christy Minstrels, and Ethiopian Serenaders—performed parodies of numbers from *The Bohemian Girl* (Mahar 3, 19, 42, 44, 45, 53, 145–53, 373n33; Hamm, *Yesterdays* 133).

52 See Paul D. Sanders's *Lyrics and Borrowed Tunes of the American Temperance Movement,* a compilation of temperance versions of popular songs: "Old Dan Tucker" becomes "Old Sir Toddy," "The Temperance Car," and "The Prohibition Train" (the latter two more directly drawn from "Get off the Track"). Sanders includes twenty-five temperance versions of "Yankee Doodle," including "A Lanky Dude" and "Temperance Yankee Doodle."

53 The three poems that Dickinson allowed to be published in the Brooklyn *Drum Beat* in 1864 to help raise money for the United States Sanitary Commission, a civilian charity that provided medical and other supplies to the Union Army, all dwell on natural scenes and images: "Blazing in gold and quenching in purple" (F321), "Flowers — Well — if anybody" (F95), and "These are the days when birds come back" (F122). See Karen Dandurand's "New Dickinson Civil War Publications" for a detailed account of what she calls Dickinson's "contribution to the Union cause."

CHAPTER THREE: DICKINSON AND MINSTRELSY

1 For discussions of the inception of the Virginia Minstrels, see Nathan 113–22; Cockrell, *Demons of Disorder* 149–55; Toll 30; Wittke 42–46.

2 In her discussion of "It makes no difference abroad," Helen Vendler parenthetically notes the banjo, remarking that it "may be making the Blackbird into an American Black Banjo-Player, the antithesis of the warbling English nightingale" (287).

3 Lott states that "the heedless (and ridiculing) appropriation of 'black' culture by whites in the minstrel show, as many contemporaries recognized, was little more than cultural robbery" (*Love and Theft* 8).

4 See Book Ten of Ovid's *Metamorphosis* for the story of Orpheus and Eurydice. In her *Orpheus in Nineteenth-Century Symbolism*, Dorothy M. Kosinski examines of the importance of the Orpheus myth in nineteenth-century culture.

5 Animal lore predominates in many verses of "Old Dan Tucker." As an example, in one verse of "De Bran New Old Dan Tucker," "De toads dey jumped, an' de tadpoles danced, / De hogs dey squealed an de possums pranced," apparently at the sight (and sound) of Dan Tucker (*Dandy Jim* 5).

6 For a history of the visual representation of the banjo in American art and artifacts, see Mazow's *Picturing the Banjo*. Gura and Bollman's study addresses the manufacture and marketing history of the banjo, especially its "centrality to nineteenth-century American music and culture" (3).

7 Also see folklorist Dorothy Scarborough's chapter on animal lore in her *On the Trail of Negro Folk-Songs*, 161–205.

8 Nathan quotes an anecdote from the 1833 *Sketches and Eccentricities of Col. David Crockett of West Tennessee* in which a jaybird song was deemed inappropriate for women: "A story is told of a woman at a country frolic in Tennessee who asked 'for her favorite tune of a jaybird; but she was admonished that she had once been before the church for the same profanity, and was ordered to be seated'" (quoted in Nathan 91). For the song "High Daddy," also see Nathan 395–400. Nathan suggests that lines in the song "Jumbo Jum" (1840) depict a dance step: "Here is the Jay Bird wing! / And the back action spring" (quoted in Nathan 88).

9 In his *The Battle for Christmas,* Nissenbaum delineates the social agitations regarding Christmas and explores its controversial evolution into a major holiday in America. Also see Cockrell, *Demons of Disorder* 32–37.

10 The Christmas stocking quotation is from a letter to Abiah Root dated January 12, 1846. In the same letter, Dickinson writes that "Old Santa Claus was very polite to me the last Christmas" (Letter 9). This phrasing suggests that Santa Claus may not always be counted on to be so "polite," and like the comment in Letter 425, hints at the provocative character of Santa Claus.

11 For example, Sable Brothers, Sable Harmonizers, Southern Opera Troupe of Sable Harmonists, Sable Sisters, Sable Brothers and Sisters, Campbell Sable Brothers, Sable Minstrels, Sable Serenaders, and several groups called Sable Harmonists (Mahar 22, 105, 363; Wittke 57, 81; Hamm, *Yesterdays* 132–33).

12 See poems F333, F575, F721, F741, F895, F935, F1104, F1312.

13 Alfred, Lord Tennyson appears to have been much admired by Dickinson. She refers to Tennyson in a number of letters throughout her life (see, for example, Letters 23, 320, 353, 486, 506). Capps notes that the Dickinson family library had "at least eight assorted volumes of Tennyson" (92). In a letter of early 1883 to Mrs. Holland, Dickinson thanks her for "Christmas Munificence" and quotes from "In Memoriam," in apparent mourning for Charles Wadsworth, who had died the previous April (Letter 801).

14 Several historians and scholars, including Toll, Lott, and Finson, assert that in the 1850s, the minstrel show assumed a three-part structure that became standard (Toll 52–57; Lott, *Love and Theft* 5–6; Finson 184). Lott describes the structure of the minstrel show at the "height of its popularity" in this way: "The first part offered up a random selection of songs interspersed with what passed for black wit and japery; the second part (or 'olio') featured a group of novelty performances (comic dialogues, malapropistic 'stump speeches,' cross-dressed 'wench' performances, and the like); and the third part was a narrative skit, usually set in the South, containing dancing, music, and burlesque" (Lott, *Love and Theft* 5–6). Mahar, who understands the minstrel show as musical theater, states that "variety was the primary feature of the minstrel show's organization" during the antebellum period and discredits the description of the typical minstrel show as a three-part program. According to Mahar, the "styles of different companies" were far more important in shaping the minstrel show program than the three-part formula (332).

15 See Mahar 2, 101–56, 353; Toll 56, 142; Cockrell, *Demons of Disorder* 75, 88, 93, 160; Winans 160; Robert Allen 163–77.

16 For accounts of the origins of the character and song "Jim Crow" and a description of the dance, see Nathan 50–52; Wittke 21, 23–25; Cockrell, *Demons of Disorder* 62–65; Finson 162–63; Dennison 45–47; Nevin 608–10.

17 Winter considers Juba to be the "most influential single performer of nineteenth-century American dance" (223), a view bolstered by the widespread influence of Juba on other dancers and the success of his international career. Winter also records that Juba had a "curious" effect on the style of English circus clowns: "The minstrel dance changed the clowns' entree, adding splits, jumps and cabrioles, as well as black-face make-up, to form a new type" (232). In his 1842 *American Notes,* Charles Dickens includes a description of "a regular break-down" and of a particular dancer, "the greatest dancer known" and purported to be Juba, whom he observed in the Five Points in New York: "Every gentleman sets as long as he likes to the opposite lady, and the opposite lady to him, and all are so long about it that the sport begins to languish, when suddenly the lively hero dashes in to the rescue. Instantly the fiddler grins, and goes at it tooth and nail; there is new energy in the tambourine; new laughter in the dancers; new smiles in the landlady; new confidence in the landlord; new brightness in the very candles. Single shuffle, double shuffle, cut and cross-cut; snapping his fingers, rolling his eyes, turning in his knees, presenting the backs of his legs in front, spinning about on his toes and heels like nothing but the man's fingers on the tambourine; dancing with two left legs, two right legs, two wooden legs, two wire legs, two spring legs—all sorts of legs and

no legs—what is this to him? And in what walk of life, or dance of life, does man ever get such stimulating applause as thunders about him, when, having danced his partner off her feet, and himself too, he finishes by leaping gloriously on the bar-counter, and calling for something to drink, with the chuckle of a million of counterfeit Jim Crows, in one inimitable sound!" (Dickens 107–8).

18 See, for example, F13, F45, F86, F364, F513, F571, F1088, and F1593.

19 See, for example, Eberwein, *Strategies* 130; Pollak, *Dickinson* 239–40; Anderson 22–23; Juhasz, "Big Tease" 55–58; Mossberg 157–58; Miller, "Sound" 206.

20 Some of these minstrel theaters were White's Opera House, the Fellow's Opera House and Hall of Lyrics, Hooley and Campbell's Opera House, Bryant's Opera House, Grand Opera House, Perhams's Burlesque Opera House, Palmo's Opera House (all in New York City); Eleventh Street Opera House and Sanford's Opera House (both in Philadelphia); and Pike's Opera House, Wells' Ethiopian Opera House, and the Grand Opera House (in Cincinnati). See Wittke 66, 67, 68, 69, 72, 74, 75, 105, 107; Toll 32, 103nn45&49; Hamm, *Yesterdays* 131; Lott, *Love and Theft* 73.

21 The song "Lucy Long" is often identified as the source of the prima donna role, made famous by George Christy in the 1840s. Toll notes that "on playbills and sheet music of the late 1840s [Christy] and other male minstrels were frequently pictured as well-dressed, even elegant, females dancing with male-attired partners" (140).

22 Habegger suggests that the letter may date from August or October 1860 (391).

23 The content of *The Bobolink Minstrel* is the same as for *Hutchinson's Republican Songster, for the Campaign of 1860*. Like Samuel Bowles, the Hutchinsons were strong supporters of Lincoln.

24 The opening verse of George W. Bungay's "The Bobolink's Campaign Song" clearly suggests that voices of freedom have been silenced in the South:

When I am at the sunny South

I dare not sing my mellow strains

A song of freedom from my mouth

Would drown amid the din of chains;

So I think-on — think-on — think-on,

Until my visit there is spent.

Now Abe Lincoln — Lincoln — Lincoln

Is to be our President.

25 The presence of Banks reinforces the political climate of the August

Amherst visit: Bowles and his newspaper had initially supported Banks for the presidential party nomination, and when that went to Lincoln, Bowles hoped that Banks would be the choice for vice president (Merriam 1: 263, 303).

26 The description in *Harper's Weekly* (January 12, 1867) of the show put on by the "Fantasticals" at the New York Christmas Day parade reports that the company of "jolly maskers" included "dancing girls with thick ankles, bunion-toed, and professionally awkward, marching arm in arm with cowled priests, and followed by Hamlet in greasy, sables, carrying on a dialogue with a colored gentleman of Jim Crow peculiarities" ("Holiday Mummeries").

27 Verses such as the following indicate Jim Crow's affinity with the tall-tale tradition: "I wip de lion ob de west, / I eat de Allegator; / I put more water in my mouf, / Den boil ten load ob tator" (Damon). Toll observes that "as blackface roarers, rivaling the likes of Davy Crockett, minstrel characters trumpeted their own boasts" (41). Also see Nathan 52, 54–57.

28 Through his observation that blackface minstrelsy signified working class whites as well as "blackness" (even as it marked as "inauthentic" the minstrel representation of blackness), Lott addresses the tangle of meaning encountered in the minstrel show (*Love and Theft* 63–64, 68–71, 138–42).

29 For verses see "Jimmy Crow" in Damon (no. 15) and "Jim Crow Complete in 150 Verses."

30 Eberwein references Tennyson's "The Lord of Burleigh" and notes parallels to Tennyson's "Beggar Maid" (*Strategies* 101). The story is echoed also in Balfe's 1843 *The Bohemian Girl* in which a young woman who had been abducted as a child and brought up among gypsies is discovered to be the long-lost daughter of aristocrats (Dizikes 95–96). The Burleigh tale has similarities as well to the legend of King Arthur, *Tom Jones*, *Oliver Twist*, and other narratives that depict a person, living simply or servilely, whose natural nobility is authenticated when his or her true family becomes known.

31 A further allusion may be to Catherine of Aragon's arrival in England in 1501 for the purpose of marriage to Arthur, Prince of Wales and expected future king (being the elder brother of Henry). Catherine came ashore in Plymouth rather than in Southampton, where a welcoming party was waiting. In order to proceed to London with the proper ceremony, it was decided that Catherine would be met at Exeter, a point between Plymouth and Southampton (Starkey 40–41).

32 The *Hampshire and Franklin Express* reported on appearances by both blackface troupes and black minstrel troupes. For example, on May 17, 1866, in the "Amherst Matters" section, the paper reported that "Parker's Negro Minstrel Troupe delighted a small audience in Agricultural Hall

on Friday evening last" (2). In September 1869, the Morris Brothers Minstrels, blackface entertainers for over twenty years, played to a "full house" in Amherst ("Amherst Matters," *Hampshire and Franklin Express* September 30, 1869: 2). For information on the Morris Brothers, see Rice 64. Daniel Lombardo describes the April 1886 appearance of Hi Henry's Minstrel Troupe in Amherst in his *Tales of Amherst* (58–59). In addition, blackface performers likely appeared in Amherst with the circus, since blackface minstrel entertainments were a regular part of the sideshow acts that were attached to virtually all of the big circuses in America in the nineteenth century (Thomas Frost 248–51; Wittke 64–65).

CHAPTER FOUR: CAPTIVITY AND LIBERTY

1 The statistics related to slave life compiled by the southern churches recorded a population of 3,250,364 slaves residing in the southern states in 1850; by 1860 the number was close to 4 million (Blassingame 344).

2 Steering the nation on a course full of switchbacks and crossroads, the governing bodies mapped the nation's direction relying on political compromise and interpretations that shifted and clashed with passing years. For a detailed discussion of the political views and maneuvering, see Sean Wilentz, David Herbert Donald, and Allan Nevins.

3 Ronald Takaki discusses the "metaphysics of Indian-hating" in the nineteenth century, which included casting the killing, enslavement, and removals of Indians into a moral framework (80–107). See Slotkin's *Regeneration through Violence*, an examination of "captivity mythology" in colonial America and the early Republic.

4 In addition to Foner, see Dublin and Takaki. Songs, letters, and other writings of the "factory girls" often compared their situation as mill workers to slavery, imprisonment, or a death sentence (Clinton 28–29; Foner, *Factory Girls*). Songs such as "The Lowell Factory Girl," "The Little Factory Girl," "The Factory Girl's Come-All-Ye," and "Song of the Factory Girls" describe and decry the terrible conditions, poor pay, and curtailed lives (Foner, *Factory Girls* 5–9, 25, 326). For an extensive discussion of the history of American protest songs, see Greenway.

5 On the history of nineteenth-century mills and factories in Amherst, see Carpenter (286–307). Also see Rand's *The Village of Amherst* (61–69) and Lombardo's *A Hedge Away* (103–4, 135–36, 254–55).

6 In 1852 Leonard's son Henry started in the family business and later became president of the Hills Company in 1877. The Hills families— Leonard, Henry, and Henry's wife, Adelaide—were friends of the Dickinsons and then their neighbors after the Dickinsons moved back to the Homestead on Main Street in 1855. Adelaide corresponded with Emily; some letters from between 1871 and 1884 still survive. Henry and

Adelaide's daughter, Caroline, was playmates with Gib Dickinson until his death in 1883. In a short essay published in 1957, Caroline reminisces on her childhood in Amherst and recalls the friendship between her mother and Lavinia, and her mother's "love and regard for Emily" (Caroline Allen 30–34).

7 In addition to the Brontës, Eliot, and Rossetti, Dickinson read many of Charles Dickens's novels (Capps 171–72). The Dickinson family library included verse collections by Ralph Waldo Emerson, Henry Wadsworth Longfellow, and John Greenleaf Whittier (Capps 111). For discussions of Dickinson's reading in addition to Capps, see Habegger 222–27, 246–50; Sewall, *Life* 2: 668–705; Keller 327–34; and Stonum. In Eliza Richards's *Emily Dickinson in Context,* see essays by Petrino 98–108; Finnerty 109–18; Miller 119–28; Loeffelholz 129–38; and Kirkby 139–47.

8 Eric Schocket discusses the correlation of the wage slave and the chattel slave in "Life in the Iron Mills." David Reynolds commends Davis's metaphors and "tonal grimness" in "Life in the Iron Mills" as especially effective in depicting the lives of factory workers, a topic that was not unusual in novels and poems of the nineteenth century (Reynolds, *Beneath* 411).

9 In a letter to Austin dated April 2, 1853, Emily writes: "Father was very severe to me; he thought I'd been trifling with you, so he gave me quite a trimming about 'Uncle Tom' and 'Charles Dickens' and these 'modern Literati' who he says are *nothing,* compared to past generations, who flourished when *he was a boy*" (Letter 113; Leyda 1: 268).

10 Rand, Leyda, and Keller all note the 1854 production of *Uncle Tom's Cabin* that played in Amherst and nearby Northampton (Rand 213; Leyda 1: 320; Keller 104). Leyda quotes part of a letter from Mrs. Elizabeth Hannum, a neighbor of the Dickinsons, to her brother Ira Goodale of New York, dated October 29, 1854: "There is something a going on in Amherst almost all of the time such as Shows Conserts Uncle Toms Calbin performed Musters Festivals Fairs Liceums Exebitions Letures Commencements and Cattle Shows" (Leyda 1: 320). Despite the misspellings and lack of punctuation, it is clear that Mrs. Hannum is including a production of *Uncle Tom's Cabin* among the amusements and events offered in Amherst.

11 Hedrick says that Stowe returned to Amherst in late November (384). Stowe's reading in Amherst roused tremendous interest: "By the time Stowe spoke in Amherst, her tour had become a major event. Tickets for the October 7th engagement were in such high demand that a limit was placed on the number each person could buy. People came from several area towns to fill College Hall, and an extra train had to be scheduled from Belchertown" (Lombardo, *Hedge* 19).

12 Susan writes in "Annals of the Evergreens":

It was about that time that I met Mrs. Stowe very pleasantly at
the house of her daughter Mrs. Allen, the wife of our Episcopal
Rector. She was in a fascinating and talkative mood, and fell into
some talk of her prolonged stay in Paris, and dwelt with great enthusiasm over the simple, but artistic French plays, she constantly
heard there, relating the plots of several, describing the stage ac-
cessories, and the audiences, with much interesting detail. Later
on in the evening she seemed a little more on her native heath,
as she told stories of old New England deacons, and their slips
into impulsive profanity, betrayed by native temper, not wholly
subdued—Yankee courting, and truth compels me to say, hinting
of her own family in fine caricature. I remember her distinctly as
the light from the chandelier fell upon her mobile face, her eyes
twinkling with fun and merriment, her forehead covered with
soft brown curls, confined with a band of black velvet, as seen in
her pictures. I invited her to drive, a day or two afterward, and as
I knew she was taciturn at times, I took no pains to draw her out,
allowing her the freedom of her larger nature undisturbed. The
glory of the October morning was too much for her—she clapped
her hands in her joy over the yellow maples, begging me to stop,
now and then that we might sit longer in the golden glory. I never
pass the little cemetery at So. Amherst, without recalling her interest in the clean, cared for, look of it, quite insisting that the
dove finishing one of the marble slabs at the top, was a real feath-
er bird, and she would only be convinced to the contrary when I
strolled through the grass and put my hand upon it. I realize more
and more as I have met persons who knew her much better than
I, who described her silent way, for the most part in society, that
I was most fortunate in her moods, for she talked constantly until
we reached home. I can but count it a choice memory and a real
honor to have been so long with an ideal New England woman,
who under the stress of heavy burdens, wrote a book which tells
its story in twenty different languages. (Susan Dickinson 25–26;
also see Pollak, *Dickinson* 195n4; Smith, *Rowing* 177).

13 Bianchi includes the story in *Face to Face,* with an altered account of
how Emily conveyed her messages to Susan: "It was here [in a hallway
next to the kitchen] that Sue gave Emily the fantastic and unique story
of the Indian Devil by Harriet Prescott Spofford, called 'Circumstance,'
which had just appeared in the *Atlantic Monthly*—and here that Emily
gave it back saying: 'Sue, it is the only thing I ever read in my life that I
didn't think I could have imagined myself!'" Bianchi continues, "Later
came these two lines—'You stand nearer the world than I do, Susan.
Send me everything she writes.' And the selfsame early *Atlantics* of Sue's

sent in response are still in extant" (Bianchi, *Face to Face* 28). In his account, Leyda raises the possibility that Dickinson praises Spofford's "The Amber Gods," published in two installments in earlier issues of the *Atlantic Monthly* (January and February 1860), and not "Circumstance" (2: 6). Following Leyda, Reynolds identifies the story as "The Amber Gods" ("Emily Dickinson" 186), though both Susan Dickinson and Bianchi clearly identify the story as "Circumstance."

14 Spofford (Prescott until 1865) published stories regularly in the *Atlantic Monthly*, beginning in 1859 with the appearance of her detective story "In a Cellar" in February. Before 1868, she published numerous stories, the collection of short fiction in *The Amber Gods and Other Stories*, the novel *Sir Rohan's Ghost: A Romance*, and *Azarian: An Episode*. In a list that she says is "far from complete," Spofford's biographer Elizabeth Halbeisen counts "eight volumes and 374 periodical appearances, including short stories, novels, poems, and articles" produced during the especially "fruitful" years from 1868 to 1890 (120). For more detailed information on Spofford's publishing history, see Halbeisen's bibliography of "The Writings of Harriet Prescott Spofford" (in Halbeisen 223–58) and Bendixen's introduction and additional prefatory materials (Halbeisen ix–xxxix).

15 Fetterley, too, aligns the woman with Scheherazade, noting that, like the queen, the "woman's life literally depends on her art" (264). Considering the popularity of the *Arabian Nights* in the nineteenth century (Ali 59–60), it would not be surprising if Spofford knew the stories. Dickinson's references in letters to Austin, Sue, and Samuel Bowles (across three decades) indicate that she was captivated by the tales' imaginative power (see Letters 19, 22, 335, 438, and 698).

16 In his account of a hiking expedition in the White Mountains, Thomas Wentworth Higginson includes the guide's information on the animal life found in the region (bear, deer, various cats) and on what is not found ("that half-mythical beast known among the Maine lumbermen as the 'Indian devil'") ("A Search" 658).

17 See Faery; Namias; Castiglia; Derounian-Stodola; Ebersole 216–36.

18 Also see Showalter, Moers (90–110), and the introduction and essays in Fleenor's *The Female Gothic*.

19 Gaul proposes that the woman's bloody ordeal is a "scene of figurative childbirth" and that the beast is "her newborn" (Gaul 36), a part of herself to which she gives birth against her own preferences (Gaul 40).

20 In her reading of "Circumstance," Judith Fetterley notes the story's reflection of Rowlandson's ordeal in the woods of colonial New England, arguing that the Indians in Spofford's story *are* devils. St. Armand asserts that "Circumstance" is "based on an incident in Cotton Mather's *Magnalia Christi Americana*" (*Emily Dickinson* 173).

21 There are many narratives that recount the extreme physical and spiri-

tual trials of people taken captive by Indians in the Maine wilderness. See, for example, accounts of Hannah Swarton, Robert Forbes, and John W. Johnson.

22 Spofford's tale fits well the patterns that Christopher Castiglia has noted in captivity narratives. Castiglia asserts that a woman's survival is dependent on her "reconstitution of identity" and on her "manipulation of language" (12, 25).

23 Rosemary Jackson argues that the compulsion of fantastic literature is to express desire, even if it also "tells of the impossible attempt to realize desire," with the recognition of desire leading to its "expulsion" (4).

24 The description of the beast as a "fabulous flying-dragon" further links Spofford's story to the Orpheus myth. In several late-fourteenth-century and fifteenth-century illustrations of the Orpheus story, a dragon is among the animals bewitched by Orpheus's music and, in some manuscripts, it is a dragon that attacks and kills Eurydice, sending her to Hades (Friedman 156–57, 174, 181–83). John Friedman writes that these medieval illustrations "were trying to paint Satan in his popular guise as the draconpede, a medieval man-headed dragon" (183). The correlation of dragons with devils resonates with the biblical description offered by John: "And I saw an angel come down from heaven, having the key of the bottomless pit and a great chain in his hand. And he laid hold on the dragon, that old serpent, which is the Devil, and Satan, and bound him a thousand years" (Rev. 20:1–2).

25 See for example, "'Tis so appalling it exhilarates" (F341), "The first day's night had come" (F423), "They shut me up in prose" (F445), "Where thou art that is home" (F749), and "I sing to use the waiting" (F955).

26 See Mary Elizabeth Massey's detailed study of the vast problem of shortages, including the dire scarcity of food, in the South during the Civil War. For personal accounts of the poverty of supplies and food during the Civil War see, for example, John D. Billings's 1887 *Hardtack and Coffee: The Unwritten Story of Army Life;* Henri Garidel's wartime journal published as *Exile in Richmond;* and Cornelia Hancock's letters published in 1937 as *Letters of a Civil War Nurse.* Patricia B. Mitchell's booklet *Cooking for the Cause* documents some of the ways that soldiers and civilians in the South dealt with food shortages during the war.

27 Since the publication of Shira Wolosky's *Emily Dickinson: A Voice of War* in 1984, many fine Dickinson scholars have examined Dickinson's writing in the context of the Civil War. See, for example, Barrett, Bergland, Dandurand, Friedlander, Hoffman, Marcellin, Miller, Shoptaw, and essays by Wolosky.

28 As additional examples of critical analysis of deprivation in the poems see John Cody 39–47; Eberwein, *Strategies* 62–69; Mossberg 135–46; Wilbur 53–61.

29 A story in *Harper's Weekly* on December 10, 1864, reports on Andersonville: "At Andersonville there were, a few weeks ago, from twenty-five to
   thirty thousand prisoners. So dreadful was the pestilence engendered
   from the close contact of the men, from filth, and from starvation, that
   eleven thousand of these were thrown uncoffined into the trenches
   around the stockade" ("Our Exchanged Prisoners" 789); later reports
   in 1865 put the number of dead at Andersonville at fourteen thousand.
   On April 30, 1864, *Harper's Weekly* reprinted a brief report from the
   Savannah Republican that "Union prisoners at Andersonville, Georgia
   are dying at the rate of 20 to 25 a day" ("Domestic Intelligence" 275). In
   Harper's Weekly, also see "Rebel Cruelties" (June 17, 1865: 379–81); "The
   Prison-Pen at Andersonville" (September 9, 1865: 562); "National Burial-
   Ground at Andersonville" (October 7, 1865: 634). B. S. Calef's "Prison-
   life in the Confederacy," a personal account of being held prisoner, was
   published in *Harper's New Monthly Magazine* (July 1865: 137–50); Louise
   E. Chollet's fictional account of life at Andersonville, "At Andersonville,"
   was published in the *Atlantic Monthly* (March 1865: 285–96).
30 By the 1860s, newspapers and magazines were also full of reports and
   stories related to the turmoil of the Civil War and other traumatic and
   incendiary situations, such as the five-part series on "The Horrors of
   San Domingo" written by John Weiss that ran in the *Atlantic Monthly* in
   1862 and 1863.
31 Weisbuch notes the cat imagery in his discussion of "As the starved
   maelstrom laps the navies" ("Prisming" 201).
32 "'Twas like a maelstrom with a notch" is the key poem in Daneen Wardrop's study of Gothicism in Dickinson's verse (*Gothic*).
33 The scalping image brings to mind Dickinson's definition of poetry that
   Higginson includes in a letter to his wife after visiting with Dickinson in
   August 1870: "If I feel physically as if the top of my head were taken off,
   I know *that* is poetry" (Letter 342a).
34 For additional information regarding Higginson's connections with
   Spofford, see his *Letters and Journals of Thomas Wentworth Higginson*
   (103–11); Halbiesen 40, 43, 52–58; Wells 114–15; Higginson, *Cheerful*
   129–30; and Rodier.
35 This discussion permeates Morrison's *Playing in the Dark*. As an example, she addresses the primacy of slavery in shaping a mythologized
   American identity: "Africanism is the vehicle by which the American
   self knows itself as not enslaved, but free; not repulsive, but desirable;
   not helpless, but licensed and powerful; not history-less, but historical; not damned, but innocent; not a blind accident of evolution, but a
   progressive fulfillment of destiny" (52).
36 See Canney, Symonds, and Fowler for discussions of American warships
   during the Civil War.

CHAPTER FIVE: THE EXHIBITION OF EMILY DICKINSON

1 In her letter, Todd offers her observations: "I must tell you about the *character* of Amherst. It is a lady whom the people call the *Myth*. She is a sister of Mr. Dickinson, & seems to be the climax of all the family oddity. She has not been outside of her own house in fifteen years, except once to see a new church, when she crept out at night, & viewed it by moonlight. No one who calls upon her mother & sister ever see her, but she allows little children once in a great while, & one at a time, to come in, when she gives them cake or candy, or some nicety, for she is very fond of little ones. But more often she lets down the sweetmeat by a string, out of a window, to them. She dresses wholly in white, & her mind is said to be perfectly wonderful" (Leyda, 2: 357).

2 Narratives crafted as literary fictions overtly illustrate the project of creating a comprehensible portrayal of "Emily Dickinson," the designation of fiction not completely displacing facts. See, for example, Judith Farr's *I Never Came to You in White,* Jerome Charyn's *The Secret Life of Emily Dickinson*, Joanne Dobson's *Quieter Than Sleep*, Nuala O'Connor's *Miss Emily*, and Susan Snively's *The Heart Has Many Doors*. The collection *Visiting Emily: Poems Inspired by the Life and Work of Emily Dickinson,* edited by Sheila Coghill and Thom Tammaro, contains poems by seventy-eight authors. Writer and director Terence Davies says that he aims for "narrative truth" in his 2016 film *A Quiet Passion* (see William Nicholson's review, "*A Quiet Passion* won't solve the mystery of Emily Dickinson—but does the truth matter?" in the April 1, 2017, issue of *The Guardian*).

3 In her last letter to her "little cousins" Louise and Frances Norcross in May 1886, Dickinson wrote "Called back" (Letter 1046).

4 "Parents sometimes forget the faces of their own children in a separation of a year of two. But the unfading artificial retina which has looked upon them retains their impress, and a fresh sunbeam lays this on the living nerve as if it were radiated from the breathing shape" (Holmes, "Sun-Painting" 170).

5 In 1995 John Felix presented a case for Otis H. Cooley as the photographer of Dickinson. Felix compares the "furnishings" seen in the photograph—the book, the chair, and especially the tablecloth—to a few other photographs possibly taken by Cooley. Felix ascertains that Cooley had a studio in Springfield, Massachusetts, between 1844 and 1855. In 1999, Mary Elizabeth Kromer Bernhard identified William C. North as the "Daguerrian Artist," as he advertised himself, who took this image of Dickinson; she dates the Dickinson daguerreotype between December 10, 1846, and late March 1847 (Bernhard 596).

6 See, as example, "New Photo of Emily Dickinson?" (*Boston Globe:* September 6, 2012) and "Is This Emily Dickinson and Her Female Lover?" (Kinser: September 9, 2012).

7 See the Dickinson Electronic Archives for links to several news sources. A posting on the Dickinson Electronic Archives announces that "On September 4, 2013, the Collector who discovered it deposited the 1859 daguerreotype at Amherst College Special Collections."

8 Among his findings, Nickell reports that the photograph, a carte de visite, was bought from a bookseller of "dubious reputation," the signature is fraudulent, and the photograph has "no provenance whatsoever." In addition, a forensic anthropologist who compared the carte de visite image and the 1846/1847 daguerreotype identified significant differences of the skull and facial features.

9 Bingham retells this story in Appendix I to her *Emily Dickinson's Home* 519–20.

10 Lavinia wrote to Niles: "I can not report any thing very favorable about Emily's picture quite yet but I hope a likeness may be secured by the suggestion of a child portrait & the picture at sixteen." Lavinia adds that she thinks Niles "would not be interested in either (as they are)" (Bingham, *Ancestors'* 225).

11 See accounts in Bingham *Emily Dickinson's Home* 519–20; Longsworth, *World* 124–25; Longsworth, "'Whose'" 13; Bernhard 598–99.

12 There are four modified portraits archived with the *Louise B. Graves collection of reproductions of the Emily Dickinson daguerreotype* at the Houghton Library, Harvard College. The manuscripts guide to the *Graves collection* includes the statement that "reproductions of this image [the original daguerreotype portrait of Dickinson] were retouched by Laura Coombs Hills, circa 1897." The annotations for the contents of each container are more ambiguous, with Laura Hills specifically mentioned in connection with only two of the altered versions, a "first stage" and an "intermediate stage." The most dramatically altered version (the one in which Emily has curled hair and the "stand-up ruffled collar")— "the final altered version"—is not specifically credited to Hills.

13 McCauley draws on the views of various eighteenth- and nineteenth-century thinkers regarding portraiture, particularly noting the influence of Johann Caspar Lavater. With his studies regarding physiognomy and the revelation of character ("discovering the interior of Man by his exterior"), Lavater "became a model for the portrait photographer" (McCauley 3).

14 In her essay "'The Inconstant Daguerreotype': The Narrative of Early Photography," Susan Williams discusses several fictional works of the 1840s and 1850s in which "magical" and "truth-telling" daguerreotypes have agency, displaying remarkable allure and openness to experiences not usually (or safely) available to women and so serving as active doubles for the female sitter. Also see Williams's *Confounding Images*.

15 Werner posits that the Dickinson daguerreotype "disappeared almost

as soon as it was developed," perhaps lost when the Dickinsons moved from Pleasant Street back to the Homestead in 1855 (Werner, "'Flash'" 481).

16 In a later letter, Wallace Keep acknowledges that his memory of the occasion is a little "beclouded," but he recalls Lavinia taking him into Emily's bedroom in the spring of 1892 and giving him the "priceless daguerreotype" (Bingham, *Home* 522).

17 Also see Bingham, *Ancestors'* 224; Aífe Murray 205.

18 Bernhard states that Lavinia "asserted her power in blocking publication" of the image by giving the daguerreotype to Wallace Keep (600).

19 See, as example, the portraits of Catharine Beecher, Harriet Beecher Stowe, Clara Barton, Dorothea Dix, Mary Todd Lincoln, and Lucy Ware Webb Hayes in Pfister (105, 110, 131, 134, 177, 180).

20 Citing Longsworth's observation of the sameness of the objects in the two photographs, Felix examines particularly the tablecloth, which he traces to other photographs by Otis H. Cooley.

21 In *Emily Dickinson Face to Face,* Bianchi tells tales of Emily the "rascal" who engaged in games of "elfing it." Bianchi writes, "It is this element of drollery in her, the elfin, mischievous strain, that is hardest for those who never knew her to reconcile with her solemn side" (63). Stating that Dickinson "could be whimsical about the things that mattered most," Bingham also refers to Emily and Austin's shared sense of humor and their penchant for "joking together" (*Home* 29, 101). In a letter of June 1892 to Lavinia, Anna Kellogg refers to Emily as "full of 'fun' & 'tease'" as a young woman (Bingham, *Ancestors'* 206).

22 Hubbard also discusses references to the daguerreotype or stereograph in "Of nearness to her sundered things" (F337), "It was not death, for I stood up" (F355), and "The soul's distinct connection" (F901).

23 Also see Adam Frank's discussion of the effects of photography on Dickinson's ideas and experience of "looking" and identity.

24 See, for example, F313, F349, F395, F554, F430, F705, F834, F1071.

25 Drawing on Adrienne Saint-Pierre's own account, Wardrop tells the story of Saint-Pierre's painstaking work to produce the copies of Dickinson's white dress (*Labor* 32–34).

26 In a letter to her mother in May 1886, Todd records that "the pallbearers took out the dainty, white casket into the sunshine, where it was lifted by the stout arms of six or eight Irish workmen, all of whom have worked about the place or been servants in the family for years. . . . They carried her through the fields, full of buttercups" (Leyda 2: 474).

WORKS CITED

Adams, Bluford. *E Pluribus Barnum: The Great Showman and the Making of U.S. Popular Culture.* Minneapolis: U of Minnesota P, 1997.

Ali, Muhsin Jassim. *Scheherazade in England: A Study of Nineteenth-Century English Criticism of the Arabian Nights.* Washington, D.C.: Three Continents, 1981.

Allen, Caroline C. "The Homestead in Amherst." *Horn Book Magazine,* Feb. 1957, 30–34.

Allen, Robert C. *Horrible Prettiness: Burlesque and American Culture.* Chapel Hill: U North Carolina P, 1991.

"Amherst Matters." *Hampshire and Franklin Express,* May 17, 1866, 2; Sept. 30, 1869, 2.

Anderson, Charles R. *Emily Dickinson's Poetry: Stairway of Surprise.* New York: Holt, Rinehart and Winston, 1960.

Applegate, Debby. *The Most Famous Man in America: The Biography of Henry Ward Beecher.* New York: Doubleday, 2006.

Bakhtin, Mikhail. *Rabelais and His World,* translated by Helene Iswolsky, 1968, Bloomington: Indiana UP, 1984.

Barnum, P. T. *The Life of P. T. Barnum.* New York: Redfield, 1855.

———. *Struggles and Triumphs: Or, Forty Years' Recollections.* Hartford: J. B. Burr, 1870.

Barrett, Faith. "Addresses to a Divided Nation: Images of War in Emily Dickinson and Walt Whitman." *Arizona Quarterly* 61.4, 2005, 67–99.

———. "'Drums off the Phantom Battlements': Dickinson's War Poems in Discursive Context." *A Companion to Emily Dickinson,* edited by Martha Nell Smith and Mary Loeffelholz, Oxford: Blackwell, 2008, 107–32.

Bean, Annemarie, James V. Hatch, and Brooks McNamara, editors. *Inside the Minstrel Mask: Readings in Nineteenth-Century Blackface Minstrelsy.* Hanover, NH: Wesleyan UP, 1996.

Bendixen, Alfred. Introduction. *The Amber Gods and Other Stories,* by Harriet Prescott Spofford, New Brunswick: Rutgers UP, 1989, ix–xxxiv.

Benfey, Christopher. "Introduction: A Lost World Brought to Light." *The Dickinsons of Amherst,* by Jerome Liebling, Hanover: UP of New England, 2001, 1–13.

———. *A Summer of Hummingbirds: Love, Art, and Scandal in the Intersecting Worlds of Emily Dickinson, Mark Twain, Harriet Beecher Stowe, and Martin Johnson Heade.* New York: Penguin, 2008.

Bennett, Paula. *Emily Dickinson: Woman Poet.* Iowa City: U of Iowa P, 1990.

———. *My Life a Loaded Gun: Female Creativity and Feminist Poetics.* Boston: Beacon, 1986.

———. "'The Negro never knew': Emily Dickinson and Racial Typology in the Nineteenth Century." *Legacy* 19.1, 2002, 53–61.

Bergland, Renee. "The Eagle's Eye: Dickinson's View of Battle." *A Companion to Emily Dickinson,* edited by Martha Nell Smith and Mary Loeffelholz, Oxford: Blackwell, 2008, 133–56.

Bernhard, Mary Elizabeth Kromer. "Lost and Found: Emily Dickinson's Unknown Daguerreotypist." *New England Quarterly* 72.4, 1999, 594–601.

Bhabha, Homi K. "The Other Question." *Screen* 24.6, 1983, 18–36.

Bianchi, Martha Dickinson. *Emily Dickinson Face to Face: Unpublished Letters with Notes and Reminiscences.* Boston: Houghton Mifflin, 1932.

———. Introduction. *The Single Hound: Poems of a Lifetime,* by Emily Dickinson, Boston: Little, Brown, 1914.

———. *The Life and Letters of Emily Dickinson.* Boston: Houghton Mifflin, 1924.

Billings, John D. *Hardtack and Coffee: The Unwritten Story of Army Life.* 1887, edited by Richard Harwell, Chicago: R. R. Donnelley/Lakeside, 1960.

Bingham, Millicent Todd. *Ancestors' Brocades: The Literary Debut of Emily Dickinson.* New York: Harper & Brothers, 1945.

———. *Emily Dickinson's Home: Letters of Edward Dickinson and His Family.* New York: Harper & Brothers, 1955.

"A Black Affair." *Harper's Weekly,* Jan. 28, 1865, 58–59.

Blassingame, John W. *The Slave Community: Plantation Life in the Antebellum South.* Oxford: Oxford UP, 1979.

Bode, Carl. *The Anatomy of American Popular Culture, 1840–1861.* Berkeley: U of California P, 1959.

Bogdan, Robert. *Freak Show: Presenting Human Oddities for Amusement and Profit.* Chicago: U of Chicago P, 1988.

The Book of Brothers; (Second Series) Being a History of the Adventures of John W. Hutchinson and His Family in the Camps of the Army of the Potomac. Boston: S. Chism, Franklin Printing House, 1864.

Boziwick, George. "'My Business Is to Sing': Emily Dickinson's Musical Borrowings." *Journal of the Society for American Music* 8.2, 2014, 130–66.

Bradlee, Francis B. C. *Blockade Running During the Civil War, and the Effect of Land and Water Transportation on the Confederacy.* 1925. Philadelphia: Porcupine P, 1974.

Brink, Carol. *Harps in the Wind: The Story of the Singing Hutchinsons.* 1947. New York: Da Capo P, 1980.

Brown, William W., compiler. *The Anti-Slavery Harp: A Collection of Songs.* Boston: Bela Marsh, 1848.

Bungay, George W., compiler. *The Bobolink Minstrel: or, Republican Songster, for 1860.* New York: O. Hutchinson, 1860.

"Business Notices." *New-York Daily Tribune,* Aug. 13, 1850.

Calef, B. S. "Prison-life in the Confederacy." *Harper's New Monthly Magazine,* July 1865: 137–50. *HarpWeek,* harpweek.com.

Canney, Donald L. *Lincoln's Navy: The Ships, Men and Organization, 1861–65.* Annapolis: Naval Institute P, 1998.

Capps, Jack L. *Emily Dickinson's Reading, 1836–1886.* Cambridge: Harvard UP, 1966.

Carpenter, Edward Wilton. *The History of the Town of Amherst, Massachusetts.* Amherst: P of Carpenter and Morehouse, 1896, *UMass Amherst Libraries,* archive.org/details/historytownamheoomoregoog. Accessed March 19, 2019.

Castiglia, Christopher. *Bound and Determined: Captivity, Culture-Crossing, and White Womanhood from Mary Rowlandson to Patty Hearst.* Chicago: U of Chicago P, 1996.

A Century of Population Growth: From the First Census of the United States to the Twelfth, 1790–1900. Washington, D.C.: GPO, 1909; Baltimore: Genealogical Publishing, 1970.

Charyn, Jerome. *The Secret Life of Emily Dickinson.* New York: Norton, 2010.

Chollet, Louise E. "At Andersonville." *Atlantic Monthly,* March 1865: 285–96.

"To the Citizens of Baltimore." *The Liberator* [Boston], March 26, 1852, col. F. *America's Historical Newspapers,* infoweb.newsbank.com.

Clark, George W. *The Harp of Freedom.* New York: Miller, Orton and Mulligan; Boston: J. P. Jewett, 1856.

———. *The Liberty Minstrel.* New York: Leavitt and Alden; Boston: Saxton and Miles, 1845.

Clinton, Catherine. *The Other Civil War: American Women in the Nineteenth Century.* New York: Hill and Wang, 1984.

Cockrell, Dale. *Demons of Disorder: Early Blackface Minstrels and Their World.* Cambridge: Cambridge UP, 1997.

———, editor. *Excelsior: Journals of the Hutchinson Family Singers, 1842–1846.* Stuyvesant, NY: Pendragon P, 1989.

Cody, David. "'When one's soul's at a white heat': Dickinson and the 'Azarian School.'" *Emily Dickinson Journal* 19.1, 2010, 30–59.

Cody, John. *After Great Pain: The Inner Life of Emily Dickinson.* Cambridge: Belknap P of Harvard UP, 1971.

Coghill, Sheila and Thom Tammaro, editors. *Visiting Emily: Poems Inspired by the Life and Work of Emily Dickinson.* Iowa City: U Iowa P, 2000.

Cook, James W., Jr. "Of Men, Missing Links, and Nondescripts: The Strange Career of P. T. Barnum's 'What is It?' Exhibition." *Freakery: Cultural*

Spectacles of the Extraordinary Body, edited by Rosemarie Garland Thomson, New York: New York UP, 1996, 139–57.

Cooley, Carolyn Lindley. *The Music of Emily Dickinson's Poems and Letters: A Study of Imagery and Form.* Jefferson, NC: McFarland, 2003.

Cornelius, Steven H. *Music of the Civil War Era.* Westport, CT: Greenwood P, 2004.

Crawford, Richard. *America's Musical Life: A History.* New York: Norton, 2001.

Dalke, Anne. "'Circumstance' and the Creative Woman: Harriet Prescott Spofford." *Arizona Quarterly* 41.1, 1985, 71–85.

Damon, S. Foster, curator. *Series of Old American Songs: Reproduced in Facsimile from Original or Early Editions in the Collection of American Poetry and Plays, Brown University.* Providence: Brown U Library, 1936.

Dandurand, Karen. "New Dickinson Civil War Publications." *American Literature* 56.1, 1984, 17–27.

Dandy Jim and Dan Tucker's Jawbone, or Cool White's Nigga Minstrel. New York: Turner and Fisher, 1844.

Davis, Ronald L. *A History of Music in American Life*, vol. 1, Malabar, FL: Robert Krieger, 1982.

"Declaration of Sentiments." *The Feminist Papers,* edited by Alice S. Rossi, New York: Bantam, 1973, 413–21.

Defoe, Daniel. *The Life and Adventures of Robinson Crusoe,* edited by Angus Ross, New York: Penguin, 1965.

Dennett, Andrea Stulman. *Weird and Wonderful: The Dime Museum in America.* New York: New York UP, 1997.

Dennison, Sam. *Scandalize My Name: Black Imagery in American Popular Music.* New York: Garland, 1982.

Derounian-Stodola, Kathryn Zabelle, editor. *Women's Indian Captivity Narratives.* New York: Penguin, 1998.

Dickens, Charles. *American Notes for General Circulation and Pictures from Italy.* New York: Charles Scribner's Sons, 1910.

Dickinson, Emily. *The Complete Poems of Emily Dickinson.* Boston: Little, Brown, 1924.

———. *Emily Dickinson's Herbarium: A Facsimile Edition.* Cambridge: Belknap P of Harvard UP, 2006.

———. *Emily Dickinson's Poems: As She Preserved Them*, edited by Cristanne Miller, Cambridge: Belknap P of Harvard UP, 2016.

———. *The Letters of Emily Dickinson,* edited by Thomas H. Johnson and Theodora Ward, Cambridge: Belknap P of Harvard UP, 1958, 3 vols.

———. *Letters of Emily Dickinson,* edited by Mabel Loomis Todd, Boston: Roberts Brothers, 1894, 2 vols.

———. *Letters of Emily Dickinson,* edited by Mabel Loomis Todd, New York: Harper & Brothers, 1931.

————. "Music: A Bound Volume of Miscellaneous Sheet Music, Without Title Page." EDR 469, Houghton Library, Harvard U, Cambridge.

————. *The Poems of Emily Dickinson: Including Variant Readings Critically Compared with All Known Manuscripts,* edited by Thomas H. Johnson, Cambridge: Belknap P of Harvard UP, 1955, 3 vols.

————. *The Poems of Emily Dickinson: Variorum Edition,* edited by R. W. Franklin, Cambridge: Belknap P of Harvard UP, 1998, 3 vols.

————. *The Single Hound: Poems of a Lifetime,* edited by Martha Dickinson Bianchi, Boston: Little, Brown, 1914.

Dickinson, Susan Huntington. "Harriet Prescott's Early Work." *Springfield Republican,* Feb. 1, 1903, 19.

Dickinson, Susan Huntington Gilbert. "Annals of the Evergreens." Dickinson Family Papers (MS AM 1118.95), Houghton Library, Harvard U, Cambridge.

Dickinson Electronic Archives, edited by Martha Nell Smith, Marta Werner, Jessica Beard, Julie Enszer, Ellen Louise Hart. University of Maryland, College Park. emilydickinson.org.

Dickinson Family Artifacts, circa 1785–1880 (Dickinson Room). Houghton Library, Harvard University. https://id.lib.harvard.edu/ead/hou01551/catalog.

Dizikes, John. *Opera in America: A Cultural History.* New Haven: Yale UP, 1993.

Dobson, Joanne. *Dickinson and the Strategies of Reticence: The Woman Writer in Nineteenth-Century America.* Bloomington: Indiana UP, 1989.

————. *Quieter Than Sleep.* New York: Bantam, 1998.

"Domestic Intelligence." *Harper's Weekly,* April 30, 1864: 275. *HarpWeek,* harpweek.com.

Donald, David Herbert. *Lincoln.* New York: Simon and Schuster, 1995.

Doriani, Beth Maclay. *Emily Dickinson: Daughter of Prophecy.* Amherst: U of Massachusetts P, 1996.

Douglass, Frederick. "The Hutchinson Family—Hunkerism." *North Star,* Oct. 27, 1848, 2.

————. Introduction. *Story of the Hutchinsons (Tribe of Jesse),* by John Wallace Hutchinson, compiled and edited by Charles E. Mann, vol. 1, Boston: Lee and Shepard, 1896; New York: Da Capo P, 1977, xv–xviii.

Dublin, Thomas. *Women at Work: The Transformation of Work and Community in Lowell, Massachusetts, 1826–1860.* New York: Columbia UP, 1979.

Dunson, Stephanie. "The Minstrel in the Parlor: Nineteenth-Century Sheet Music and the Domestication of Blackface Minstrelsy." *ATQ* 16.4, 2002, 241–56.

Ebersole, Gary L. *Captured by Texts: Puritan to Postmodern Images of Indian Captivity.* Charlottesville: UP of Virginia, 1995.

Eberwein, Jane Donahue. *Dickinson: Strategies of Limitation.* Amherst: U of Massachusetts P, 1985.

Eberwein, Jane Donahue, Stephanie Farrar, and Cristanne Miller, editors. *Dickinson in Her Own Time: A Biographical Chronicle of Her Life, Drawn from Recollections, Interviews, and Memoirs by Family, Friends, and Associates.* Iowa City: U of Iowa P, 2015.

Edelstein, Tilden G. *Strange Enthusiasm: A Life of Thomas Wentworth Higginson.* New Haven: Yale UP, 1968.

Edmonds, Anne Carey. *A Memory Book of Mount Holyoke College, 1837–1987.* South Hadley, MA: Mount Holyoke College, 1988.

Eliot, T. S. "Tradition and the Individual Talent." *Selected Essays.* New York: Harcourt, Brace, and World, 1964, 3–11.

Ellis, Kate Ferguson. *The Contested Castle: Gothic Novels and the Subversion of Domestic Ideology.* Urbana: U of Illinois P, 1989.

England, Martha Winburn, and John Sparrow. *Hymns Unbidden: Donne, Herbert, Blake, Emily Dickinson and the Hymnographers.* New York: New York Public Library, 1966.

Enszer, Julie. "Is This a Photo of Emily Dickinson? And Will It Tell Us Who She Loved?" *Ms. Magazine*, Sept. 11, 2012. msmagazine.com.

Erkkila, Betsy. *Mixed Bloods and Other Crosses: Rethinking American Literature from the Revolution to the Culture Wars.* Philadelphia: U of Pennsylvania P, 2005.

Faery, Rebecca Blevins. *Cartographies of Desire: Captivity, Race, and Sex in the Shaping of an American Nation.* Norman: U of Oklahoma P, 1999.

Farr, Judith. *The Gardens of Emily Dickinson.* Cambridge: Harvard UP, 2004.

———. *I Never Came to You in White.* Boston: Houghton Mifflin, 1996.

———. *The Passion of Emily Dickinson.* Cambridge: Harvard UP, 1992.

Felix, John. "A Daguerreian Detective Story. Otis H. Cooley: Possible Photographer of the Only Known Emily Dickinson Daguerreotype." *Journal: New England Journal of Photographic History* 146/147.3–4, 1995, 10–14.

Fetterley, Judith. "Harriet Prescott Spofford." *Provisions: A Reader from Nineteenth-Century American Women,* edited by Judith Fetterley, Bloomington: Indiana UP, 1985, 261–78.

Finnerty, Páraic. "Transatlantic Women Writers." *Emily Dickinson in Context,* edited by Eliza Richards. Cambridge: Cambridge UP, 2013, 109–18.

Finson, Jon W. *The Voices That Are Gone: Themes in Nineteenth-Century American Popular Song.* New York: Oxford UP, 1994.

Fitzgerald, William G. "Side-Shows III." *Strand Magazine,* June 1897, 521–28.

Fleenor, Juliann E., editor. *The Female Gothic.* Montreal: Eden, 1983.

Flood, Alison. "Emily Dickinson Gets a New Look in Recovered Photograph." *Guardian*, Sept. 5, 2012. guardian.co.uk.

Folsom, Ed and Kenneth Price. "Dickinson, Slavery, and the San Domingo Moment." *The Classroom Electric,* 2001, whitmanarchive.org/resources/teaching/dickinson/index.html. Accessed March 20, 2019.

Foner, Philip S., editor. *The Factory Girls: A Collection of Writings on Life and Struggles in the New England Factories of the 1840s by the Factory Girls Themselves.* Urbana: U of Illinois P, 1977.

———. *The Life and Writings of Frederick Douglass,* vol. 1, New York: International, 1950.

[Forbes, Robert and] Arthur Bradman. *A Narrative of the Extraordinary Sufferings of Mr. Robert Forbes, his wife, and five children; during an unfortunate journey through the wilderness, from Canada to Kennebec-River, in the year 1784.* Norwich: John Trumbull, 1793. *Readex Digital Collections. Early American Imprints, Series 1. Evans, 1639–1800.*

Fowler, William M. *Under Two Flags: The American Navy in the Civil War.* New York: Norton, 1990.

[Franconi's Hippodrome] "New York, April 30, 1853." *Daily Evening Transcript* [Boston], May 2, 1853, 2. *America's Historical Newspapers,* infoweb.newsbank.com.

Frank, Adam. "Emily Dickinson and Photography." *Emily Dickinson Journal* 10.2, 2001, 1–21.

Franklin, R. W. "Emily Dickinson to Abiah Root: Ten Reconstructed Letters." *Emily Dickinson Journal* 4.1, 1995, 1–43.

———, editor. *The Master Letters of Emily Dickinson.* Amherst: Amherst College P, 1986.

Friedlander, Benjamin. "Emily Dickinson and the Battle of Ball's Bluff." *PMLA* 124.5, 2009, 1582–99.

Friedman, John Block. *Orpheus in the Middle Ages.* Cambridge: Harvard UP, 1970.

Frost, Linda. "The Circassian Beauty and the Circassian Slave: Gender, Imperialism, and American Popular Entertainment." *Freakery: Cultural Spectacles of the Extraordinary Body,* edited by Rosemarie Garland Thomson, New York: New York UP, 1996, 248–62.

———. *Never One Nation: Freaks, Savages, and Whiteness in U.S. Popular Culture, 1850–1877.* Minneapolis: U Minnesota P, 2005.

Frost, Thomas. *Circus Life and Circus Celebrities.* London: Chatto and Windus, Piccadilly, 1881.

Gac, Scott. *Singing For Freedom: The Hutchinson Family Singers and the Nineteenth-Century Culture of Reform.* New Haven: Yale UP, 2007.

Garber, Marjorie. *Vested Interests: Cross-Dressing and Cultural Anxiety.* New York: HarperCollins, 1992.

Garbowsky, Maryanne M. "A Maternal Muse for Emily Dickinson." *Dickinson Studies* 41, 1981, 12–17.

Garidel, Henri. *Exile in Richmond: The Confederate Journal of Henri Garidel,* edited by Michael Bedout Chesson and Lesie Jean Roberts, Charlottesville: UP of Virginia, 2001.

Gaul, Theresa Strouth. "Captivity, Childbirth, and the Civil War in Harriet Prescott Spofford's 'Circumstance.'" *Legacy* 19.1, 2002, 35–43.

G[eorge] F. Bailey and Co.'s Great Quadruple Combination! Advertisement. *Hampshire Express,* May 3, 1866, 3.

Geo[rge]. F. Bailey and Co.'s Metropolitan Quadruple Combination comprising under one colossal canvas! Four complete exhibitions! . . . At Worcester . . . May 21st 1866. [Worcester, MA: 1866]. Broadside. American Antiquarian Society. *Readex Digital Collections. American Broadsides and Ephemera, Series 1.*

Ghazoul, Ferial Jabouri. *The Arabian Nights: A Structural Analysis.* Cairo: Cairo Associated Institution, 1980.

Gilbert, Sandra M. and Susan Gubar. *The Madwoman in the Attic: The Woman Writer and the Nineteenth-Century Literary Imagination.* New Haven: Yale UP, 1979.

Gleason, George. "Is It Really Emily Dickinson?" *Emily Dickinson Journal* 18.2, 2009, 1–20.

Gosset, Thomas F. *"Uncle Tom's Cabin" and American Culture.* Dallas: Southern Methodist UP, 1985.

Graves, Gertrude M. "A Cousin's Memories of Emily Dickinson." *Boston Sunday Globe,* Jan. 12, 1930, 41.

Graves, Louise B., collector. Louise B. Graves Collection of Reproductions of the Emily Dickinson Daguerreotype, circa 1897 and 1978. MS Am 1118.15, Houghton Library, Harvard U.

Green, Clara Bellinger. "The Sketch Book: A Reminiscence of Emily Dickinson." *Bookman: A Review of Books and Life* 60.3, 1924, 291–93.

Greenway, John. *American Folksongs of Protest.* Philadelphia: U Pennsylvania P, 1953.

Gura, Philip F., and James F. Bollman. *America's Instrument: The Banjo in the Nineteenth-Century.* Chapel Hill: U of North Carolina P, 1999.

Gyles, John. *Memoirs of Odd Adventures, Strange Deliverances, etc. in the Captivity of John Gyles, Esq. Written by Himself.* 1736. *The Garland Library of Narratives of North American Captivities,* vol. 6, arranged by Wilcomb E. Washburn, New York: Garland, 1977.

Habegger, Alfred. *My Wars Are Laid Away in Books: The Life of Emily Dickinson.* New York: Random House, 2001.

Halbeisen, Elizabeth K. *Harriet Prescott Spofford: A Romantic Survival.* Philadelphia: U of Pennsylvania P, 1935.

Hall, Stuart. "Ethnicity: Identity and Difference." *Radical America* 23.4, 1991, 9–20.

Hamm, Charles. Liner notes. *There's a Good Time Coming and Other Songs of the Hutchinson Family as Performed at the Smithsonian Institution.* LP. Smithsonian Institution, 1978, 4–14.

———. *Yesterdays: Popular Song in America.* New York: Norton, 1979.

Hancock, Cornelia. *Letters of a Civil War Nurse, Cornelia Hancock, 1863–1865,* edited by Henrietta Stratton Jaquette, Lincoln: U of Nebraska P, 1998.

Hannaford, Ivan. *Race: The History of an Idea in the West.* Baltimore: Johns Hopkins UP, 1996.

Harris, Neil. *Humbug: The Art of P. T. Barnum.* Boston: Little, Brown, 1973.

Hedrick, Joan D. *Harriet Beecher Stowe: A Life.* New York: Oxford UP, 1994.

Higginson, Thomas Wentworth. *Cheerful Yesterdays.* Boston: Houghton, Mifflin, 1898.

———. "Emily Dickinson's Letters." *Atlantic Monthly* Oct. 1891, 444–56.

———. *Letters and Journals of Thomas Wentworth Higginson, 1846–1906,* edited by Mary Thacher Higginson, Boston: Houghton Mifflin; Cambridge: Riverside, 1921.

———. "Ought Women to Learn the Alphabet?" *The Magnificent Activist: The Writings of Thomas Wentworth Higginson,* edited by Howard N. Meyer, New York: Da Capo, 2000, 266–82.

———. "Negro Spirituals." *Atlantic Monthly* 19, June 1867, 685–94.

———. "A Search for the Pleiades." *Atlantic Monthly* 46, Nov. 1880, 657–64.

Higginson, Thomas Wentworth and Henry Walcott Boynton. *A Reader's History of American Literature.* Boston: Houghton, Mifflin, 1903.

"The Hippodrome." *National Aegis* [Worcester, MA], June 8, 1853, 2, 3. *America's Historical Newspapers,* infoweb.newsbank.com.

[Hippodrome, Boston]. *San Francisco Evening Journal,* Sept. 8, 1853, 2. *America's Historical Newspapers,* infoweb.newsbank.com.

Hoffman, Tyler B. "Emily Dickinson and the Limit of War." *Emily Dickinson Journal* 3.2, 1994, 1–18.

"Holiday Mummeries." *Harper's Weekly,* Jan. 12, 1867, 28–29.

Holifield, E. Brooks. *Theology in America: Christian Thought from the Age of the Puritans to the Civil War.* New Haven: Yale UP, 2003.

Holly, Carol. "'Grand and Sweet Methodist Hymns': Spiritual Transformation and the Imperialistic Vision in Harriet Prescott Spofford's 'Circumstance.'" *Legacy,* 18.2, 2001, 153–66.

Holmes, Oliver Wendell. "The Stereoscope and the Stereograph." *Soundings from the Atlantic.* Boston: Ticknor and Fields, 1864, 124–65.

———. "Sun-Painting and Sun-Sculpture; with a Stereoscopic Trip across the Atlantic." *Soundings from the Atlantic.* Boston: Ticknor and Fields, 1864, 166–227.

Holy Bible, Containing the Old and New Testaments. King James Version, American Bible Society.

Homans, Margaret. *Women Writers and Poetic Identity: Dorothy Wordsworth, Emily Bronte, and Emily Dickinson.* Princeton: Princeton UP, 1980.

"Home and Foreign Gossip." *Harper's Weekly,* Dec. 1, 1866, 759.

Howe, Susan. *My Emily Dickinson.* Berkeley: North Atlantic Books, 1985.

Howitt, William. "The Hutchinson Family." *Boston Daily Atlas,* June 25, 1846, col. B. *America's Historical Newspapers,* infoweb.newsbank.com.

Hubbard, Melanie. "'Turn it, a little': The Influence of the Daguerreotype

and the Stereograph on Emily Dickinson's Use of Manuscript Variants."
Mosaic 38.1, 2005, 115–32.

Hutchinson, John Wallace, editor. *Hutchinson's Republican Songster, for the Campaign of 1860.* New York: O. Hutchinson, 1860.

———. *Story of the Hutchinsons (Tribe of Jesse)*, compiled and edited by Charles E. Mann, Boston: Lee and Shepard, 1896; New York: Da Capo P, 1977, 2 vols.

Hutchinson, Joshua. *A Brief Narrative of the Hutchinson Family: Sixteen Sons and Daughters of the "Tribe of Jesse."* Boston: Lee and Shepard, 1874.

"The Hutchinson Family." *Bangor Daily Whig & Courier*, Jan. 1, 1855, col. B. *America's Historical Newspapers*, infoweb.newsbank.com.

"The Hutchinson Family." *Mississippi Free Trader and Natchez Gazette*, June 18, 1851, col. D. *America's Historical Newspapers*, infoweb.news bank.com.

Hutchinson Family Scrapbook. Wadleigh Memorial Library, Milford, NH.

[Hutchinsons]. *Boston Daily Atlas*, March 27, 1845, 2. *America's Historical Newspapers*, infoweb.newsbank.com.

"The Hutchinsons." *Hampshire and Franklin Express*, Nov. 25, 1859, 2.

Itzkoff, Dave. "Still No New Pynchon Photo, But Here's Emily Dickinson." *New York Times*, Sept. 5, 2012. nytimes.com.

Jackson, Richard, editor. *Popular Songs of Nineteenth-Century America: Complete Original Sheet Music for 64 Songs.* New York: Dover, 1976.

Jackson, Rosemary. *Fantasy: The Literature of Subversion.* New York: Methuen, 1981.

Jackson, Virginia. *Dickinson's Misery: A Theory of Lyric Reading.* Princeton: Princeton UP, 2005.

Jeffries, John P. *The Natural History of the Human Races, with Their Primitive Form and Origin, Primeval Distribution, Distinguishing Peculiarities; Antiquity, Works of Art, Physical Structure, Mental Endowments and Moral Bearing.* New York: Jenkins, 1869.

Jenkins, MacGregor. *Emily Dickinson: Friend and Neighbor.* Boston: Little, Brown, 1930.

"Jim Crow Complete in 150 Verses." *American Song Sheets*, America Singing: Nineteenth-Century Song Sheets, series 1, vol. 5, [n.p.], [n.d.], Rare Book and Special Collections Division, Library of Congress, https://www.loc.gov/item/amss.as106700/. Accessed March 23, 2019.

Johnson, John W. *Life of John W. Johnson, Who Was Stolen by the Indians.* 1861; reprint, *The Garland Library of Narratives of North American Indian Captivities*, vol. 111, arranged by Wilcomb E. Washburn, New York: Arno, 1977.

Johnson, Thomas H. *Emily Dickinson: An Interpretive Biography.* Cambridge: Belknap P of Harvard UP, 1955.

———. Introduction. *The Letters of Emily Dickinson*, edited by Thomas H.

Johnson and Theodora Ward, Cambridge: Belknap P of Harvard UP, 1958, 3 vols., xv–xxii.

Johnson, Thomas H. and Theodora Ward, editors. *The Letters of Emily Dickinson.* Cambridge: Belknap P of Harvard UP, 1958, 3 vols.

Jordan, Philip D. *Singin' Yankees.* Minneapolis: U of Minnesota P, 1946.

Jordan, Philip D. and Lillian Kessler. *Songs of Yesterday: A Song Anthology of American Life.* Garden City, NY: Doubleday, Doran, 1941.

Juhasz, Suzanne. "The Big Tease." *Comic Power in Emily Dickinson,* edited by Suzanne Juhasz, Cristanne Miller, and Martha Nell Smith. Austin: U of Texas P, 1993, 26–62.

———. *The Undiscovered Continent: Emily Dickinson and the Space of the Mind.* Bloomington: Indiana UP, 1983.

Kahn, Eve M. "Where a Poet's Feet Trod." *New York Times,* May 22, 2014. nytimes.com.

Keller, Karl. *The Only Kangaroo among the Beauty: Emily Dickinson and America.* Baltimore: Johns Hopkins UP, 1979.

Kelly, Gary. "General Introduction." *Varieties of Female Gothic,* edited by Gary Kelly, vol. 1, London: Pickering & Chatto, 2002, xi–lx.

Kelly, Mike, Carolyn Vega, Marta Werner, Susan Howe, and Richard Wilbur. *The Networked Recluse: The Connected World of Emily Dickinson.* Amherst: Amherst College P, 2017.

Kinser, Jeremy. "Is This Emily Dickinson and Her Female Lover?" Advocate. com, Sept. 9, 2012.

Kirkby, Joan. "Periodical Reading." *Emily Dickinson in Context,* edited by Eliza Richards. Cambridge: Cambridge UP, 2013, 139–47.

Kolve, V. A. *The Play Called Corpus Christi.* Stanford: Stanford UP, 1966.

Kosinski, Dorothy M. *Orpheus in Nineteenth-Century Symbolism.* Ann Arbor: UMI Research, 1989.

Kunhardt, Philip B., Jr., Philip B. Kunhardt III, and Peter W. Kunhardt. *P. T. Barnum: America's Greatest Showman.* New York: Knopf, 1995.

Landman, Neil H., Paula M. Mikkelsen, Rüdiger Bieler, and Bennet Bronson. *Pearls: A Natural History.* New York: American Museum of Natural History and the Field Museum, 2001.

Lent's Great National Circus. Advertisement. *Hampshire and Franklin Express,* May 31, 1861, 3.

Levine, Lawrence W. *Highbrow/Lowbrow: The Emergence of Cultural Hierarchy in America.* Cambridge: Harvard UP, 1988.

Leyda, Jay. *The Years and Hours of Emily Dickinson.* New Haven: Yale UP, 1960, 2 vols.

Liebling, Jerome. *The Dickinsons of Amherst.* Hanover: UP of New England, 2001.

Lindfors, Bernth. "Circus Africans." *Journal of American Culture* 6.2, 1983, 9–14.

————. "'The Hottentot Venus' and Other African Attractions in Nineteenth-Century England." *Australasian Drama Studies* 1.2, 1983, 82–104.

————. "P. T. Barnum And Africa." *Studies in Popular Culture* 7, 1984, 18–27.

"Living Curiosities at Barnum's Museum." Advertisement. *Harper's Weekly,* Dec. 15, 1860, 799.

Loeffelholz, Mary. "U.S. Literary Contemporaries: Dickinson's Moderns." *Emily Dickinson in Context,* edited by Eliza Richards. Cambridge: Cambridge UP, 2013, 129–38.

Loesser, Arthur. *Men, Women and Pianos: A Social History.* New York: Simon and Schuster, 1954.

Lombardo, Daniel. *A Hedge Away: The Other Side of Emily Dickinson's Amherst.* Northampton, MA: Daily Hampshire Gazette, 1997.

————. *Tales of Amherst: A Look Back.* Amherst: Jones Library, 1986.

Longsworth, Polly. "'Whose But Her Shy—Immortal Face': The Poet's Visage in the Popular Imagination." *Language as Object: Emily Dickinson and Contemporary Art,* edited by Susan Danly, Amherst, MA: Mead Art Museum, Amherst College/U Massachusetts P, 1997, 34–41.

————. *The World of Emily Dickinson: A Visual Biography.* New York: Norton, 1990.

Lott, Eric. "Blackface and Blackness: The Minstrel Show in American Culture." *Inside the Minstrel Mask,* edited by Annemarie Bean, et al., Hanover, NH: Wesleyan UP, 1996, 3–32.

————. *Love and Theft: Blackface Minstrelsy and the American Working Class.* New York: Oxford UP, 1993.

Lowenberg, Carlton. *Musicians Wrestle Everywhere: Emily Dickinson and Music.* Berkeley, CA: Fallen Leaf P, 1992.

Luce, William. *The Belle of Amherst.* New York: Samuel French, 2007.

Mahar, William J. *Behind the Burnt Cork Mask: Early Blackface Minstrelsy and Antebellum American Popular Culture.* Urbana: U of Illinois P, 1999.

Marcellin, Leigh-Anne Urbanowicz. "Emily Dickinson's Civil War Poetry." *Emily Dickinson Journal* 5.2, 1996, 107–12.

Marien, Mary Warner. *Photography and Its Critics: A Cultural History, 1839–1900.* Cambridge: Cambridge UP, 1997.

Martineau, Harriet. "The Hutchinson Family in London." *Littell's Living Age,* 9, April 25, 1846, 179. *Hathi Trust Digital Library,* babel.hathitrust.org.

Mason, Lowell and George James Webb, compilers and arrangers. *The Vocalist: Consisting of Short and Easy Glees, or Songs, in Parts.* Boston: Wilkins, Carter, 1846.

Massey, Mary Elizabeth. *Ersatz in the Confederacy: Shortages and Substitutes on the Southern Homefront.* 1952, introduction by Barbara L. Bellows, Columbia: U of South Carolina P, 1993.

Mazow, Leo G., editor. *Picturing the Banjo.* University Park: Palmer Museum of Art/Penn State UP, 2005.

McCauley, Elizabeth Anne. *Likenesses: Portrait Photography in Europe, 1850–1870*. Albuquerque: Art Museum/U of New Mexico, 1980.

McLean, Sydney R. "Emily Dickinson at Mount Holyoke." *New England Quarterly* 7.1, 1934, 25–42.

McMurtry, R. Gerald. *Lincoln and the Hutchinson Family Singers*. Harrogate, TN: Lincoln Memorial U, 1944.

McNamara, Brooks. "'A Congress of Wonders': The Rise and Fall of the Dime Museum." *ESQ* 20, 1974, 216–32.

———. *Step Right Up*. Garden City, NY: Doubleday, 1976.

Meer, Sarah. *Uncle Tom Mania: Slavery, Minstrelsy, and Transatlantic Culture in the 1850s*. Athens: U of Georgia P, 2005.

"Memorabilia of Mary Lyon." Mary Lyon Collection (MS 0500 [LD 7082.25 1837]), Mount Holyoke College Archives/Five Colleges Archives and Manuscript Collections.

Merriam, George S. *The Life and Times of Samuel Bowles*. New York: Century, 1885, 2 vols.

Miller, Cristanne. *Emily Dickinson: A Poet's Grammar*. Cambridge: Harvard UP, 1987.

———. "The Humor of Excess." *Comic Power in Emily Dickinson*, edited by Suzanne Juhasz, Cristanne Miller, and Martha Nell Smith, Austin: U of Texas P, 1993, 103–36.

———. "Immediate U.S. Literary Predecessors." *Emily Dickinson in Context*, edited by Eliza Richards. Cambridge: Cambridge UP, 2013, 119–28.

———. "Pondering 'Liberty': Emily Dickinson and the Civil War." *American Vistas and Beyond: A Festschrift for Roland Hagenbuchle*, edited by Marietta Messmer and Josef Raab, Trier: WVT Wissenschaftlicher Verlag Trier, 2002, 45–64.

———. *Reading in Time: Emily Dickinson in the Nineteenth Century*. Amherst: U of Massachusetts P, 2012.

———. "The Sound of Shifting Paradigms, or Hearing Dickinson in the Twenty-First Century." *A Historical Guide to Emily Dickinson*, edited by Vivian R. Pollak, Oxford: Oxford UP, 2004, 201–34.

Mitchell, Domhnall. *Measures of Possibility: Emily Dickinson's Manuscripts*. Amherst: U of Massachusetts P, 2005.

Mitchell, Patricia B. *Cooking for the Cause: Confederate Recipes, Documented Quotations, Commemorative Recipes*. Chatam, VA: Sims-Mitchell House, 1988.

Moers, Ellen. *Literary Women: The Great Writers*. Garden City, NY: Doubleday, 1976.

Morrison, Toni. *Playing in the Dark: Whiteness and the Literary Imagination*. New York: Vintage, 1993.

Morse, Jonathan. "Conduct Book and Serf: Emily Dickinson Writes a Word." *Emily Dickinson Journal* 16.1, 2007, 53–72.

Morton, Samuel George. *Crania Americana; or, a Comparative View of the Skulls of Various Aboriginal Nations of North and South America: To Which Is Prefixed an Essay on the Varieties of the Human Species.* Philadelphia: Dobson, 1839.

Moseley, Caroline. "The Hutchinson Family: The Function of Their Song in Ante-Bellum America." *Journal of American Culture* 1.4, 1978, 713–23.

Mossberg, Barbara Antonina Clarke. *Emily Dickinson: When a Writer Is a Daughter.* Bloomington: Indiana UP, 1982.

Murray, Aífe. *Maid as Muse: How Servants Changed Emily Dickinson's Life and Language.* Durham, NH: UP of New England, 2009.

Murray, Marian. *Circus! From Rome to Ringling.* New York: Appleton-Century-Crofts, 1956.

Namias, June. *White Captives: Gender and Ethnicity on the American Frontier.* Chapel Hill: U of North Carolina P, 1993.

Nathan, Hans. *Dan Emmett and the Rise of Early Negro Minstrelsy.* Norman: U of Oklahoma P, 1962.

"National Burial-Ground at Andersonville." *Harper's Weekly*, Oct. 7, 1865, 634. *HarpWeek*, harpweek.com.

Nevin, Robert P. "Stephen C. Foster and Negro Minstrelsy." *Atlantic Monthly* 20, Nov. 1867, 608–16.

Nevins, Allan. *The Emergence of Lincoln*, vol. 2, New York: Charles Scribner's Sons, 1950.

Newhall, Beaumont. *The Daguerreotype in America.* New York: New York Graphic Society, 1968.

"New Photo of Emily Dickinson?" *Boston Globe*, Sept. 6, 2012. boston.com.

The New Princeton Encyclopedia of Poetry and Poetics, edited by Alex Preminger and V. T. F. Brogan, Princeton: Princeton UP, 1993.

[New York: Hippodrome]. *Barre Patriot* [Barre, MA], June 3, 1853, 4. *America's Historical Newspapers*, infoweb.newsbank.com.

Niblo and Sloat's New York Circus!! Advertisement. *Hampshire and Franklin Express* June 22, 1860, 3.

Nicholson, William. "'A Quiet Passion' Won't Solve the Mystery of Emily Dickinson—But Does the Truth Matter?" Review of *A Quiet Passion,* directed by Terence Davies. *Guardian*, April 1, 2017. https://www.theguardian.com/books/2017/apr/01/a-quiet-passion-wont-solve-the-mystery-of-emily-dickinson-but-does-the-truth-matter-. Accessed May 5, 2019.

Nickell, Joe. "A Likeness of Emily? The Investigation of a Questioned Photograph." *Emily Dickinson International Society Bulletin* 5.2, 1993, 1–3, 15.

Nissenbaum, Stephen. *The Battle for Christmas.* New York: Knopf, 1996.

North American Circus will exhibit at Springfield. . . . The Apollonicon! The greatest musical invention of the age! . . . [Springfield, MA, 1850]. Broadside. American Antiquarian Society. *Readex Digital Collections. American Broadsides and Ephemera, Series 1.*

Nott, Josiah C. "Two Lectures on the Natural History of the Caucasian and Negro Races." *The Ideology of Slavery: Proslavery Thought in the Antebellum South, 1830–1860,* edited by Drew Gilpin Faust, Baton Rouge: Louisiana State UP, 1981, 206–38.

Oates, Joyce Carol. "Soul at the White Heat: The Romance of Emily Dickinson's Poetry." *Critical Inquiry* 13, 1987, 806–24.

O'Connor, Nuala. *Miss Emily.* New York: Penguin, 2015.

[Old Granite State.] *Daily Evening Transcript* [Boston], June 3, 1843, 2. *America's Historical Newspapers,* infoweb.newsbank.com.

"Our Exchanged Prisoners." *Harper's Weekly,* Dec. 10, 1864, 789. *HarpWeek,* harpweek.com.

Ovid. *Metamorphoses.* Translated by Rolfe Humphries, Bloomington: Indiana UP, 1955.

Paley, Morton D. "Tyger of Wrath." *PMLA* 81.7, Dec. 1966, 540–51.

"Palm Leaf Hats." *New-England Magazine* 1.2, Aug. 1831, 177–78. *HathiTrust Digital Library,* hdl.handle.net/2027/chi.55220605. Accessed March 19, 2019.

"Panther Captivity: A Surprising Account of the Discovery of a Lady Who Was Taken by the Indians." *Women's Indian Captivity Narratives,* edited by Kathryn Zabelle Derounian-Stodola, New York: Penguin, 1998, 81–90.

Parton, James, et al. *Eminent Women of the Age; Being Narratives of the Lives and Deeds of the Most Prominent Women of the Present Generation.* Hartford: S. M. Betts, 1869.

Pascoe, Judith. "'The House Encore Me So': Emily Dickinson and Jenny Lind." *Emily Dickinson Journal* 1.1, 1992, 1–18.

Patterson, Rebecca. "Emily Dickinson's 'Double' Tim: Masculine Identification." *Critical Essays on Emily Dickinson,* edited by Paul J. Ferlazzo, Boston: G. K. Hall, 1984, 167–75.

———. *Emily Dickinson's Imagery,* edited by Margaret H. Freeman, Amherst: U of Massachusetts P, 1979.

———. *The Riddle of Emily Dickinson.* London: Victor Gollancz, 1953.

Petrino, Elizabeth A. "British Romantic and Victorian Influences." *Emily Dickinson in Context,* edited by Eliza Richards. Cambridge: Cambridge UP, 2013, 98–108.

Pfister, Harold Francis. *Facing the Light: Historic American Portrait Daguerreotypes.* Washington, D.C.: Smithsonian Institution, 1978.

Phillips, Elizabeth. *Emily Dickinson: Personae and Performance.* University Park: Pennsylvania State UP, 1988.

Piersen, William D. *Black Yankees: The Development of an Afro-American Subculture in Eighteenth-Century New England.* Amherst: U Massachusetts P, 1988.

Pollak, Vivian R. *Dickinson: The Anxiety of Gender.* Ithaca: Cornell UP, 1984.

———. "Thirst and Starvation in Emily Dickinson's Poetry." *Emily Dickinson:*

A Collection of Critical Essays, edited by Judith Farr, Upper Saddle River, NJ: Prentice-Hall, 1996, 62–75.

Porter, David T. *The Art of Emily Dickinson's Early Poetry.* Cambridge: Harvard UP, 1966.

"The Prison-Pen at Andersonville." *Harper's Weekly,* Sept. 9, 1865: 562. *HarpWeek,* harpweek.com.

A Quiet Passion. Directed by Terence Davies. Soda Pictures/Music Box Films, 2017.

Rand, Frank Prentice. *The Village of Amherst: A Landmark of Light.* Amherst: Amherst Historical Society, 1958.

"Raymond and Waring's Unrivaled and Long Established Menagerie." Advertisement. *Hampshire and Franklin Express,* July 29, 1847, 3.

"Rebel Cruelties." *Harper's Weekly,* June 17, 1865: 379–81. *HarpWeek,* harpweek.com.

Rehin, George F. "Blackface Street Minstrels in Victorian London and its Resorts: Popular Culture and its Racial Connotations as Revealed in Polite Opinion." *Journal of Popular Culture* 15.1, 1981, 19–38.

————. "Harlequin Jim Crow: Continuity and Convergence in Blackface Clowning." *Journal of Popular Culture* 9.3, 1975, 682–701.

Reiss, Benjamin. *The Showman and the Slave: Race, Death, and Memory in Barnum's America.* Cambridge: Harvard UP, 2001.

"Researchers Find Picture of Emily Dickinson." *CBS Evening News,* reported by Scott Pelley, CBS, Sept. 6, 2012. cbsnews.com.

Reynolds, David S. *Beneath the American Renaissance: The Subversive Imagination in the Age of Emerson and Melville.* Cambridge: Harvard UP, 1988.

————. "Emily Dickinson and Popular Culture." *The Cambridge Companion to Emily Dickinson,* edited by Wendy Martin, Cambridge: Cambridge UP, 2002, 167–90.

Rice, Edward LeRoy. *Monarchs of Minstrelsy, From "Daddy" Rice to Date.* New York: Kenny, 1911.

Richards, Eliza, editor. *Emily Dickinson in Context.* Cambridge: Cambridge UP, 2013.

————. "'How News Must Feel When Traveling': Dickinson and Civil War Media." *A Companion to Emily Dickinson,* edited by Martha Nell Smith and Mary Loeffelholz, Oxford: Blackwell, 2008, 157–79.

Roberts, Brian. "'Slavery Would Have Died of That Music': The Hutchinson Family Singers and the Rise of Popular-Culture Abolitionism in Early Antebellum-Era America, 1842–1850." *Proceedings of the American Antiquarian Society.* Worcester, MA: American Antiquarian Society, 2006, 301–68.

Rockwood and Stone's Mammoth Circus. Advertisement. *Hampshire and Franklin Express,* July 4, 1845, 3.

Rodier, Katharine. "'Astra Castra': Emily Dickinson, Thomas Wentworth Higginson, and Harriet Prescott Spofford." *Separate Spheres No More:*

Gender Convergence in American Literature, 1830–1930, edited by Monika M. Elbert, Tuscaloosa: U of Alabama P, 2000, 50–72.

Rosenbaum, S. P., editor. *A Concordance to the Poems of Emily Dickinson.* Ithaca: Cornell UP, 1964.

Rozinek, Erika. "Trembling for the Nation: Illinois Women and the Election of 1860." *Journal of Illinois History* 5.4, 2002, 309–24.

Runzo, Sandra. "Dickinson, Performance, and the Homoerotic Lyric." *American Literature* 68.2, 1996, 347–63.

Ryan, Mary P. "Gender and Public Access: Women's Politics in Nineteenth-Century America." *Habermas and the Public Sphere,* edited by Craig Calhoun, Cambridge: MIT P, 1992, 25988.

Sablosky, Irving. *American Music.* Chicago: U of Chicago P, 1969.

———. *What They Heard: Music in America, 1852–1881, from the Pages of Dwight's Journal of Music.* Baton Rouge: Louisiana SUP, 1986.

Sanders, Paul D., compiler and editor. *Lyrics and Borrowed Tunes of the American Temperance Movement.* Columbia: U Missouri P, 2006.

Sanjek, Russell. *American Popular Music and Its Business: The First Four Hundred Years,* vol. 2, New York: Oxford UP, 1988.

[Sarah Sands; Plymouth]. *Boston Daily Atlas,* June 14, 1853, 2. *America's Historical Newspapers,* infoweb.newsbank.com.

Saxon, A. H., editor. *Selected Letters of P. T. Barnum.* New York: Columbia UP, 1983.

———. *P. T. Barnum: The Legend and the Man.* New York: Columbia UP, 1989.

Scarborough, Dorothy. *On the Trail of Negro Folk-Songs.* 1925. Hatboro, PA: Folklore Associates, 1963.

Schocket, Eric. "'Discovering Some New Race': Rebecca Harding Davis's 'Life in the Iron Mills' and the Literary Emergence of Working-Class Whiteness." *PMLA* 115, Jan. 2000, 46–59.

Scott, Derek. *The Singing Bourgeois: Songs of the Victorian Drawing Room and Parlour.* Milton Keynes: Open UP, 1989.

Sewall, Richard B. *The Life of Emily Dickinson.* New York: Farrar, Straus and Giroux, 1974, 2 vols.

———. *The Lyman Letters: New Light on Emily Dickinson and Her Family.* Amherst: U of Massachusetts P, 1965.

Shakespeare, William. *The Tragedy of Antony and Cleopatra. The Riverside Shakespeare,* edited by G. Blakemore Evans, Boston: Houghton Mifflin, 1974, 1343–91.

Sherwood, William R. *Circumference and Circumstance: Stages in the Mind and Art of Emily Dickinson.* New York: Columbia UP, 1968.

Shoptaw, John. "Dickinson's Civil War Poetics: From the Enrollment Act to the Lincoln Assassination." *Emily Dickinson Journal* 19.2, 2010, 1–19.

Showalter, Elaine. *Sister's Choice: Tradition and Change in American Women's Writing.* Oxford: Clarendon, 1991.

Silber, Irwin, compiler and editor. *Songs of the Civil War.* New York: Columbia UP, 1960.

"Sketch of the Life of Miss Millie Christine; or Christine Millie." *Biography, Medical Description and Songs of Miss Millie Christine, the Two-Headed Nightingale.* New York: Torrey & Clark, 18–. 3–25.

Slotkin, Richard. *Regeneration through Violence: The Mythology of the American Frontier, 1600–1860.* Middleton, CT: Wesleyan UP, 1973.

Small, Judy Jo. *Positive as Sound: Emily Dickinson's Rhyme.* Athens: U of Georgia P, 1990.

Smith, Martha Nell. "A New Daguerreotype of Emily Dickinson?" *Emily Dickinson International Society Bulletin* 24.2, 2012, 4–5.

———. *Rowing in Eden: Rereading Emily Dickinson.* Austin: U of Texas P, 1992.

Snively, Susan. *The Heart Has Many Doors.* Amherst: White River, 2015.

Sollors, Werner. *Neither Black nor White yet Both: Thematic Explorations of Interracial Literature.* New York: Oxford UP, 1997.

Sontag, Susan. *On Photography.* New York: Farrar, Straus and Giroux, 1977.

Southern, Eileen. *The Music of Black Americans: A History,* 3rd edition, New York: Norton, 1997.

Southern, Eileen and Josephine Wright. *Images: Iconography of Music in African-American Culture, 1770s–1920s.* New York: Garland, 2000.

Speaight, George. *A History of the Circus.* London: Tantivy P; San Diego: A. S. Barnes, 1980.

Spofford, Harriet Prescott. "Circumstance." *The Amber Gods and Other Stories,* edited by Alfred Bendixen, New Brunswick: Rutgers UP, 1989, 84–96.

St. Armand, Barton Levi. *Emily Dickinson and Her Culture: The Soul's Society.* Cambridge: Cambridge UP, 1984.

———. "'I Must Have Died at Ten Minutes Past One': Posthumous Reverie in Harriet Prescott Spofford's 'The Amber Gods.'" *The Haunted Dusk: American Supernatural Fiction, 1820–1920,* edited by Howard Kerr, John W. Crowley, and Charles L. Crow, Athens: U of Georgia P, 1983, 99–119.

Stanton, Elizabeth Cady, "Abby Hutchinson," *Eminent Women of the Age; Being Narratives of the Lives and Deeds of the Most Prominent Women of the Present Generation,* edited by James Parton, et al., Hartford: S. M. Betts, 1869, 387–89.

Starkey, David. *Six Wives: The Queens of Henry VIII.* New York: Harper Collins, 2003.

Stonum, Gary Lee. "Dickinson's Literary Background." *The Emily Dickinson Handbook,* edited by Gudrun Grabher, Roland Hagenbüchle, and Cristanne Miller. Amherst: U Massachusetts P, 1998, 44–60.

Swarton, Hannah. "'A Narrative of Hannah Swarton Containing Wonderful Passages Relating to Her Captivity and Deliverance,' Related by Cotton

Mather." *Puritans among the Indians: Accounts of Captivity and Redemption, 1676–1724,* edited by Alden T. Vaughan and Edward W. Clark, Cambridge: Belknap P of Harvard UP, 1981, 147–57.

Symonds, Craig L. *Lincoln and His Admirals: Abraham Lincoln, the U.S. Navy, and the Civil War.* Oxford: Oxford UP, 2008.

Takaki, Ronald. *Iron Cages: Race and Culture in Nineteenth-Century America.* New York: Oxford UP, 1990.

Talley, Thomas W. *Negro Folk Rhymes: Wise and Otherwise.* 1922. Port Washington, NY: Kennikat P, 1968.

Tennyson, Alfred Lord. *Tennyson's Poetry: Authoritative Texts, Juvenilia and Early Responses Criticism,* edited by Robert W. Hill Jr., New York: Norton, 1971.

Thomson, Rosemarie Garland. *Extraordinary Bodies: Figuring Physical Disability in American Culture and Literature.* New York: Columbia UP, 1997.

Tilton, Theodore. "Mrs. Elizabeth Cady Stanton." *Eminent Women of the Age; Being Narratives of the Lives and Deeds of the Most Prominent Women of the Present Generation,* edited by James Parton, et al., Hartford: S. M. Betts, 1869, 332–61.

Todd, John Emerson. *Emily Dickinson's Use of the Persona.* 1965. U of Wisconsin–Madison, PhD dissertation. Facsimile, Ann Arbor: UMI, 1982.

Todorov, Tzvetan. *The Fantastic: A Structural Approach to a Literary Genre,* translated by Richard Howard, Ithaca: Cornell UP, 1975.

Toll, Robert C. *Blacking Up: The Minstrel Show in Nineteenth-Century America.* New York: Oxford UP, 1974.

Trachtenberg, Alan. "Likeness as Identity: Reflections on the Daguerrean Mystique." *The Portrait in Photography,* edited by Graham Clarke, London: Reaktion, 1992, 173–92.

———. "Mirror in the Marketplace." *The Daguerreotype: A Sesquicentennial Celebration,* edited by John Wood, Iowa City: Iowa UP, 1989, 60–73.

Turco, Lewis. *The New Book of Forms: A Handbook of Poetics.* Hanover: UP of New England, 1986.

Tyler, W. S. *History of Amherst College During its First Half Century, 1821–1871.* Springfield, MA: Clark W. Bryan, 1873.

"The United States and the Barbary States." *Atlantic Monthly,* Dec. 1860, 641–57.

Van Amburgh and Co.'s Great Golden Menagerie! . . . Prof. Davis . . . The following is a complete list of animals. . . . [June 8, 1868] . . . [Worcester, MA: 1868]. Broadside. American Antiquarian Society. *Readex Digital Collections. American Broadsides and Ephemera, Series 1.*

Vendler, Helen. *Dickinson: Selected Poems and Commentaries.* Cambridge: Belknap P of Harvard UP, 2010.

Walsh, John Evangelist. *Emily Dickinson in Love: The Case for Otis Lord.* New Brunswick: Rutgers UP, 2012.

Ward, Theodora. *The Capsule of the Mind: Chapters in the Life of Emily Dickinson.* Cambridge: Belknap P of Harvard UP, 1961.

Wardrop, Daneen. *Emily Dickinson and the Labor of Clothing.* Durham: U of New Hampshire P, 2009.

———. *Emily Dickinson's Gothic: Goblin with a Gauge.* Iowa City: U of Iowa P, 1996.

———. "'That Minute Domingo': Dickinson's Cooptation of Abolitionist Diction and Franklin's '*Variorum Edition.*'" *Emily Dickinson Journal* 8, 1999, 72–86.

Ware, W. Porter and Thaddeus C. Lockard Jr. *P. T. Barnum Presents Jenny Lind: The American Tour of the Swedish Nightingale.* Baton Rouge: Louisiana SUP, 1980.

Webb, G. J. and Lowell Mason, compilers and arrangers. *The Odeon: A Collection of Secular Melodies, Arranged and Harmonized for Four Voices, Designed for Adult Singing Schools, and for Social Music Parties.* Boston: J. H. Wilkins and R. B. Carter, 1837.

Weinstock, Jeffrey Andrew. *Scare Tactics: Supernatural Fiction by American Women.* New York: Fordham UP, 2008.

Weir, Alison. *The Six Wives of Henry VIII.* New York: Grove Weidenfeld, 1991.

Weisbuch, Robert. *Emily Dickinson's Poetry.* Chicago: U of Chicago P, 1975.

———. "Prisming Dickinson; or, Gathering Paradise by Letting Go." *The Emily Dickinson Handbook,* edited by Gudrun Grabher, Roland Hagenbüchle, and Christanne Miller, Amherst: U Massachusetts P, 1998, 197–223.

Weisner, Stephen G. *Embattled Editor: The Life of Samuel Bowles.* Lanham, MD: UP of America, 1986.

Weiss, John. "The Horrors of San Domingo." *Atlantic Monthly,* June 1862, 732–54; Aug. 1862, 212–27; Sept. 1862, 347–58; March 1863, 289–306; June 1863, 768–85.

Welch and Mann's Mammoth National Circus! Advertisement. *Hampshire and Franklin Express,* July 30, 1846, 3.

Wells, Anna Mary. *Dear Preceptor: The Life and Times of Thomas Wentworth Higginson.* Boston: Houghton Mifflin; Cambridge: Riverside P, 1963.

Werner, M. R. *Barnum.* New York: Harcourt, Brace, 1923.

Werner, Marta L. "'For Flash and Click and Suddenness — ': Emily Dickinson and the Photography-Effect." *A Companion to Emily Dickinson,* edited by Martha Nell Smith and Mary Loeffelholz, Oxford: Blackwell, 2008, 471–89.

Werner, Marta L. and Jen Bervin. *Emily Dickinson: The Gorgeous Nothings.* New York: Christine Burgin and New Directions, 2013.

Whitman, Walt. *The Gathering of the Forces: Editorials, Essays, Literary and Dramatic and Other Material Written by Walt Whitman as Editor of the*

*Brooklyn Daily Eagle in 1846 and 1847,*edited by Cleveland Rodgers and John Black. New York: G. P. Putnam's Sons/Knickerbocker P, 1920, 2 vols.

Wilbur, Richard. "Sumptuous Destitution." *Emily Dickinson: Three Views.* Amherst: Amherst College, 1960, 35–46. Reprinted in *Emily Dickinson: A Collection of Critical Essays,* edited by Judith Farr, Upper Saddle River, NJ: Prentice Hall, 1996, 53–61.

Wilentz, Sean. *The Rise of American Democracy: Jefferson to Lincoln.* New York: Norton, 2005.

Williams, Susan S. *Confounding Images: Photography and Portraiture in Antebellum American Fiction.* Philadelphia: U Pennsylvania P, 1997.

———. "'The Inconstant Daguerreotype': The Narrative of Early Photography." *Narrative* 4.2, 1996, 161–74.

Winans, Robert B. "Early Minstrel Show Music, 1843–1852." *Inside the Minstrel Mask: Readings in Nineteenth-Century Blackface Minstrelsy,* edited by Annemarie Bean, et al., Hanover, NH: Wesleyan UP, 1996, 141–62.

Wineapple, Brenda. *White Heat: The Friendship of Emily Dickinson and Thomas Wentworth Higginson.* New York: Knopf, 2008.

Winter, Marian Hannah. "Juba and American Minstrelsy." *Inside the Minstrel Mask: Readings in Nineteenth-Century Blackface Minstrelsy,* edited by Annemarie Bean, et al., Hanover, NH: Wesleyan UP, 1996, 223–41.

Wittke, Carl. *Tambo and Bones: A History of the American Minstrel Stage.* New York: Greenwood, 1968.

Wolff, Cynthia Griffin. *Emily Dickinson.* New York: Addison-Wesley, 1988.

Wolosky, Shira. *Emily Dickinson: A Voice of War.* New Haven: Yale UP, 1984.

———. "Public and Private in Dickinson's War Poetry." *A Historical Guide to Emily Dickinson,* edited by Vivian R. Pollak, Oxford: Oxford UP, 2004, 103–31.

Wood, John. "Silence and Slow Time: An Introduction to the Daguerreotype." *The Daguerreotype: A Sesquicentennial Celebration,* edited by John Wood, Iowa City: Iowa UP, 1989, 1–29.

Workman, Nancy V. "Scheherazade at Thornfield: Mythic Elements in '*Jane Eyre.*'" *Essays in Literature* 15.2, 1988, 177–92.

General Index

Main entries in quotation marks are songs unless otherwise designated. Page references in italics refer to illustrations.

GENERAL INDEX

Bingham, Millicent Todd, 147, 155, 161–63,
195n4, 219n22; on modified ED portrait,
157–58

birds: ED as, 138, 203n35; theme, 25, 60,
72–73, 76–81, 89, 92, 108–9, 138, 145,
192n16. *See also specific birds*

blackface. *See* minstrelsy, blackface

Blackwood, Mrs. Price, 65

Blake, William, 137–38

"Blue Juniata, The" 50

Bobolink Minstrel, The, 95, 209n23

bodies. *See* aberration and normality; disability, physical

Bohemian Girl, The (M. W. Balfe), 50,
198n17, 210n30

"Bonnie Doon," 65

Boston, dime museums in, 19–21

Boston Academy, 47

*Boston Academy's Collection of Church
Music, The* (Mason), 49

Boston Anti-Slavery Society, 61

Boston Daily Atlas, 193n26

Bouve and Sharp (lithographers), 75

Bowles, Samuel, 64, 195n4, 209n24, 209–
10n25; letters to, 71, 94–96, 98–100,
205–6n49, 214n15; Master letters and,
174; Spofford and, 141

Boziwick, George, 47, 198n13

Brady, Mathew, 149–50

Brooklyn Daily Eagle, 62

Brower, Frank, 88

Brown, William Wells, 57, 65–66

Bullard, Asa, 116

Bullard, Eunice, 116

Bungay, George W., 209n24

burlesque, 83

Burns, Robert, 65

captivity and freedom: in American imagination, 1, 3–4, 110–12, 142–43, 216n35;
domestic captivity and, 111, 122, 131–32;
in ED poems, 37–38, 64, 69, 110, 129,
138–39, 143; in popular culture, 8, 12,
114, 138–39, 184; prisoners of war and,
111, 135–36. *See also* "Circumstance";
escape theme; "Life in the Iron Mills";
slavery; *Uncle Tom's Cabin*

Carpenter, E. W., 113

cartes de visite, 149–50, 218n8. *See also*
photography, early

castanets, 70, 75–76; in ED poems, 76,
79–80

Caucasians, 193n30; construction of whiteness and, 38–40, 44

CBS Evening News, 152

Chang and Eng ("Siamese twins"), 23

Chickering piano, 194n1

Chinese Museum, Boston, 47

Christmas, 6, 70, 77–79, 207n10, 207n13,
210n26

Christy, George, 209n21

Christy Minstrels, 198n18, 206n51

Circassian Beauties, 193n30, 194nn31–32

"Circumstance" (Spofford), 12, 111–12,
117–28, 131, 133–34, 141–42, 145,
213–14nn13–15, 214–15nn19–24

Circus of Niblo and Sloat, 28

circuses, 10; in Amherst, 27–30; ED's interest in, 1, 6, 29–31; theme, 2, 33, 193n27.
*See also specific circuses and circus
performers*

citizenship, 19

Civil War, U.S., 3–4, 143, 206n53, 216n30;
in ED poems, 2–3, 5, 67, 73, 134–36,
184. *See also* Andersonville prison

"Clare the Kitchen," 76

Clarke, George W., 203–4n38

Clinton, Catherine, 113

Cockrell, Dale, 11, 52, 62–63, 84, 97–98,
106, 199n21

common meter, 48–49, 197n11

common particular meter, 197n11

concerts, ED attends, 1, 47–48

Congo Melodists, 201–2n27

Cook, James, 22, 190–91n9

Cooley, Carolyn Lindley, 196–97n10

Cooley, Otis H., 150–51, 217n5, 219n20

Crania Americana (Morton), 193n30

Creation, The (Haydn), 47

Crosby, L. V. H., 198–99n19

crucifixion, 72–73

Currier and Ives (lithographers), 21–22

daguerreotypes, 7, 148–50, 186; aesthetic
effects of, 150; as "alive," 160–61, 170,
218n14; in ED poems, 167–68, 219n22.
See also Dickinson, Emily, images of;
photography, early

dance, 23, 70; minstrel, 50, 77, 88, 91–92,
100–101, 107, 207n8, 208–9n17; music,
68, 77; theme, 82, 88–93. *See also
specific dances*

"Dandy Jim," 65, 67

Davies, Terence, 189n2

INDEX OF FIRST LINES

Index of poems by first line with Franklin numbers. An asterisk denotes the full reproduction of a poem.